A Cappella Arranging

A Cappella Arranging

Deke Sharon and
Dylan Bell

Hal Leonard Books

An Imprint of Hal Leonard Corporation

Published in 2012 by Hal Leonard Books
An Imprint of Hal Leonard Corporation
7777 West Bluemound Road
Milwaukee, WI 53213

Trade Book Division Editorial Offices
33 Plymouth St., Montclair, NJ 07042

Music permissions can be found on pages 335-337, which constitute an extension of this copyright page.

Printed in the United States of America

Book design by Publishers' Design and Production Services, Inc.

Library of Congress Cataloging-in-Publication Data

Bell, Dylan.
    A cappella arranging / Dylan Bell and Deke Sharon.
        pages   cm
    Includes index.
1. Arrangement (Music)   2. Vocal music.   3. Choral music.   I. Sharon, Deke.   II. Title.
MT70.5.B45 2012
782.5'137--dc23
                                                            2012025313

ISBN 978-1-4584-1657-5

www.halleonardbooks.com

Contents

CHAPTER 6

CHAPTER 7

SECTION III

CHAPTER 8

CHAPTER 9

CHAPTER 10

Step 3: Listening to Other Versions

CHAPTER 11

Step 4: Form and Conceptualization

CHAPTER 12

Step 5: Preparing Your Materials

CHAPTER 13

Step 6: Melody and Lyrics

CHAPTER 14

Step 7: The Bass Line

CHAPTER 15

Step 8: Background Voices

CHAPTER 16

Step 9: Final Touches

CHAPTER 17

Step 10: Record/Rehearse

INTERMISSION

In-Depth Arrangement Analyses

SECTION IV

Advanced Topics in Arranging

Foreword

In the last years a cappella singing has surged in popularity. Once a niche art form practiced largely in American colleges, it has spread nationally and internationally, aided in no small part by the popularity of touring groups and television shows such as *The Sing Off*, which feature groups of diverse ages and backgrounds, all performing at a high level.

Useful for anyone from professional arrangers interested in refining their craft to amateurs looking to create their first arrangement, this book offers a practical, step-by-step guide. Through years of experience as arrangers, producers, and performers of a cappella music, the authors present a refreshingly flexible, open-minded approach that incorporates the latest trends, without losing sight of the history and traditional aspects of a cappella music.

With suggestions not only about the nuts and bolts of writing great arrangements but also about the creative process, learning to fail, and reaching your full potential as a creator of art, this book tackles issues that all musicians face. That it does so in an engaging way is a testament to the authors' sense of humor and playfulness, which is at the heart of all great creativity.

The authors' exhortation to "get out there, write, and sing" is a genuine one. As leaders at the forefront of the a cappella revolution of the last decades, their enthusiasm is infectious, and their track record is undeniable.

Joshua Habermann
Conductor, Dallas Symphony Chorus
Music Director, Santa Fe Desert Chorale

Introduction

A cappella came first. Before instruments, there was only the voice, making a cappella the earliest form of music. It was the driving force behind music notation and has played a significant role in secular as well as sacred music history ever since. You might think of today's contemporary a cappella style as something new. But from madrigals to doo-wop—and before and beyond—popular music has been performed without instruments.

As musical styles have developed over the years, so have the styles of modern a cappella arranging, leaving students and singers who would like to arrange without a definitive text to guide them. We hope to change that with this book.

Who Is This Book For?

Short answer: anyone who is interested in a cappella music.

Longer answer: anyone with an interest in learning to arrange for unaccompanied voices, or just curious about how it is done. This could include:

» Beginning arrangers of all ages
» Music students
» Community groups looking to write their own charts and find their own sound
» Professional and semiprofessional groups looking to add new ideas to their toolbox of textures and styles and freshen up their sound
» Professional vocal and instrumental songwriters, composers, and producers who are looking for genre-specific insight on a cappella writing
» Academics interested in the techniques involved in creating "contemporary a cappella," the current name for the modern a cappella idiom, which tends to emphasize the rhythmic underpinnings of current popular music through more complex textures and vocal percussion, as well as the periodic use of instrumental imitation and extended vocal techniques, all combining to create a rich sound that replicates the sound of a full band or track

This book is structured to act as a kind of self-contained arranging course, read straight through. However, it can also serve as a go-to reference manual.

Serious about learning the craft? Start at the beginning and work your way though. Looking for pointers or dealing with a specific problem with your chart? Just read the chapter that suits your needs. Couldn't find what you were looking for? Please contact us online at www.acappellaarranging.com and we'll post a reply. A cappella arranging is an evolving art, and our website is a constantly expanding addendum to this book.

Our Perspective

In our opinion, information is too often consumed as truth, swallowed whole without chewing. Unfortunately, there is rarely a qualifying "this is just my opinion" statement in almost any presentation by the media, nonfiction authors, or anyone else offering his or her own viewpoint. Pundits argue with infuriating certainty, and articles rarely pose open, unresolved questions. We live in the Age of Experts, all-knowing, infallible authorities, and we are told we should accept their word as gospel.

However, you know better; you've started at the introduction with an interest in getting the whole story and in finding out not only what will be here, but how to see it. You're interested in context. Therefore, we're probably preaching to the choir (forgive the pun) when we make the following declaration:

>> *Everything in this book is just an opinion. Take it with a grain of salt.*

It might seem strange for us to say that—after all, we believe in our own words enough to take the time to publish them—but we believe it needs to be said. There is no universal truth in art. Quality is in the eye (or the ear) of the beholder. And, lest it not be obvious, music theory is just that—theory—not a guaranteed road map to successful musical creativity.*

These words may be almost sacrilegious to some people reading this book. Having spent years studying music, taking lessons, listening to professors, reading lectures, and analyzing music as described in a variety of texts, the idea that everything you've learned up to this point isn't at least mostly "right" can be deeply unnerving. Truth is, music study no more guarantees success or quality than if you'd just gone to the symphony once a week, sat outside a jazz club on your night off, or listened to Top 40 radio whenever you drive.

---

* In case you have never considered this point, let us offer a simple example: Bach wrote music. People later studied his music, extrapolated "rules," and then began to teach those rules as if they were the "proper" way to create art. However, Bach didn't follow rules. In fact, he often went against the established practices of his day, which is part of what made him such a timeless genius.

Conventions in This Book

You'll get the most out of this book if you have the following skills:

Basic knowledge of music theory

Basic notation skills

Simple piano skills

If you don't have these, don't worry: we've included a list of supplementary resources in the appendices. Keep them on hand if things get dicey.

When discussing notes and pitches outside a notational context, we'll use what's called scientific pitch notation terminology, which is what the MIDI keyboard uses. Middle C is C4, and A440 is A4. A soprano high C is C6; a bass low E is E2, and so on. Octaves run C–C—in other words, C4 is *lower* than A4.

Terms printed in **boldface** can be found in the glossary at the back.

The Exercises and Recordings

In an attempt to continue the concepts presented, we occasionally include questions or exercises. Don't look for a list of answers at the end of the book—there aren't any. The questions are open-ended and intended to generate further thought and discussion. Do not attempt to tie up all loose ends in your mind and come to final conclusions about everything before you move on; much of what is vital in art is the conflict between different principles of music and how the artist deals with that issue in the process of making the art. If you think there's only one way to do something, do yourself a favor and look for the exception.

The principles in the book can be discussed on the page ad nauseam, but they mean very little until you actually hear them. Recorded examples can be found at http://www.acappellaarranging.com.

Listening to an arrangement while you look at the sheet music is very helpful. Sections of our website correspond directly with certain pages and principles discussed, so keep it on hand while reading. Even if you can hear in your head the music you see on the page, some things simply cannot be shown on paper. Various types of nuance, phrasing, and soul are unnotatable, and yet an individual's unique sonic character may be a determining factor in an arrangement. Considering how and why a song is different on the page than in the ear is one of the most important and difficult lessons you can learn as an arranger, for it is in that gap that your arrangement will sometimes find its most unsalvageable failure or its greatest success.

Acknowledgments

This being our first book, we have an exhaustive list of people who have helped steer us through our musical education and made a mark on our creative psyches, and so we have an exhaustive list of people to thank.

Deke would like to thank: Michael Secour (St. Mary the Virgin); Carrie Parker (Town School); William Ballard (San Francisco Boys Chorus); Bruce Lamott (San Francisco University High); Alan Fletcher (New England Conservatory); Gene Blake, Andy Cranin, Marty Fernandi, and all of my fellow Tufts Beelzebubs; Austin Willacy and the rest of my House Jacks brethren; the Contemporary A Cappella Society of America board, past and present; Gabe Rutman, Jon Ryan, and the original Ultimate A Cappella Arranging Service staff; Anne Raugh and Don Gooding; Bill Hare and Ed Boyer; the members of American Vybe and Groove 66; Straight No Chaser; the cast and crew of *The Sing-Off*; Joshua Habermann, David Buttaro, Eric Bigas, and Andrew Lovett (the original arbiters of reality); and most of all Katy, Cap, and Mimi Sharon for endless support, understanding, and love . . . plus some pretty silly family sing-alongs.

Dylan would like to thank: William Bell, Susan Bawden, Megan Bell, and Brendan Bell, who have always supported me; my teachers Marianne Liss, Mayumi Kumagai, Robin Watson, Curtis Metcalf, Casey Sokol, and the one and only Ted Duff, for helping me find my musical voice; my musical families in Cadence and Retrocity, for letting me polish my arranging skills; and the Swingle Singers and the Nylons, who inspired me while I was young and hired me when I was older. And of course my wife, Suba, for everything.

A Cappella Arranging

SECTION I

Quick Start

This section will take you through the ten basic steps of writing an arrangement. If you're planning to read this book from cover to cover, consider this section a synopsis of what is to come. It never hurts to get an overview of the forest before observing the individual trees.

On the other hand, some people like to toss the instruction manual aside and jump in with both feet. If you're such a person, this section will get you off to a running start. If you stumble, don't worry: plenty of detailed advice on each of the steps can be found later in the book.

CHAPTER 1

Basic Arranging in Ten Steps

1. Choose a Song

You're probably thinking, "Wait . . . isn't this obvious? A prerequisite? Should this even be considered a step?" We'd like you to consider song selection as your first major decision as an arranger, because so many of your subsequent decisions will proceed from this first choice.

You're probably also thinking, "OK, but deciding on a song is easy, isn't it?" If you're a freelance arranger or just arranging for fun on your own, usually either your decision is made for you or you have no restrictions. Easy.

But if you're arranging for a specific group with specific needs, you have many nuanced considerations. It's easy to come up with songs that would be fun to arrange, but usually there is a question of what is needed in the repertoire based on what is currently sung, your group's core style, untapped talent, soloist options, which artists or composers you already have in the repertoire, who you'll be singing for in upcoming performances, and so on.

We recommend avoiding songs that are performed by other a cappella groups often, since that will inevitably lead listeners to compare your group's version of the song to others, rather than listening to your group on its own merits. Conversely, your group will make a name for itself much more quickly if you develop your own sound and your own repertoire. This matters less if you're just starting out in a region with few or no other a cappella groups. If you plan on expanding your fan base and reach, it's a good idea in time to develop your own sound and style.

Regarding your current repertoire, you should be sure that your group has a great first and last song and a great encore. Usually these songs will be most effective if they are uptempo, high-energy numbers. You'll likely find your group performing these high-impact numbers most frequently, as you'll sometimes only be singing a few songs (at a party, event, on a street corner, or for friends) and want them to leave a lasting impression.

Your group should also have at least one excellent ballad at its disposal. Once you grab an audience with your energy, you want to leave an emotional impression, and one of a cappella's greatest strengths is its ability to render big, beautiful chords.

It should go without saying, but before you settle on a song, be sure you have someone in your group who can sing the solo (if you're planning on a solo line in your arrangement). A poor soloist can ruin a great arrangement of a great song and leave listeners with the impression that either the song or the arrangement (or both) are mediocre (or worse). The soloist is the most important vocalist in any song, so you had better be sure that you have the right voice to get the job done.

2. Listen to the Original—Repeatedly

This principle is the same as in foreign language study: listen over and over again until it becomes second nature. While you're concentrating, and while you're not. You will begin to hear sounds, textures, rhythms, and chords that you never heard before, some of which are very subtle and mixed quietly in the background.

Many a cappella arrangements suffer from not integrating the subtle, often almost subliminal musical elements that define a song. There are times when doing the obvious thing in an arrangement isn't the most effective approach. When you've listened to a song to the point that you can hear it in your head while it's not playing, you've fully integrated it. You want to internalize not only the specific notes and chords, but also the nuances of the song's feel. This takes time. And besides, it helps later on when you find you don't need to listen back to the original recording as often.

3. Look At—and Listen To—Other Arrangements

"What? Isn't that cheating?" Let's put it this way: would you rather spend your time reinventing the wheel by transcribing the melody and chords, or focusing on the more creative elements of arranging?

We thought so.

Stravinsky admitted to "stealing" musical ideas from others and even from himself, and he wasn't the first great musician to do so. Whereas there is a plagiarism case to be made from someone copying a paragraph out of a book, there's no ownership of a musical texture, a vocal lick, or an arranging trick. The artistry is in knowing when and where to use these various elements. It's not cheating: it's research. Conversely, by listening to what's out there, you can deliberately move in another direction with your arrangement if you wish and ensure that your version stands out.

You can find a variety of other arrangements in printed music or in recorded form. Search online for different versions in sheet music (not only a cappella, as a piano-vocal score might provide some insight and save you time if an a cappella version doesn't exist in print) and recordings.

Caveat emptor: often there are mistakes or simplifications in the printed music (yes, even the melody and/or chords), but if you've more or less memorized the song, you'll catch them. All you need is a close approximation of the solo in many cases anyway, as the soloist may want to learn the solo directly from the original recording.

You should be able to find many different recorded versions of songs (again, not only a cappella), which will provide you with a variety of different approaches to the core material. This will help you to identify which musical elements are most important to your arrangement and to assemble a list of the effective as well as the problematic choices others have made. It provides an initial road map of the song's potential pitfalls and high points.

Other arrangements of a song can be heard on various a cappella albums and can be found in a number of places (see our "Resources" section at the back). Although you don't want to lift entire passages note for note (*that* would be cheating), you can see what decisions the arranger made, appreciate what works, and learn from the less effective sections.

4. Decide on a Form

Sometimes the form is exactly right without alteration, and other times it will take a great deal of creativity to know how to sew together the important sections of a song that has too much instrumental filler. The longer the original, the more likely you'll have to cut something.

One important thing that we've learned from singing and watching a cappella throughout our lives: listening to and watching a cappella is a heightened experience. It is often more exciting, but also more exhausting. In a sense, everyone's a lead singer, and the audience has many more personalities and faces to watch than in a band, but not so many so that it's like watching a chorus. As a result of this more personal, more intimate performing experience, audience members concentrate and pay attention to a cappella more than to most instrumental musical forms, which is why less is often more. Say what needs to be said as poignantly as possible and avoid unnecessary repetition.

If you don't understand this point, bring a stopwatch to an a cappella show and compare performed song lengths with the originals. A three-minute song onstage comes across as a full four-and-a-half-minute radio tune. Performing "Hey Jude" at its entire seven-minute length would be incredibly tiresome. Or take a look at any a cappella album: many of the best a cappella albums clock in at thirty-five to forty-five minutes or even less versus fifty-plus minutes for a modern album with instruments. Your mind can more easily wander when an instrumental passage occurs, whereas your attention is drawn to the sound of voices, which can cause the listener to tire more easily.

Since many songs are written for and recorded with instruments, there are often instrumental solos, long intros, and transitional passages that may translate poorly to voices. If you've memorized your song completely (and you should have), try singing through from start to finish, and see where you lose interest. Chances are that's where your audience will as well.

Also listen for anything that won't translate well to your singers' voices. If your group is not well versed in vocal guitar solos, you may well want to abridge or skip them, unless you come up with an alternate choice for that musical passage.

If you're having a hard time keeping everything organized because there are too many changes in the song's form, you can use technology to help organize your thoughts. Anyone who's familiar with music recording software can import an audio file of the song and then cut it into individual sections. This will allow you to mix and match them, creating different "radio edits."

» *Deke says: We use this radio-edit technique on The Sing-Off before we start every arrangement (especially because we often have to choose the best ninety seconds of a four-minute song); we call them "cut-downs." Create a couple of versions and compare to see which works best.*

If you're more low-tech, write out a basic road map either on computer or on index cards and experiment with shuffling the pieces around. By now you know the song well enough that, by seeing the pieces in front of you, you can reorder or cut pieces of the song in your head.

On rare occasions—perhaps if a song is too short, doesn't have a bridge, or relies on too many long guitar passages—you'll find extreme measures are necessary. Options include weaving in another related song, possibly by the same artist, or composing a short transition. You may find that it's just not going to work, no matter what you do. Don't fret—choose another song to arrange now and put this song on the back burner until you find a solution.

5. Prepare Your Materials

Before you get started, you should know that it doesn't matter whether you notate music on paper or on computer or arrange by ear using recording software. Each method has inherent benefits and hurdles, and all can result in superior artistry. It's a matter of personal choice. Whichever method you choose to document your arrangement, it's time to set your foundation.

Before you go any further, you need to decide (at least for now) how many vocal parts your arrangement will have.

If you have a small ensemble (six or fewer), you're choice is likely made for you: you'll want as many notes as you have people, and doubling only one or two parts will likely cause an unwanted imbalance.

If you're arranging for a mid-sized ensemble (seven to fifteen members, like most college groups), consider having at least two people per part unless you really know what you're doing. You'll get a much fuller sound and hedge your bet against out-of-tune singing. Writing for more parts can get more complicated to manage: try starting with soloist/melody, bass, and two to four background parts, expanding from there as your creativity demands.

Don't forget to factor in the soloist and any extra parts, such as vocal percussion or duet lines, that need their own designated voice. Once you have your final count, consider how many staves (on paper) or tracks (in your recording program) you need. The solo should be on the top of each staff system and may be joined by duet or trio parts. You should avoid having more than two parts per staff, as the inner voices will have difficulty following which notes are theirs. If you're recording, you'll likely have your own track-management system. There is no right or wrong organizational method, although organizing tracks similar to laying out staves on a score is effective.

With two parts per staff, the upper voice should be notated with stems up throughout, and the lower voice with stems down (should you need to cross the voices, it'll be apparent). If your final count is three, four, or six staves, you'll want paper with twelve staves per page, and if you've arrived at five staves, paper with ten staves per page is also available. If you're arranging on computer, this isn't usually a concern—you can put each voice on its own line and condense later. If you're recording to computer, you can lay out the number of tracks you need in advance.

As you can probably tell by now, arranging on computer (via notation program or recording program) is far more flexible than doing so on paper, since you can make major changes once you're well into the process without much difficulty. Example: you can move everything up a half step on a computer with the click of a mouse, but on paper you have to laboriously rewrite everything.

Once you've decided on all of the above, lay out the song by counting the number of measures, and making a note of where each section begins (verse, chorus, bridge, and so on). Next, fill in your clefs and key signatures on paper, or name your tracks in your recording program. When you're done, you'll have a solid foundation that will allow you to work on sections in any order you'd like without any confusion over where you are or how the section fits formally with the rest of the music.

6. Write Out the Melody

Take your prepared paper/computer file/song file and write out/sing the solo line from the first measure through the last, including all rests. Having the solo line written down/recorded will keep you from losing your place while you're arranging—it serves as a place-keeper and a road map.

Also, for small groups, especially quartets and quintets, the soloist's pitch and rhythm are important to consider at all times. Sometimes the soloist will be the only voice on a certain chord tone, and you'll want to know exactly where the solo will be in terms of pitch, rhythm, and syllable. In these cases, it's worth the extra effort to make sure the solo line is exactly correct, inflections and all.

And remember that a soloist sometimes doesn't sing exactly the same notes and rhythms as the original or even remain consistent each time he or she sings the song in your rehearsals. For this reason, you should indicate, as you arrange, which sections of the melody need to be sung as written in order to make the arrangement work as you intend and which sections the soloist can improvise in more.

7. Write Out the Bass Line

Once you have your form and melody, the next most important vocal part is the bass (or second alto, if you're working with all female voices). You may well change the bass line as you're adding other parts, but you should at the very least create what you think you want now.

If the bass line in the original song is unique and/or memorable (that is, it has a hook or a distinctive countermelody), you're probably going to want to duplicate it as closely as possible, knowing that you'll have to leap an octave at times (when the line becomes too low to sing or too high to still be the lowest voice). You should choose carefully where to do this so that it doesn't disrupt any signature melodic contours.

If the bass line is not clearly defined, then you're free to weave one of your own. Consider vocal range, the roots of the chords, and the rhythmic feel of the original as the primary factors. The bass line is the song's "second melody" and is usually the most recognizable line after the solo, so make it melodic, catchy, and, wherever possible, fun to sing. A fully engaged singer is a better singer, and a boring bass line will likely result in a boring performance.

Don't forget to take into consideration specific vocal-production concerns, like where your bass or bass section is going to breathe, how fast your bass can articulate, and how long he (or she, in the case of all-female groups) can hold a note. If you're not familiar with bass voices and their sounds and limitations, have your bass sing for you and listen to a few of the greats, like the Bobs' Richard Greene, Take 6's Alvin Chea, the Persuasions' Jimmy Hayes, and the Nylons' Arnold Robinson. Each has a unique way of phrasing and articulating, and there's much to be learned from their recordings.

8. Write the Background Vocals

From Rockapella to Take 6 to the Nylons, the background voices (**BGs**) are usually treated as a unit in contemporary a cappella arranging, but there are a myriad of things to consider—so many, in fact, that it's impossible to go into them all in any depth here. To give you a shove in the right direction, some of your considerations should be:

Rhythmic variety: Having these voices sing different rhythms from the solo and bass

Syllabic sounds: Words versus sound syllables

Voice leading: Making the background lines melodic and avoiding unnecessary jumps

Duet/trio: Locking into the same words and rhythms as the melody

Block chords versus counterpoint: All voices acting as a single unit versus individual, separate lines

Arpeggiation: Voices working as a unit but spelling out chords by singing one note at a time, like guitar strings

Instrumental idioms: Using the voices to imitate instrumental sounds or textures

Musical styles: Using vocal conventions from classical, doo-wop, close harmony, pop, R & B, and so on

Of all of these ten steps, this will prove the most time-consuming, demanding, and ultimately most rewarding, as it's here that you get to be your most creative.

9. The Final Touches

Now is the time to go back and sing through the entire arrangement, out loud if possible (sing a specific line an octave higher or lower if need be). Where is it too empty or boring to sing? Where might it be too busy or too complicated? How do the sections fit together? Where do you breathe? Is there a sense of development throughout the **chart**? Where are the weakest passages and how can you fix them?

It's best to turn your "inner editor" off when you're originally coming up with ideas, but you do eventually need to turn it back on and look at your arrangement as a whole, and now's the time (see chapter 4 for details).

10. Record/Rehearse

If you have the capabilities to do so, it's helpful to record your own arrangement. By singing each part "for real," in more detail than you did in step 9, you'll discover whether any parts just don't work and what parts will need extra attention in rehearsal. You'll be able to spell-check your notation properly and discover any copy errors or places where the notation is unfriendly or poorly laid out. Most important, you'll finally hear your arrangement sung by real voices *before* taking it to the group. You'll discover whether it works as a whole (and save yourself some time and embarrassment if things need to be fixed), and in the process, you'll likely discover some performance nuances that you can bring to the group.

If you thought your job was complete when you copied and distributed your arrangement, you're mistaken. A great arrangement is one that grows and changes with the group that sings it, and a great arranger is one who knows that no arrangement is finished until it is tailored to a specific group. Do not let your ego get in the way of this crucial step in the arranging process; suggestions from the group and your own changes after you hear a proper sing-through will only make the chart better. You will be respected and applauded for your flexibility.

When listening to the sing-through in rehearsal, your focus should in part be on your choices, their interpretation of them, and the distance between. How does the arrangement sound in voices as opposed to in your head? What differs from your expectations, what have they improved upon, and what isn't as good as you'd hoped?

Be honest with yourself and open to trying a variety of ideas and suggestions. This is when you get to mold your clay, and it is the most valuable learning experience you'll ever have as an arranger; use this time wisely.

In case you didn't realize it, many renowned composers and arrangers have had the luxury of writing for the best orchestras and choruses in the world and could write just about anything that they could imagine; you probably can't. Like it or not, you're arranging for your group, and it's your fault, not theirs, if the arrangement doesn't work. It's your job to make them sound their best and your responsibility to maximize their potential through your choices. You can push their limits occasionally, but to push those limits you have to know them and work within them.

And just as you'll push your group's limits, you should also push your own. There are plenty of standard arrangements in the world, and you're probably not interested in adding to the pile. To be a great arranger you have to know how to write a standard arrangement and also have the creativity and drive to do something new. Most instrumental arrangers approach a song with the initial question, "What am I going to do differently?," whereas many a cappella arrangers approach a song by asking, "How can I make this sound the same, but with voices?" Consider adopting a perspective that makes the most of both ways of thinking. The best arrangements manage to maintain the successful elements of an original version and also bring to it something new.

Once you're finished and your arrangement is safely in the repertoire, it's time to go back to step 1.

Exercises

» Choose a simple song you know well (say, "Happy Birthday to You") and arrange it using this method. Notice the ways in which this differs from your usual practice. Are there valuable steps you've been skipping? Are there ways you're used to arranging that are superior to this method?

» Consider the order of these ten steps. Are there some steps you can take in a different order? Do you prefer a different order? Would you add any steps?

» Try arranging a song using a different notational method. If you usually write down your music on paper or in a notation program, try arranging through a recording program by ear, and vice versa. How does using a different notational method affect your arranging process or style?

» Look at some of the first arrangements you ever did, remember how they sounded, and analyze what you would do differently now.

» Take an arrangement you've done for one group and give it to another group. What do the two groups do differently, and what remains essentially the same between their interpretations?

Principles of Arranging

In the previous section, we gave you the "quick start." Before we delve into these steps in detail, we thought we'd step back and take a bird's-eye view of the principles behind arranging. Starting with a clear and expansive definition of the word itself, we'll discuss the different types of arranging, describe some practical skills such as transcription that are related and essential to the task at hand, and offer some helpful thoughts on the creative process. Finally, we'll shatter a few myths that may stand between you and your arranging process.

CHAPTER 2

What Is Arranging?

Now that we've laid out a basic road map—a cheat sheet, if you will, for those who want to jump right in—let's take a step back and look at the principles of arranging. And there's no better place to start than with the simple question, "What is arranging?"

The act of arranging is, in its most basic sense, the positioning of preexisting elements for maximum effect, resulting in an order that's pleasing and that suits our needs. Often arranging is associated with purely artistic or creative endeavors. Flower arranging, for instance, has a long tradition, especially in Japan, where it is so refined an art that it takes decades to understand all of the nuances.

In our twenty-first-century commerce-driven culture, flower arranging also carries a negative connotation, the pastime of someone with a lot of free time on his or her hands, someone who doesn't have to do "real" work. In our society, creation is seen as a sublime act of artistic expression, whereas arranging is sometimes considered an indulgence or a second-rate activity. This attitude is seen clearly in the language surrounding arrangements in copyright law. An arrangement is considered a "derivative work," one that, on its own merits, is of less value than an original work. According to American copyright law, there are even several cases in which an arranger does not own his arrangement; instead, all significant ownership rights belong to the songwriter.

It is easy to consider an arrangement (or an arranger) as second-rate compared to a composition (or composer). But look at the great musicians of the past—didn't Ravel arrange Debussy's music for symphony orchestra? One of Vaughan Williams's greatest successes was based on a theme by Thomas Tallis, and Gounod's *Ave Maria* remains to this day as popular as its inspiration, the Prelude in C Major from Book I of Bach's *Well-Tempered Clavier*. As for jazz, it's not usually the songwriter who's given the greatest credit, it's the arranger or performer. "Covering" songs has become almost a rite of passage for big pop stars, and many recording artists' first hit song is a cover of a tune made famous by an earlier artist. Hip-hop relies heavily on sampling. The list goes on and on.

Music arranging is a very specific art, bringing together elements of composer, conductor, producer, and performer in a single individual who decides how the music will be crafted. After all, a pop song is only a melody (which can be altered), a chord progression (which often is altered), and a set of lyrics. Everything else is up to the arranger.

A music arranger's job is to take the best of a piece of music and create and craft the rest. We say "create" because that's what happens. New countermelodies, rhythms, textures, and so on arise from the arranger's pen, and in the final product, a new arrangement often highlights the beauty of the song in different, and often deeper, ways. A song has a life of its own, and the arranger's job is to help it grow and evolve. Often a new arrangement of a song is considered even better than the original.

It can be assumed that the arranger is enamored with the beauty of the object to be arranged, but that is not always going to be the case. If you are more than a very casual arranger, you'll one day find yourself in a position to arrange a song that you don't love, be it for a group member who's excited to sing a specific solo, a well-paying commission that you aren't wild about, or a corporate gig for which you'll be required to learn the company song.

This should not distress you, for it is often in opposition that the greatest art can be created. Think about black-and-white photos you've seen of urban decay, industrial wastelands, or even scenes of war. Great truth and even aesthetic beauty can be found within that which is often thought ugly. In the case of photography, it's a matter of finding the right angle, the right perspective, and using the tools of the art (color, chiaroscuro, framing, composition, and so forth) to find an inherent beauty in the place and moment.

There is beauty in everything, and this is often the subject of the most powerful art. Death, chaos, and evil are some of the most compelling subjects for songwriters, playwrights, and moviemakers. We're not trying to tell you, of course, that every annoying tune is an opportunity to craft a musical *Schindler's List*. Some cheesy pop songs should remain cheesy pop songs. We're merely trying to point out that you, as the artist and craftsperson, are the one who creates the perspective from which everyone will hear the song. Sometimes you'll find you do your greatest work when challenged.

At its most fundamental, a song is simply a melody and lyrics. Everything else is up for grabs. In a way, you have more freedom than most artists and craftspeople. You're working with a couple of core elements; the rest is entirely up to you.

Exercises

» Consider the different ways the word "arranging" is used in our culture. How do these uses compare with the act of music arranging?
» Think about other arts—how are they similar to arranging? Also, consider crafts, art made for a specific function; how do they compare to music arranging?
» Choose something else to arrange—flowers, your desk, whatever. Think about each step while you're doing it. Why are you making the choices you do in

the order you choose? What parts of the process feel creative? What parts feel mechanical or uncreative?

» Keep a notebook of ideas and fill it with observations and thoughts drawn from other arrangements, artistic performances, and the like. Some will be very specific (a chord progression), others extremely broad (when interweaving two songs, start with large sections of each, then overlay later). The more you add to your notebook, the more of a resource it will be when you find yourself needing an idea, facing writer's block, or wondering what to do next.

CHAPTER 3

The Arranging Spectrum

The term "arranging" in music has a definition so vague as to be almost useless. Technically speaking, you can put a couple of people in a room with a **lead sheet**, shout "1, 2, 3, 4!," and whatever comes out of their mouths is an arrangement. But it's doubtful anyone would refer to it as such.

Arranging is a creative process and an organizational process; but, simply put, it's about making choices—dozens and dozens of choices, both artistic and logistical. Since there are so many ways to arrange and so many different arranging styles, it's helpful to define them a little. For the purposes of discussion, we're defining the different styles of arranging by the kinds of choices and decisions made during the process. If pushed, though, we'll be the first to admit that any delineation is somewhat arbitrary, with demarcation lines more properly considered gray areas.

In other words, in line with the "no rules, no rigid structures" philosophy of this book, we present these arranging "styles" not as hard-and-fast categories, but rather as points on a spectrum. And like colors on a spectrum, different arranging styles can be mixed and blended, even within a single work. Here are some points on our arranging Spectrum in order of the fewest to the greatest number of decisions.

Transcription

Transcription (known colloquially as **lifting**) is the process of listening to music and writing all the parts down, note for note, as accurately as possible. Truthfully speaking, transcription is not actually arranging. The transcriber is not making any choices, just writing down what he or she hears.

So why include it at all?

Even though it's not arranging in and of itself, transcription is an essential tool for the arranger. You can't arrange without being able to lift the melody, or the bass line, or that cool synth hook in the chorus. Moreover, transcription is the single second-greatest way to learn how to arrange (next to this book, of course!). Transcription allows you to peek under the hood of a great chart, get your hands dirty, and really see how it works. It allows you to step into the shoes of the masters, learn what they do, and even gain insight on their own decision-making process. More on this later.

Caveat: it is extremely unusual simply to transcribe and not make a single decision at all. When listening to a recording, unless you can pick out each individual voice from start to finish, you'll be making decisions about which voice or vocal part will be singing which of the notes you hear, who will cover vocal splits, how to handle doublings, and so on. This is still transcription: almost all decisions are already made for you, leaving just a couple of notational and divisional choices for you to make.

Adaptation

We define "adaptation" as the act of taking something already written primarily for voices and altering its format. Examples could include:

» Taking a TTBB (all male voices) chart and writing it for SATB (mixed voices)
» Taking a voices-and-rhythm section chart and "a cappella-fying" the rhythm section (for instance, an electric bass line would be sung an octave higher in most cases, and vocal percussion would be simplified to something that can be done by a single voice rather than an entire drum kit)
» Adjusting someone else's arrangement to suit your group (your tenors are a bit weak in their upper range so you split your altos and give them the first tenor notes, you remove the final chorus because their version is too long for your purposes, and so on)
» Condensing a multipart arrangement into fewer parts (for smaller groups who write arrangements in the studio and want to perform them live, this is an essential skill).

When adapting, decisions are usually more logistical than creative. Nothing or very little new is added or changed: the form, tempo, harmonic information, and overall vibe remain the same. Decisions and changes might include such things as transposing the key or swapping a few vocal lines from one part to another for better voice allocation. Put it this way: if you can play the two arrangements one after the other and say, "They're basically the same thing," that's adaptation. It may not really feel like arranging to some since it doesn't involve much of a creative element, but it requires many of the same practical, logistical techniques found in any arranging style.

Translation

This is what we often think of when talking about a cappella arranging, particularly in the contemporary genre: taking a song written for a band and arranging it for voices. Often the idea behind this arranging style is to replicate the feel and style of the original piece as closely as possible, so that the novelty for the listener lies in hearing something familiar recreated with voices.

Some may consider this style of arranging to lack creativity, but we disagree. Truth be told, it *can* lack creativity, but it also can be very creative and fun. No one criticized the Kronos Quartet when they arranged and performed Jimi Hendrix's "Purple Haze" as an encore, and that was pure translation.

There are countless decisions to be made. Which instruments do you replicate and which do you leave behind? What sounds and syllables do you use? How do you keep the energy moving forward? How on earth will my singers replicate that crazy sound effect in the bridge? There's a pretty wide spectrum here for creative work, and although throughout the book we'll be showing you some tricks to keep it interesting, at best we'll be scratching the surface. The best contemporary a cappella arrangements often drive off-road and return with a sound or choice no one has used before.

A good, simple guide to writing an interesting translational arrangement is this: instead of focusing on the original piece and how to push that onto voices, *focus on your group sound* and imagine what sounds you want to pull from the original into your sound. Even if you think you're just translating, using this approach will drive your creative decision making, and you and your group will define the final sound.

》 *Deke says: When working on The Sing-Off I often find myself telling a group "Don't go to the song, bring the song to you!" In other words, rather than going out of your way to use your voices to sound exactly like the original recording, rely on your group's core sound and style, and make arranging choices based on your strengths so in the end you'll be performing your version of a song rather than trying to imitate someone else's.*

Transformation

Transformation or "compositional" arranging is the term we use for taking a piece of music and substantially changing how it sounds. This may come from adding new elements, significantly changing the harmonies or form, or other large-scale changes. Often it is achieved through deconstruction and reconstruction: breaking the song down to its basic elements of melody and lyrics (you'll notice that the bass line and chords are not included here) and rebuilding it into something new or considerably different. With this approach, depending on how far away from the original style the arranger goes, he or she can almost feel like the piece's second composer. If you get comments like, "I love what you did with that song," it usually means someone heard something new, and your arrangement probably contains transformative elements. A really good transformational arrangement may even sound better to some than the original!

Mixing the Elements

Most arrangements land somewhere in the middle of the spectrum, written with a combination of translational and transformational approaches. They may start by keeping the "bones" of the song the same (translation) but then add a few completely new elements, or they might take a rock song and treat the voices more like a string quartet (transformation). There is plenty of room for all types of arranging even in a single chart.

Often arrangers will change their approach over time. They start out transcribing arrangements by their favorite a cappella artists, then they start tweaking those arrangements to fit their own group. Then they start writing their own charts, intending them to sound like the original. As they get more comfortable with their skill set, they start adding and changing the pieces, melding their creativity with that of the original artist. As they develop their own signature sound, their arrangements will feel more and more like creative works in their own right. This is why being a vocal arranger is so rewarding: once you've developed your craft well enough, your arrangement may become one of the best-known or best-loved versions of a song.

It's easy to ascribe a value judgment to this: more creativity = "good" arrangement, less = "bad." But not only is this not valid, it doesn't even make any sense. Music is subjective, and in some cases a very transcriptive, straightforward arrangement will result in a very powerful performance, whereas a very clever, unusual arrangement will fall flat.

Remember that the success of your arrangement will not be judged by how complicated it is or how far you've taken it from the original; it will be judged by how well it allows a group to make music that's powerful, moving, and exciting. It doesn't matter how creative a football coach is in his drills and plays; it only matters whether the team wins the game. Bringing an audience to its feet is winning the game. People want to hear some songs or styles sound close to the way they remember them; twist the song into something unrecognizable and they won't be happy.

And it's important to make sure the creative elements of the arrangement serve the song, rather than the song serving your need to show off your arranging chops or creative masterwork. If all you want is a platform for your own creative skills, take the leap, go all the way, and write your own music!

» *Dylan says: I sing in an a cappella group devoted to music of the 1980s, and the big kick for the audience (and for us) is hearing all the guitar and synth bits that are the signatures of the songs reproduced vocally, note for note. Most of my arrangements for this group are pretty translational; but I'll use some of the "transformational" vocabulary to add some extra sparkle, remove a passage that seems dull, or come up with a crazy new way of representing a guitar solo. The result is a chart that satisfies both the audience's desire to hear what they know and my desire to create something interesting, different, and new.*

Arranging Formats

So far we are talking about the basic principles and concepts behind arranging. When it comes down to the actual work, there are a number of approaches you can take. Here's a quick rundown, along with the pros and cons of each. Knowing these will help you discover which format is best for you, your group, or any given song or situation.

Arranging by Ear

This is the original arranging style: getting some people together and working out the parts. Most doo-wop groups arranged like this, and it still happens in just about any situation: parts are often worked out on the fly during recording sessions, for example, or just for fun when jamming. Some groups are famous for their ability to work out a song and perform it on the spot.

» *Deke says: While on tour with the House Jacks several years ago in Germany, an especially drunk audience kept yelling out songs for us to sing. In frustration we decided to try one, then another, and by the end of the show we realized we were able to take requests and work out arrangements in real time, in front of an audience. It's not easy, but it's loads of fun, provided you have a group that's able to think on its feet and is both rather fearless and just the right amount of stupid. Note to those willing to try: you don't have to be perfect. In fact, it's better if you're not, because if you're too good, song after song, people stop believing you're actually making up the arrangement by ear as you go.*

Pros

  » It's fast, easy, and fun
  » No theory, harmony or notation skills needed, beyond your own ears
  » Allows for spontaneous and collaborative creativity

Cons

» Arrangements are usually limited in their complexity: it's harder to build complex musical structures
» Lack of a written record makes it easy to forget parts and harder to teach them to newer members (this can be partially mitigated by recording yourselves after each session)

If we told you Take 6's incredibly complex arrangements were arranged and taught by ear, would you believe us? Mark Kibble usually arranges while sitting at a piano so he can figure out how the chords will be voiced, then stands up and feeds parts to the other members one at a time. In fact, they sometimes take a few words and a simple melody from an audience member during a show and work out an arrangement in front of the audience in real time.

Arranging by Recording

This style is sometimes used by people with limited notational or theoretical skills, but also by those who prefer hearing a piece develop along the way, rather than trying to hear whole structures in their head. This is commonly done with a computer and recording software. The arranger can sing a melody, maybe the bass line, and work out parts as he or she goes.

Pros

» Combines the natural simplicity of arranging by ear with the advantage of having a record of what's been done
» Immediate, on-the-go feedback on the arrangement: no need to wait to hear it sung by a group
» Charts are often user-friendly, since all the parts were created through singing

Cons

» It can be labor-intensive: making a single change often means re-singing all parts in that section
» Arrangement is likely to be limited by the range/ability of the arranger's own voice
» Like arranging by ear, it's a little harder to write complex charts this way

Rockapella is a great example of a group that creates fun, clever arrangements using a recording. Scott Leonard or Sean Altman would sing into a four-track recorder, and once things were just right, he'd send out the individual tracks to each group member; they'd assemble the tracks in rehearsal.

Notational Arrangement

This is the standard method: writing parts down in a fully notated score.

Pros

» The most flexible and powerful method, allowing arrangements from simplest to most complex
» Still the best method for transmitting and disseminating an arrangement to other groups
» Not time-and-place-centered like arranging by ear: your chart can be learned and sung anywhere at any time

Cons

» Notating is time-consuming and sometimes dull work
» Relies on a group's (or at least the director's) ability to sight-read
» Complex arrangements can be harder to memorize

These methods also can be mixed-and-matched. An arrangement worked out by ear can be notated later, or a notated arrangement can be tweaked in rehearsal by working out new parts by ear. Recording as you go can provide a good intermediate step between by-ear musings and final notation. You may discover a personal preference for one style over the other.

For the purposes of this book, we will be primarily talking about notational arranging. However, all the tips, tricks, and techniques discussed will work with any arranging format. Moreover, you should not feel bound to one method while working. If you're stuck while arranging on paper or computer, step away and start singing until you come up with something that works well, or take the passage to your group with a rough outline and work it out during rehearsal. A great arranger will use all the tools at his or her disposal.

One last important thought: get out of the way. The arrangement is not about you, and if you're making choices to draw attention to yourself as arranger, stop. A selfish movie director will make choices that draw attention to his or her cleverness, hoping the audience will appreciate the craft and intelligence in evidence, whereas a great director wants the audience to forget they're in a movie, to get swept away in the moment and perhaps only later look back in wonder at what artistry and craft allowed for such an immersive, moving film. Help your singers make great music, and in time word will spread that the person behind the curtain is you.

CHAPTER 4

The Dreamer, the Editor, and the Critic: Discovering Your Toolkit and Developing Your "Inner Ear"

It's nearly impossible to describe the creative process in any meaningful terms, but, foolishly enough, we're going to try anyway.

We can talk all we want about quantifiable skills such as theoretical knowledge, or the ability to voice lead or transcribe—all necessary skills—but if that were enough, we'd be able to write computer programs that followed rules to create great art.

There are other, "fuzzier" skills that we all possess and develop over time which lie somewhere between the art and the science of arranging (or any creative process, for that matter). Rather than describe them as specific skills, we prefer to think of them as three distinct characters or archetypes. They're present in all of us, and if we can help them to get along, there's no limit to what they can do together.

Enter the Dreamer, the Editor, and the Critic.

If you studied twentieth-century psychology, this might remind you of the id, the ego, and the superego. Or, if you prefer, try Jung's archetypes.

The Dreamer

The Dreamer is raw, unpolished creativity. The Dreamer is the part of you that generates ideas, simple or crazy. The Dreamer isn't practical: he's not the type to figure out how to make things work. Someone else can do that.

The Dreamer needs a lot of space and time to do his thing. He doesn't understand time or deadlines: sometimes he only works when he feels like it. And the Dreamer is a sensitive soul. Interrupt him, analyze his work, or criticize him, and he'll run out of the room and disappear for a while. And you don't want that:

without the Dreamer, you have nothing to work with. He can create something from nothing, and that is his greatest power.

The Editor

We all know the Editor well: she gets things done and makes things go. She's practical and logical (if a little stodgy and boring sometimes). The Editor loves to tinker and execute, and this is her big skill. The Editor has an eye for the big picture and is excellent at assimilating different ideas and making them work together.

But the Editor is useless without something to work on. And she's not the one who creates it: that's the Dreamer's job. Sometimes the Editor is a little myopic: she can't see beyond what's in front of her. She needs help on either side to make things go: raw material to work with as well as someone to look it over and help make it better.

The Critic

The Critic looks for faults. Like a detective with a magnifying glass, or a tax auditor, he's looking for things that aren't right. He's looking for weakness, and if it's there, he'll find it.

Sounds like a nasty character. Why include him at all?

At first glance, the Critic seems like a negative type—but really, he's not. His end goal is the same as the Dreamer's and the Editor's: he wants to make the best arrangement possible. He just has a very specialized tool set, useful at very specific times. Unlike the Editor, who's simply working with what she has, the Critic can see what's missing and thus help to find it. But he's like a guy with a chainsaw, so you want to be careful about letting him loose.

Making Them Work Together

All these characters are essential to the creative process; the trick is to know when and where to let them play. We imagine the creative process as being a room where two people can work together (occasionally three, but it tends to get crowded). Different people will come in and out at different stages of the game.

Let the Dreamer Start

Let the Dreamer into the room first. Tell the Editor and the Critic to come back later. When? When the Dreamer says so, and no sooner (unless you're on a deadline). Give the Dreamer plenty of time and space to create. For you, this means wild, vague brainstorming. Write all your ideas down (mostly in word form only, since you're not getting specific yet) on a piece of paper or some kind of portable recorder. Don't worry if the ideas are incomplete, don't try to make the ideas fit together, and most important, *don't judge them.* These steps happen later. Go crazy, try stupid things, and give yourself permission to come up with lousy ideas. *Do not let the Critic into the room.* Although both essential to the process, the Dreamer and the Critic are essentially at odds with each other. If you let the Critic in, you will immediately start judging your half-formed ideas, extinguishing them before they have a chance to grow. This is probably the single most common cause of creative blocks and the reason so many people feel as though they've been stopped before they even start. We'll talk about strategies for dealing with this later.

Eventually the Dreamer will get tired, and the raw ideas will stop flowing. If all is well, you've got a bunch of vague, unconnected scribblings. This is the stuff that art is made from, and now it's time to let the Editor in to turn them into something tangible.

Let the Editor In

You've got your creative mess: now let's make something of it. The Editor in you can take a look at the raw material, make connections, and decide which pieces can work together well and which pieces should be left behind. The Dreamer can stay on, occasionally explaining what he was trying to do or why he came up with the idea. This is important for the Editor: even if an idea isn't used, the artistic impulse that generated the idea might show its face in another way.

> *The Dreamer:* I want something sparkly-sounding. I know—an angel choir!
>
> *The Editor:* No angel choir ... we don't have enough parts. But you want sparkly, right? Let's borrow the sopranos for a bar to do something sparkly. The tenors can take over during this section to fill it out.

Much of the actual writing of parts happens at this point, and this process will take a while. But this is where you'll feel a lot of progress as scribblings become actual notes on paper.

Invite the Critic

Once you've got a section mostly done, it's time to let the Critic in. Now you can look it over with an eagle eye and spot weaknesses, such as bad voice leading or a lack of movement and energy, or a dull passage that should be cut. At this point, most of the dialogue happens between the Critic and the Editor.

> *The Critic:* This section has your sopranos too high for too long. It's going to sound shrill.
>
> *The Editor:* OK, then I'm going to revoice them lower.

There will be times when the Editor and the Critic are at an impasse: the Critic sees a weakness, and the Editor can't figure out a solution. What to do? Ask the Dreamer. Be prepared to go in a completely new direction:

> *The Critic:* This section is too repetitive. It sounds like the last section. Do something new.
>
> *The Editor:* I can't keep it continuous-sounding AND do something new. I don't know how!
>
> *The Critic and the Editor sit glumly, staring at each other.*
>
> *The Dreamer:* Those guys are always singing guitar parts, right? What about a new sound … like strings or something?
>
> *The Editor:* I suppose I could turn this section into a vocal "string quartet" instead. Let's see what happens.

You'll probably identify with each character to some extent, and you may find you lean more toward one than another. This is very helpful to know and shows a strong sense of creative self-awareness. Do you come up with a dozen ideas effortlessly but find it hard to actually get anything finished? You have a strong Dreamer. Are you great at working with ideas but can't get started easily? You probably have a strong Editor tendency. Can you see/hear the "improvables" in any chart right away but tend to shoot down your own work? You have a good Critic. Keep in mind that no one of these archetypes is better than either of the others: they're all valuable, all essential to the creative process.

All this talk about fictional characters may seem a little goofy to some. But trust us—it really helps to separate the different personalities that come into play in the creative process. If you distinguish them this way, you'll have more control over each aspect and a stronger ability to call upon the different strengths of each *when you need it.* And this is the key to a successful creative process.

» *Deke says: Even though I've done over two thousand arrangements, I still like to try something new in every arrangement, especially when I'll be the one teaching it, since I can quickly make changes as needed. I usually describe this to others as*

"I'm taking a risk here" or "the bridge of this song is risky." I almost always have an easy, risk-free fallback position should the risk not pay off, but sometimes the risk results in the best passage in the arrangement. Using the above terminology, sometimes you have to hold off the Editor and Critic and try an idea the Dreamer has dreamed up, however loudly the other two complain.

The "Inner Ear"

Your "inner ear," simply put, is your ability to hear music in your head. This skill is essential in arranging: not only do you want to hear music you already know without having to play the recording every time (for example, the original recording of a song you're arranging), but you also want to hear *your* version as you're making it. You want to be able to hear ideas in your head (even if they're not really clear yet), then write them down and change them as you go.

Many beginning arrangers will play ideas on the piano or notate things on a computer and play them back, then make most of their decisions based on what they are hearing coming *back* to them, rather than hearing the sound in their head first. They try something, play it back, try something again, play it back, and on and on until something clicks. Most people who arrange this way find it slow and frustrating, and they often give up part of the way through; or they arrange charts very rarely, knowing that it takes a long time. They attribute this to a lack of arranging skills or even talent and just give up.

Hearing music with your inner ear may sound like one of those innate, Mozart-genius skills that the Gifted Few possess. It isn't. While it does come more easily to some, anyone can do it. It just takes some training.

>> *Dylan says: Hearing music in your head is not always connected to talent or formal musical training. There are some people who don't know much about music but seem to find it easy to arrange. Conversely, I've sung in high-level professional groups with guys that find arranging to be like pulling teeth. These guys have more training and experience than the former types; they just haven't learned to arrange with their inner ear.*

Think you don't have much of an inner ear? Try this: you'll probably be surprised.

Think of a specific recording of your favorite song. Play it in your head; skip back and forth if you want to. Imagine the melody—you can probably sing most of it already. Think of the guitar or keyboard hook. Now imagine the guitar: focus on the actual sound quality, whether it's sweet and silky or hard and gnashing. Listen to the drums: focus on the crack of the snare drum, or that killer drum fill just before the chorus. Think of those little bits of sonic "candy" that make the piece interesting—the place where the singer's voice cracks a little, or the guitar feeds back, or the cool delay effect that shows up somewhere.

This is an awful lot of information. And it's not abstract notes-and-chords information either: you're actually playing back a recording of the song in your head.

And that's how the inner ear works. It's like a digital recorder: it records pieces of sounds around you—musical and otherwise—that you can play back later. It may seem now as though all you can remember is random assortments of sounds that occur around you, but the more your work with singers and your arrangements, the more you'll start to hear those in your head. You can also use this the other way: to put together chords and voices in your head and then write them down. Don't worry: you're not going for full-on Divine Transcription, where you can dream up full symphonies and just write them down. You'll be changing stuff afterwards, filling it out as you go. But the trick is to get it *started* in your head.

So, let's practice. Try this:

1. Hear a Note

Pick a note and sing "ahhhh." Sing it again. Now stop singing and remember what that sound sounded like. Listen for the note, but listen also to the actual sound of your voice. Your brain is playing back your "sampled" singing. Don't fret if it doesn't happen right away: just sing the note a few times until you can hear it clearly without singing. If a sung note seems too tough, start by simply saying "hello" and then repeating that sound.

» *Deke says: During my freshman year at New England Conservatory, our first few months were spent memorizing melodies from around the world. Different forms, different scales, different styles. And it wasn't enough to simply sing a collection of notes; we had to get the phrasing correct, memorize improvised passages and the like. (How do you think jazz musicians through the decades learned to play and improvise?) If you'd like to strengthen your musical memory, this is a great first step. But don't just choose a few CDs from your library. Search for musical traditions from around the world and memorize songs you've never heard before.*

2. Manipulate That Note in Your Head

With computer 3-D modeling, you make a shape, then virtually turn it around onscreen. You can do the same with sounds in your head. Try it with the note you just sang before. In your head, virtually play with it. Make it twice as long, or short and staccato. Move it up a half step. Move it up by step until you've sung a whole scale in your mind. Have your voice sing Handel's "Hallelujah" Chorus high and low, fast and slow.

3. Add More Voices

Start with something simple—a whole note. Sing a C with the syllable "la" in your head for three slow beats. Once you've got that locked in, try playing it back in your head while singing E, F, and E slowly, again using the syllable "la" for each note, for one beat each. Now try hearing both in your head together. This isn't necessarily easy and may require practice. Once that's set, add G, A, and G over the top. When you have that down, you'll be using your inner ear to play triads with good voice leading.

Your mind is a powerful tool, and as an arranger, you're going to be developing a new way of thinking. Don't expect it to happen overnight; like a muscle, it needs development over time to grow. But if you've gotten this far, you're now starting to arrange in your head, with nary a keyboard, computer program, or piece of staff paper in sight.

Exercises

> » Pick a song you know well. Play it back in your head. Can you hear the chord progression? The lyrics? The instrumentation? Try starting your inner-ear playback in different places in the song (the second verse, the bridge, and so on.)
> » Pick a song that you've always liked but don't know very well and listen to it repeatedly while focusing on it. How many times does it take to have the song memorized?
> » Take a vocal arrangement you know pretty well. Read through the bass part without singing; instead, hear a voice in your head singing it. Choose a distinctive voice—maybe a bass singer in your choir, or a famous singer, or an actor, such as James Earl Jones (the guy who did the Darth Vader voice in the *Star Wars* movies). Don't be afraid to try something crazy: the stranger it is, the more easily your brain will remember the sound. Try it with a soprano singing low, or a cartoon character, or some heavy-metal singer. The stranger, the better! Try the same with each vocal part.

CHAPTER 5

Transcription

Since the Renaissance, a central part of a visual artist's training was copying the works of master artists: by painstakingly recreating a masterwork by da Vinci, an advanced art student would learn all the master's theories and techniques first-hand: light and shade, color mixing, form, and composition. The same is true in arranging: transcribe a great arrangement, and you'll learn these techniques in a way that no class or book can ever teach.

» *Dylan says: In all my years of music training, I have never taken a vocal arranging course. Instead, I got a summer job transcribing vocal parts for a musical: I was given the original Broadway recordings and asked to score the parts for the four singers. It was challenging and exhausting, but I learned more about four-part TTBB harmony there than I had anywhere else. When directing my university jazz choir, I started lifting Take 6 charts, and this is where I learned almost everything I know about vocal jazz writing.*

Transcription is basically a learning-by-doing process, but there are a few tips and tricks to make it easier.

Preparation

To begin with, *buy a good pair of headphones*. You'll want to really hear "inside the music" to grab those inner parts, and reduce outside distraction. You'll be listening to the same five seconds of music over and over again, and if you don't have headphones, your roommate or spouse will hurt you.

Next, *give yourself a good chunk of time*. Transcribing is one of those things where it takes a while to get in the zone, and once you're there, you'll want to stay there. Until you're experienced, it's not easy to leave in the middle and come back.

Then, *assemble your materials*: a big pad of score paper (preferably with large staves), pencils (no pens! You'll be doing a lot of scribbling and correction here), erasers, and sharpeners. And, yes, you're going old-school here: no computer notation. You need to be able to scribble things down quickly and messily, while listening, before your short-term memory loses it. Computer notation, even if you're fast, is still too slow and clunky for this.

Now, *prep the score*. Score preparation usually involves carefully measuring out the number of bar lines per page and that sort of thing, but we don't suggest doing that here. This isn't a final product: it's a rough sketch, and you'll need whatever amount of space you need for a complicated bar of music. Just do the basics: designate staves, systems, and key and time signatures. If the piece has parts that move around all over the place (guitars in the verse, keyboards in the chorus), don't do this yet; wait until you've done the structural listening described below.

Next, *have a keyboard at the ready*. It is usually easiest to check a part by singing it back in your head, but you'll probably want to final-check things, especially harmonies, against a keyboard.

Choose Your Song

You may already be planning to lift a specific piece, but if you're doing this for practice, we'd suggest choosing a piece of music, or something by a particular group, with a fixed number of parts. It's much easier to transcribe if you know how many parts there are. A lot of transcribing is about filling in the missing pieces, so if you know how many pieces there should be, it's all the easier. Try something like a barbershop quartet or an early Nylons recording, where there are almost always four parts and the harmonies are straightforward. If you're a jazzer with a good ear, try Take 6. Their writing structure is almost always the same: bass, melody, and four BGs. If you try to lift a complex, who-knows-how-many-overdubs contemporary recording, your roommate or spouse will probably find you hours later in the fetal position, headphones still strapped to your head, the same four bars on endless repeat.

Although not entirely legal, you can sometimes find other people's transcriptions of a cappella arrangements and recordings through the internet. If you do get your hands on one, we strongly recommend that you not look at it until you have completed your work, or at most look at only a page at a time once you're done. The temptation will be great, but you're not going to learn as much if you rely entirely on someone else's work. And there's no guarantee that their transcription is accurate anyway.

Listening

Next, start listening. You'll be doing this in a number of different ways, with different objectives.

Shallow Listening

Listen to the song a few times over and over, just to get a feel. Don't analyze just yet; let your mind unconsciously absorb the bigger-picture elements such as form, key, any major changes in texture, and so on. Your subconscious will absorb a lot more than you think: if you listen a few times over and get a sense of the chord changes, lifting the bass line will seem easy. Harmonic changes won't take you by surprise, and you'll be aware of little changes in the inner parts or where the lead part changes.

Structural Listening

Now it's time to listen a little deeper and take note of any structural changes in the parts. In a **homophonic** chart, it's pretty straightforward, and you may be able to skip this step. In an instrumentally based vocal chart, take a note of who's doing what and how many parts are involved. Your thinking might run something like: "Verse has 'guitars' . . . sounds like three parts. The chorus adds a 'keyboard' part—sounds like two more voices. In the bridge, it's all vocal, four parts." Take your time and write everything down as point-form notes. You'll need this information to know how to score the piece and to help with the detective work described later.

Lift the Outsides: Melody, Then Bass

Do this first. The melody and bass are the heart of the song, they're the easiest parts to hear, and the other parts are determined by them. You can lift the melody in sections, but for most pieces, we recommend doing it all the way through. Same with the bass. With these lines, it's good to stay focused on a single voice or part.

An important note: work in small sections. And we mean really small, like one or two bars at a time. Listen over and over, and make sure it's right before you move on. Our brains are pretty sophisticated predictive machines—which can work either for us or against us. On first listen you might hear something, and say, "I've got it." But your brain has filled in whatever you *didn't* get with something close, something that makes sense—but something that isn't actually right. This is especially true with melodies, but it's also the case with bass lines: you might hear the chord progressions correctly but connect them incorrectly. And remember: even if what you wrote works just as well, in transcription accuracy is the name of the game. Years from now some smug smart-aleck will find your chart and sniff, "Ha! A mistake! What a fool! And get a load of me: I noticed it!"

Lift the BGs, in Sections

You could do these all the way through, but we recommend going section by section. The inner parts are both harder to hear and dependent on each other. So if you've spent half an hour lifting one part in one section, you've also spent that time hearing the other part(s), and they'll come to you more easily. Also, if you can't get through the whole piece in one session, you'll at least have a few completed sections, rather than a whole unfinished thing. You'll have a better sense of accomplishment, and it will be much easier to get back into it later on.

Start with the second-from-the-top part: next to the outsides, it's the easiest to hear and to cross-check against the melody. Get a verse (or maybe a verse and chorus) down and move on to the next part.

In a four-part chart, there's only one more part. Knock yourself out.

If there are more parts, it's usually easiest to just keep going down to the next lower part. Make sure you don't just go for the part you hear the most easily: it may not be the next part down, and you'll be left with mysterious holes in your chart. In some charts, it's easier to work "outside in": go for the part directly above the bass, then keep alternating next-highest, next-lowest, until you've got them all.

If you've chosen a piece where the voices are imitating instruments, go by instrument. Lift the guitar (or whatever the instruments are) parts, highest to lowest. Fortunately, you made notes earlier, right? They may not be 100 percent correct, but they're a good start.

Vertical Transcribing: Being a Harmonic Detective

Ever watched a movie where a cop is chasing a bad guy? The cop's got him clearly in his sights. He turns a corner . . . and the bad guy's gone. Disappeared into thin air.

Vocal parts do this too. You'll be happily lifting someone's part, and it will seem to disappear. Don't worry: with some harmonic detective work, you'll probably find it.

Much of the time, you'll be doing **horizontal** transcription, lifting one vocal part at a time, following its melodic contour. When you get to more complex inner parts, especially if the music's relatively homophonic, it can be harder to hear an individual line, and you'll need to do some **vertical** transcription. In this case, you're listening for chords and sonorities and looking for the missing pieces.

For example, you've got a big-band style shot: quick, dense, and hard to grab. You managed to catch this much so far:

Soprano 1	E5
Soprano 2	C♯5
Alto	?

Tenor	?
Baritone	G♯3
Bass	E2

Remember all those seemingly pointless, out-of-context ear-training exercises? Naming intervals, major and minor chords, and all that? Here's where it actually helps (and if someone had actually told you that, or realized it themselves, maybe those exercises would have made more sense at the time . . .). Go back and listen to that shot, over and over. Don't worry about picking out individual notes just yet. Instead, absorb the overall sound, and ask yourself some questions.

Is It Major or Minor?

Answer: since your baritone is singing a major chord tone, you think it's major. (If it turns out it sounds minor, it's possible your baritone transcription is wrong. More on cross-checking later).

Is There a Seventh Sound in There Somewhere?

If so, does it sound major or dominant? Major seventh chords tend to sound happy and sunshiny, while dominant seventh chords come off as a little more meaty and bluesy. Let's say you hear meaty/bluesy and conclude there's a dominant seventh in there. This looks like a E-something chord, so it's probably a D♮. Got one so far? No—which means it's one of your mystery singers. Which one? Let's say that D sounds as if it's nestled in there somewhere. Well, if your second soprano is singing a C♯, a D would be squashed right up beside it. You'd hear that friction as being pretty strong, so it's probably not the alto.

Play what you've got so far on the piano. This is a great way to cross-check, because you can actually *see* the holes. Where's a good place for that D? How about above the G♯? That puts it in a logical place for the tenor, and nestled in the chord just as you hear it. The tenor has the D. Sweet. One down, one to go.

So, this chord is an E7 "something something." What are the somethings? Well, you've already covered the third and seventh, and your second soprano is singing the thirteenth. What's left? Ninths, seconds, fourths, and fifths . . . or doubled notes. If your ears are used to the sounds, you might be able to pick out these color notes. If not, here's a simple process of trial-and-error:

Your alto's note is somewhere between D♯3 and C4. So, just play the chord on the piano with all those possibilities.

D♯3—doesn't fit.

E4—could be, but it really sounds like there's more going on.

F4—interesting sound—check it against the recording. No, too dissonant.

F♯4—possibly.

G4—like the F: interesting, but too funky.

G♯—it doesn't add anything, and it's in the chord elsewhere. Probably not.

A4—doesn't fit.

A♯4—too dissonant.

B4–like the E, it fits . . . but there's still something missing.

C4—nope.

Now you know that it's either a doubled note (E, G♯, or B) or the F♯. So go back and listen just for the F♯. It sounds as though it's there. So, the alto's an F♯, and your chord is built. Break out the champagne.

But wait—let's check the whole chord to be sure.

We know you're exhausted. But remember Mr. Smug Found-Your-Mistakes Guy? Let's not give him any ammunition.

Cross-checking is fairly simple. Listen to the chord and play it on the piano. Anything sticking out as wrong? No? Good. Now, play the chord from the recording and hum the soprano note softly. Is it there? Does it fit? Yes? Move on to the second soprano. Make sure you're not adding any new notes—just because it sounds nice doesn't mean it's right. Once you've done the whole chord, pop the cork on that champagne.

This may have seemed painful, but it's not very likely you'll need to do this a lot. And sometimes a completed vertical stack is like an oasis in the desert of a partially finished transcription and can help with the horizontal part too. If you know the second soprano line ends on a C♯4, you can trace the part backward and forward from there—sort of like musical forensics.

Yes, unless you're captivated by obsessive detail work, transcription can be boring. And you will likely break your pencil in two out of frustration. However, like a budding engineer who takes apart an engine to see how it is built, there is no better way to understand the inner workings of an arrangement. Pick a song you like and an arrangement you respect, then use the process of transcribing to figure out what makes it great.

When you've done this a few times, your ears will develop a vocabulary. You'll hear the quality of a chord without having to go through all the trial-and-error. Fortunately, a lot of arrangers use the same **voicings** over and over: there are only so many combinations that work with any given number of parts, and you'll start to hear them as whole units. More important, these voicings, sounds, and techniques will start to make their way into your own writing. And if you're a real nerd, you may become hooked on transcribing.

CHAPTER 6

Five Myths about Music Making

An artist must start with a blank piece of paper and a clear mind. Unless you've been living under a rock for the past century, there's no way you could have avoided the barrage of false information and unsubstantiated axioms that make up most people's musical perspective. If you're a highly trained musician, you may find yourself bogged down by the weight of your rules and knowledge, unable just to sit and create. If you're less experienced, you may be intimidated by the task ahead, afraid of breaking a rule or making something awful, ripe for judgment and ridicule. Either way, there may be roadblocks in the way, myths about music making that stop you in your tracks. Time for some myth busting.

Myth No. 1: There's Good, There's Bad, and There's a Hierarchy

The logic goes something like this: The most complicated, sophisticated, and difficult-to-execute music is High Art. It sits at the top of the pile. The simplest music sits at the bottom. Everything else sits in a pretty well-defined order in between. At the top is Western European art music (what we tend to call "classical" music, usually forgetting that many cultures have their own classical music), and for many people, jazz. At the bottom is Low Art music such as folk music and Top 40 pop. "Good" and "bad" judgments are usually thrown in here as well.

Let's call this what it is: musical and cultural snobbery.

We challenge anyone who believes this to take a good look at their own music collection. Is it filled with nothing but Stockhausen anthologies and/or 1950s bebop? If so, we suggest you've limited your tastes. If your collection contains some popular music CDs or "simple" singer-songwriters, you've just busted your own myth.

Music is a little like food: it nourishes us, it satisfies our senses, and everyone loves it and needs it in their lives. Most of us enjoy an amazing variety of food, from fancy French cooking to a simple hamburger to Indian and Thai dishes. Rarely would someone say, "I only eat northern Italian cuisine," and eschew all other types of food. While there's something to be said for an exquisite work of *haute cuisine*, sometimes you just want that good old burger: if it satisfies you, if it nourishes you, then it's "good." Simple as that. If you like pop music, don't consider it a guilty pleasure. Keep your ears and mind open: Bach may fill you with a sense of wonder, Led Zeppelin may get your motor running, and Josh Groban may make you weep. Dump the good/bad baggage and embrace it all.

» *Deke says: Upon graduating from the New England Conservatory of Music, I believed in my heart that there was fundamentally good and bad music, and that I could tell the difference. It took me years to fully realize that music is 100 percent subjective. Good music has to be in tune, doesn't it? Debunked: our Western musical system is built on compromise, trading perfect tuning for harmonic flexibility (all half steps on the piano are the same, but they're not in nature). More complex music is better, isn't it? Debunked: twelve-tone music was brilliant conceptually but largely unlistenable and heartless. The more a person knows about music, the better the music he or she makes, right? Debunked: Luciano Pavarotti didn't and Paul McCartney doesn't read music, and many of the greatest musicians of the past hundred years never studied music. I could go on and on. In short, enjoy the music you like, and turn the dial when you hear something you don't (unless you want to learn from it, in which case sit tight).*

» *Dylan says: I went to York University, where I studied everything from jazz piano to twentieth-century electronic music to south Indian percussion . . . while playing in R & B bands on the side. Even with a wide variety of music in my background, I still walked out with the "musical hierarchy" mentality. It was only in my professional career, where I started playing and singing with any musicians I could find, that I learned that there are masterful practitioners and beauty and value to be found in any type of music.*

Myth No. 2: Music Has Rules, So Learn Them and Stick to Them

Many people seem to believe in music theory as some sort of Ten Commandments to guide and define the process. "Thou shalt resolve thy dominant chord," "thou shalt not write parallel fifths"—that sort of thing. Here's the truth:

» *There are no rules, only contexts.*

Music theory is just that—a theory as to how and why things work in music. It's a tool, an academic study, and a language. However, it is not a law. In fact, the most appreciated and popular music through the ages has usually defied the rules, bent them, ignored them, or been ignorant of them. The theorists step in later and explain what makes the music pioneering and take a stab at explaining what makes it "good." A theorist is kind of like a technical historian, and historians usually have some idea about what we should and shouldn't do now as a result of what we know about the past. The information is helpful, but it's not definitive. Historians are rarely the people who are making history. The people making history—in this case music history—are usually people laying waste to the rules.

Think about it: when was the last time you studied "hip-hop theory" or "death-metal theory"? When you think theory and rules, you're usually thinking of classical music. The theories applied retroactively to this specific type of music do indeed explain it well—but not all the "rules" will fit other musical genres. As for the other types of music . . . well, the theorists will get to it, once the snobs from Myth No. 1 consider it a "legitimate" genre. Back when jazz was at its most popular, the snobs would never have put it in the same echelon as classical music, and no one would have dreamed of teaching "jazz theory." Now most music schools offer an accredited course in just that.

You say you need rules? Can't live without them? Well, there *are* guidelines and conventions that can be learned. Go ahead and learn them, but remember that they are just that: guidelines. Conventions are useful, but if you never look beyond them your music may sound, well, conventional.

Myth No. 3: Music Should Be Left to the Experts

This is one that bothers us the most. It's a product of our Age of Experts. Once upon a time, regular, everyday people sang while they worked and played. They played instruments at home for fun and sometimes gathered around to hear each other perform. Then, civilization became more specialized, and knowledge became more fragmented. We saw the rise of conservatories (basically Expert-training schools) and public concerts, where the Expert got onstage and did his or her thing, figuratively and literally separated from the listeners. The listeners just sat and listened, having been relegated to the status of passive consumers of the Expert's product. This was further exacerbated by the advent of recorded music: music became something you bought, not something you made yourself. Regular people stopped making music as much, and if they did make music, they certainly wouldn't dare put on a formal concert like an Expert.

We're not suggesting that the expert mentality as a whole is flawed. We need experts in some fields: after all, you wouldn't place your medical care in the hands of a devoted amateur. Some disciplines have important rules that must be followed, and a lack of knowledge can be dangerous. But music is not one of those; no one dies when a chord is out of tune or a melodic line is weak. We're also not denying that there are those who devote their entire lives to music and therefore have greater facility at it. We're just suggesting that it's an artificial divide, with an artificial value judgment attached.

Consider the words "professional" and "amateur." Most people would automatically rank them: professional anything is better than amateur anything.

Now, go back and look at the true meaning of the words. A "professional" does something for money. The word "amateur" is from the French for "lover of." Now rephrase "amateur" and "professional" as "making music for the love of it" and "making music for money." Does that change your perception at all?

Have you ever wondered why karaoke is so popular, or why folk music saw a revival in the early 1960s—or even why a cappella music is so rewarding? What do they all have in common? They're all examples of everyday people making music. Ever wondered why some cultures, countries, or traditions just seem to be "naturally musical"? It's not biology, or even the nature of the music. If you take a closer look, "musical" cultures are those that engage everyone in music making. There is no real divide between experts and ordinary folks. In these cultures, music is something that permeates all facets of life, rather than being distilled in concert settings. Music is made and expressed, not bought and consumed.

Myth No. 4: There Is One Great Path to Studying Music

Every person is different. Some learn best from books, others need a teacher, and still others have to grasp concepts through experience. A formal music education is often a structured path of study that stresses elements of music theory, music history, and private lessons, This is perfect for a violinist looking to be the concertmaster of a symphony orchestra; it would be largely unsatisfying to an a cappella singer, writer, or arranger. One's time would be much better spent singing in a group, transcribing arrangements from great recordings, and writing a song a day.

There are a few schools that offer a flexible course of study and more progressive topics, but why is it assumed that spending $40,000 or more a year and sitting in a classroom is going to imbue an individual with a divine spark? Find a great local a cappella group or musician and pay one of those members for private lessons; it will cost far less and you'll learn much more that's relevant to your music and technique.

If you look at the great musical advances of the twentieth century, you'll see that almost none of them involve anything resembling conservatory training. Louis Armstrong blended musical forms and created jazz through doing, not studying. Many great artists don't read music, including the late, great a cappella arranger Gene Puerling. Barbershop and doo-wop quartets created harmony through improvisation and were almost exclusively amateur, untrained singers. The list goes on.

Of course, you can always find great musicians who have studied formally, but there's no clear connection between their training and their pioneering. And for every one of them who has a degree, there are three others of equal merit who never spent a day in a classroom.

This is not a wholesale dismissal of formal instruction. There is a use for formal musical training in our culture—primarily if the student is looking for a career in the study, preservation, and propagation of a historical music. Classical groups, for example, would be of lower quality and accuracy if there weren't places where music of previous centuries could be studied, understood, and put into context. They're called conservatories—places where things are conserved—for exactly that reason.

A cappella singers, for the most part, are exploring new territory, and until there's a great pan-stylistic a cappella program offered at a school somewhere, there's more to be learned outside the classroom. And once there is such a program, it should be understood that it's providing only a fraction of the tools you need to make great music.

》 *Deke says: The summer before I graduated from Tufts and NEC, I knew that I only had some of what I needed to know about starting a professional a cappella group. I was graduating with four years in the Beelzebubs and a bachelor of music degree, yet neither of those was going to find members or book gigs for me. So I decided to gather some friends, create a quintet for the summer, and sing all over the San Francisco Bay Area. It was low stress (since it had a finite end date and no real do-or-die needs or goals), lots of fun, and one of the best learning experiences of my life: no books, no rules, just some guys who wanted to sing. In case you're wondering, we called ourselves the Mach-5 (after Speed Racer's car).*

Myth No. 5: Creativity Can Be Measured

This assumes that creativity is some quantifiable thing. You can have more or less of it. If you don't have it, you can get it, learn it, or buy it.

Or—and this is worse—creativity is something some of us are born with, like double-jointed thumbs or green eyes. Some of us are blessed with creativity; for the rest of us, no such luck. We may as well give up now.

Are we saying that creativity can't be learned? Or that if you're not born "creative," you will never be? Absolutely not on both counts.

Creativity is the act of creating or trying something new. It does not have to be something that's never been tried, and in fact most creativity is far from new. As children we have countless small and large victories throughout our development as we learn how to read, write, sing, draw, and dance.

And if you're frustrated, feeling as though you'll never have a creative thought, remember that almost nothing is unique, and nearly every thought has been thought before. The point is not to create a completely new flavor or color or word, but rather to take elements that already exist and put them in a new order. The pieces are not new, the act of arranging is not new, yet like a kid with a pile of Legos and an hour, you end up with something unlike anything that has existed before. Just as a journey of a thousand miles begins with one step, if you keep taking steps and making small decisions, the end result will likely be unique and very creative.

» *Dylan says: I liken creativity to an energetic force, like gravity or electricity. If you're a Star Wars fan, it's something like, well, The Force. It's both inside us and all around us. And although you can't learn creativity the way you can learn math or geography, you can learn how to tap into this force flowing around you.*

» *Deke says: Let the record show that it's the pragmatic Canadian who referenced The Force, not the northern Californian who grew up near George Lucas and countless hippies. I would have used an example along the lines of an octopus figuring out how to open a jar, but at this point I think it's best we just move on.*

Creativity is in our DNA. It's an essential part of the human condition: creativity is what has driven humankind from the first stone tools to the technical and creative marvels we see today. If you don't think you are creative, just think of the last time you had a bright idea of any sort or thought of the perfect gift to buy a loved one. It's in you: all it takes is some "training" to learn how to access it when you need it. We've provided some tools in the next few chapters to get you started.

Final Thoughts Before We Start

If you believed any of the above myths to be true, we understand. We have believed them all at one point or another. Sometimes, the more training we receive, the more these myths seemed to be true, and the more constrained we've felt when trying to be creative, or expressive. It took a long time to shake off that baggage, and it's not as though we don't still carry misconceptions with us to this day (yes, we can occasionally be overheard griping, "that is the *worst* song . . .").

If you believe that music is, above all, a language (and we do), then consider this: don't spend all your time as a linguist, studying and worrying about grammar, syntax, and spelling, or even about what makes a great linguist. Spend your time learning how to express "I love you," and then make sure you tell someone every day.

Exercises

» Pick up a music book, turn to a random page, and read a paragraph. Now, consider the exact opposite to be true. Can it be true? What validity can you find in any perspective other than that of the author?

» Choose a piece of music you consider to be bad and listen to it repeatedly. What makes it bad, in your opinion? Who holds your opinion, and who might disagree? As you listen to it more and more, do you find it less or more unappealing?

» Consider: does it matter to you what other people think of music you like? Can you enjoy music that all your friends hate? How much of your music taste is purely aesthetic—and how much is related to your image or identity?

» The next time you're stuck when arranging a piece of music or writing a song, consider doing something you're not supposed to do (a "bad" vocal leap, a clichéd or nonsense lyric, a dissonant chord). Can you make it work?

» Sit down at a piano or pick up a guitar or other musical instrument and start playing with no regard to the rules of music—only emotion. Play with your elbows. Make chords with your fists. Create a two-minute piece that's humorous, angry, or contemplative, without any rules—only emotion—to guide you.

» Charles Ives's father would have two marching bands march toward each other playing different pieces of music. John Cage wrote pieces of music for multiple radios turned to different stations. Make music out of combinations of music that already exist, overlaying CDs, radio stations, and the sounds of the street. Listen to how they play, how they interact.

» Go to a concert of music you love with the express intention of "studying" the music. With great focus and attention, just as you would in a lecture, listen to how the music is created, expressed, and performed. Think about how the sound is telling you the truth, and how words describing the music are only approximating that experience.

CHAPTER 7

Vocal Conventions: Ranges, Breaks, and "Sweet Spots"

In most books, this would consist of a couple of charts showing instruments and their ranges. You could just as easily find this sort of thing on the internet. Here, we'll get into more depth, specifically with a cappella in mind. Rather than simply talk about vocal ranges, we'll talk a bit about vocal nuances in order to give you more insight into some of the norms and boundaries for vocal writing.

Think Outside the (Voice) Box

For some people, especially those familiar with instrumental arranging, writing for voices may seem like quite a limitation compared to writing for a big band, orchestra, or any instrumental ensemble. We beg to differ.

When most people talk about "vocal range," they assume standard choral singing and associated technique. But much of contemporary cappella arranging is about using the voice as an instrument. Far beyond singing words, this can include instrumental imitation, which opens up a whole world of unexpected and unfamiliar sounds. It also includes the "extended techniques" found in avant-garde and world music. Examples include Tuvan-style throat singing and modern a cappella lip buzzing (giving extended bass range comparable to a bass guitar or bass trombone), whistle tones (getting into piccolo range—think early Mariah Carey), overtone singing (making possible multiple simultaneous tones from one singer), clicks, pops, squeaks, and shrieks. The list is extensive. And let's not forget vocal percussion, from standard drum imitation to electronica- or hiphop-influenced beat boxing.

There is no more dynamic and versatile instrument than the human voice. First of all, with the exception of a powerful synthesizer, no instrument can make as many sounds as a voice. Even so, who cares? Is any instrument as capable of expressing emotion? Only a voice can make you laugh, cry, or feel any other emotion with such speed, power, and nuance. Music is expression, and even all instruments used together cannot touch the power or the human voice.

If you're still not convinced of the flexibility of the voice, consider the trad-eoffs and strengths of various instruments:

» Chordal instruments such as pianos and guitars can play multiple notes simultaneously. But most are limited to twelve equal-tempered semitones. Pianos offer no sliding, no vibrato or pitch inflections, no control over the notes once the keys have been struck. Guitars can slip and slide a little but can't alter dynamics or timbre very well after the note is struck, even with the use of pedals.

» Brass and woodwinds can offer pitch variation and strong dynamic con-trasts. So can voices. Brasses as a whole have a wider pitch range, but most are subject to pitch and tuning limitations. The voice, from the perspective of physics, is a "perfect instrument": it can slip and slide continuously anywhere around its entire vocal range.

» Percussion instruments are a powerful sonic presence, yet most of their sounds can be well approximated by the human voice, especially when amplified, and in the past twenty years there have been great advances in vocal percus-sion and beat boxing to the extent that it's sometimes impossible to tell the difference.

» Strings can offer nearly infinite note length and exciting timbres, but they are dynamically and timbrally limited compared to voices.

» And let's not forget the vocal ace-in-the-hole: we can sing words. Find an instrument that can do that!*

In short, the voice can equal or approximate almost any instrument you can name. From a subsonic kick-drum sound to a nearly supersonic whistle, the voice can cover practically the entire musical spectrum of notes and most of the spectrum of human hearing. It's not a limited instrument—it's the most flexible.

Vocal Range Conventions

First, a slew of disclaimers. The conventions listed here are just suggestions; for every one of them you will find exceptions. These guidelines will suit you well if you don't know the voices you're writing for: stick to them and you pretty much guarantee that anyone will be able to sing your chart. For now, we'll assume you're writing for mixed voices: all-male, all-female, and other styles are explained in greater detail later in the book. Also, even though we've discussed the extreme range possibilities of the human voice, right now we are going to work within the standard range of choral singing, since many of the extended technique skills are specialized. Alas, you can't assume that any choir will have a Tuvan throat singer at its disposal!

---

*What's that? A vocoder/keyboard can? Sure—but you still need a voice to "talk" the words into it.

Next, some definitions. These assume amateur singers with a little training and experience. Professional singers will have a more developed voice, meaning a near-inaudible **break**, wider range, and wider sweet and power spots.

Full range: represents safe extremes for each voice part

Average range: represents where you'll want to focus most of the writing; you can "dip" into higher and lower ranges, but may not want to keep people outside the average range for very long, especially on the lower end if the voices aren't amplified

Break: varies greatly from singer to singer, but this represents a reasonable average. Singing up, down, around, or through the break often means changes in timbre. You may want to avoid this for a main melody part for example, or you may want to exploit this timbre change, such as when arranging a song by a singer who deliberately changes his or her voice over the break for a yodeling-like sound

Sweet spot: where a given voice part sounds most natural and lyrical; good for melodic writing

Power spot: where the voice starts to sound full to slightly strained in **chest voice**; good for a strong rock or pop lead, where the singer is typically at the top of his or her chest-voice range

These timbral ranges are good to know since voice parts have quite a bit of crossover. What sounds sultry for an alto may sound bright and rockin' for a tenor; and what sounds sweet for a soprano may sound full and powerful for an alto. Knowing these differences means that you can make artistic choices based on what sound you're after.

Soprano

Full range:	G3–C6
Average range:	C4–G5
Break:	G4–B♭4 (some high sopranos will have a second, higher break around D4)
Sweet spot:	G4–E5 (primarily in **head voice**)
Power spot:	G4–D5 (chest voice)

Alto

Full range:	F3–G5
Average range:	G3–D5
Break:	G4–A4 (some low altos and female tenors will have a second, lower break around A3–C4)

Sweet spot:	C4–A4
Power spot:	F4–C5

Tenor

Full range:	A2–A4 (up to D5–E5 with falsetto)
Average range:	C3–G4
Break:	D4–F4
Sweet spot:	G3–F4
Power spot:	C4–G4

Bass

Full range:	D2–F4 (notes below F2 will require either amplification or lots of basses to come through)
Average range:	F2–C4
Break:	C4–D4 (lower basses may have a second, lower break around F2–G2)
Sweet spot:	A2–A3
Power spot:	F3–D4

You'll notice there are no definitions for "in-between" vocal parts such as soprano 2, alto 2, or baritone. As a general rule, for the in-between parts, treat the average range as their full range, and leave the extreme ranges for the outer parts. You can also move the "average range" of these in-between parts down a third for soprano 2 and alto 2 and up a third for baritone.

These ranges are typical of standard singers, but if you find yourself dealing with professionals, you should get their specific ranges. For example, a rock tenor spends more time in what would be considered standard alto range than tenor range. In fact, plenty of pop music lives in the high tenor range for men and the alto range for women—essentially the same place, which is why women can sometimes sing along to the radio more effortlessly than men can.

Exercise

» Survey the singers in your own group and write our their ranges as above. Have them sing a note in each part of their range to help you familiarize your ear with their timbre.

The Ten Steps Expanded

Early in the book, we gave you a "Quick Start." Now we'll get to the heart of it and go into some real detail. For the time being, we're going to assume that we're arranging a song that is in a Western popular contemporary format, including (but not limited to) pop, rock, folk, jazz . . . even polka, and that we're writing for a mixed ensemble with a minimum of four parts. Most of what we explain here will apply to other types of music—but not all. A melody +bass + BGs format may not suit a madrigal, for example, or a new-music aural sound-scape, or many types of world music. Later on in the book we delve into some more specifics about different musical genres and ensemble configurations.

All that said, here we go!

» *Deke says: Melody + bass + BGs is not always the best choice for a song, but it is an easy way to think about the fundamental sound of contemporary a cappella. Madrigals and barbershop rely heavily on the sound of homophony (all parts singing the same words in the same rhythm much of the time), and doo-wop usually features a melody soaring over the background voices, which are treated as a single unit. Contemporary a cappella is structured to create a full sound reminiscent of modern pop music, which at its core requires a bass line that is in rhythmic opposition to other parts, lest it all sound too simple. Layers are needed to create a full sound, and at a bare minimum the bass and BGs should be doing different things.*

CHAPTER 8

Step 1: Song Selection

You won't always have the opportunity to choose the song you'll be arranging. Maybe your group will hand you a mandate, or maybe you'll be commissioned to arrange for a group with their heart set on a specific song. Nonetheless, knowing the importance of song selection, and the common pitfalls to avoid, is an important first step to creating an arrangement for the ages.

Does It Fit?

First of all, you want to choose a song that will complement the other songs in your or the group's repertoire. You don't want something that's exactly the same as another song, but you probably don't want something that's wildly different either.

You should also consider how well the song is going to translate to voices. This is, understandably, one of the first things new arrangers want to know. There are no easy answers, but in general, you know that a Crosby, Stills, Nash, and Young song that is already vocal will probably make an easy transition, whereas a guitar-based heavy metal tune will demand much more of your skills, and a group's extended vocal techniques, in order to work.

It's important to be realistic about your abilities as an arranger and to have a good sense of the limitations of the performing group you're writing for. You always want to pick songs that are challenging but not too close to functionally impossible. By finding songs that are "a reach, but within reach," both you and your group will constantly grow and develop. Considerations include the song's harmonic and rhythmic complexity, its harmonic rhythm (the rate at which the chords change, be it once every eight measures or six times every measure), the orchestration of the original (number of parts, instruments, and sound effects), and your familiarity with the song. Don't think for a moment that a better arrangement is a more complex one; the best arrangements are effective renditions of songs that suit a particular group perfectly.

The important question is, "Will this sound good?" And the answer always lies, at least in part, in the performing group's ability. In other words, find a song that will play up their collective strengths and play down their weaknesses.

>> *Deke says: During season one of The Sing-Off, we initially considered having the last round before the finale be "Judges' Challenge," which was to be a song that was chosen to be difficult for the group. When asked for suggestions, I replied, "Do you want songs that seem hard but are actually attainable, or should I come up with something that is extremely difficult for a group?" After much discussion, we decided to go with "Judges' Choice" (a song that a group will excel at), because after all, who wants to watch an hour of a cappella groups flailing and failing?*

Why *That* Song?

There should always be a reason—a central idea—that drives your song choice besides "My group wants to sing it." A cappella arranging, certainly more than most types, often alters a song radically, but there should always be some aspect that is improved upon or brought out of the original. If you have the time, after making your choice, spend a couple of days considering the song and all its parts from different perspectives. You may find that there's a particular section or motif that you want to expand upon musically. Maybe your concept for the arrangement will come from a certain vowel sound, chord voicing, or rhythm. Your central idea will make your arrangement a real, individual artwork and keep you from merely translating the song to voices.

When you're first arranging, you're drawn to songs because you like them. Look deeper into the mechanics and message of the song to find why you're drawn to it, then make choices in the arrangement that will draw others to it as well.

Love It or Leave It

You'll find that some songs fill your mind with possibilities, while others leave you unexcited. If the choice is yours, avoid arranging a song you don't like, because you'll almost certainly just be going through the motions, and people may very well hear that in the chart. If you really love a song, it will show in ways you can never explain. Trust us on this. If you don't like the song, get the person who suggested it to arrange it himself or herself.

That said, if you don't initially like a song, give it a chance. The familiarity factor is important to consider: sometimes "I don't like it" really means "I don't know it." So give the song a few spins. Often, once you delve into a song, you'll find more and more that you like about it. The more you arrange, the more your tastes will expand. If you still think it isn't appropriate (or you still just don't like it), move on.

And if you *have* to arrange a song, you'd better learn to like it. If it's not your cup of tea, at least consider this: *someone* likes it, and if it's a popular song, clearly there's something in it that appeals to many people. Your job is to figure out what that is—the groove, a melodic hook, the lyrical sentiment. Discovering this will not only help you appreciate (if not actually like) the song; it will help inform your arranging choices as you discover the signature elements and inherent strengths of the song.

Moreover, by identifying its weaknesses, you'll be able to create a version of the song that people like you will perhaps prefer to the original!

Consider Anything—and Be Different

Shouldn't an extremely popular song be a perfect choice? Not always. Your group may want to perform a song that's at the top of the charts right now, but there is an inherent danger to that strategy: your version will likely want to be close to the original, prompting comparison—which might not be favorable. Furthermore, the more popular the song, the more likely people will tire of it soon, rendering it less useful six months from now. It is hard to put your stamp on something very new; it's also difficult to avoid the "burnout" phase during which a song is overplayed, before it hits classic status—if it ever does.

You may want to hit the sweet spot between a song your audience knows and one that hasn't been overdone. Your listeners may hear the song, remember it but not be tired of it, and appreciate your version, without comparing it to the original. An additional upside to this angle is that the less popular a song, the greater the chance that it's not being overdone by other a cappella groups (not a problem for some groups that sing recreationally, but perhaps a concern for a college group on a campus with a dozen other groups, or a pro group that's looking to make a mark).

» *Dylan says: The Nylons made their mark by rebranding well-known tunes (such as "Happy Together" and "The Lion Sleeps Tonight"), to the point where their versions came to be nearly as well-known as the originals. So when choosing songs for the latest Nylons record, we had to walk the fine line between popular and overdone songs. My solution: we came up with some artists that the guys loved, chose their ten best-known songs—and eliminated the first five. Songs six though ten were still well-known, yet they provided us with an opportunity to rebrand them for the Nylons.*

Have a Soloist in Mind

There's nothing more discouraging than having a wonderful arrangement fizzle because no one can sing it properly. There may be more than one member of your group with the song in their range, but make sure there's at least one. This is particularly true of so many deceptively high rock tenor songs. If you're not sure, diplomatically ask a couple of members to sing it for you, alone, before you begin. Most of your questions will be answered right there, and you'll also know in advance if any alterations (in tempo or key) will be needed.

And vocal range isn't even the biggest concern. More important is the emotional message and impact a song carries. Who in your group is the best conduit for the song, if anyone? Not everyone can sell every solo, and if you don't have the right person, pick a different song.

Gabe Rutman (former arranger for the University of Southern California a cappella group the SoCal VoCals, and one of the first arrangers for Deke's company TotalVocal; now a respected Los Angeles composer and producer and member of the Rescues) put it bluntly: "You can have the best doo-wah-dippities in the universe. Slap a crap solo on top and wait for people to hit 'skip track.'"

On the other hand, there is a great solo for every person on the planet. The key is to find it. By working backward—starting from your singer's personality, range, and style—you are more likely to find a song that ends up being extremely impactful.

Variety Is the Spice . . .

By nature, a cappella groups are capable of performing many different styles of music in the same set. Some groups take advantage of this, but many don't. A great song is one that makes the group look great, and few things make a group look better than versatility. If you're singing mostly pop, consider choosing a jazz tune. If you're stuck in the 1970s, try something that was on the charts during the past year. Singing the same types of songs not only causes the group to stagnate; it also takes its toll on an arranger's creativity. Arranging a different type of song will lead you to encounter problems that you usually don't and force you to find new, interesting, and effective solutions.

And remember, there's a whole world of music out there, from rock to barbershop, from jazz to South African township jive, from drum-and-bass to Inuit throat singing. You might want to say to yourself, "We perform a wide variety of styles already," but before you do, put your remark in context.

To be clear, this doesn't mean a classical group should sing a Nirvana song just to prove a point. Every arrangement should be custom tailored to the group's style and needs, and a song well outside a group's wheelhouse needs to be carefully considered and treated, lest it come across as a joke—and an unintended one at that.

I Can't Think of Anything!

Music is so widely available that the amount of choice can be paralyzing. If you're stuck and can't for the life of you come up with possibilities, here are a few places to narrow the search:

- » Your own recordings
- » Friends' playlists
- » Jazz fakebooks or "Greatest Hits" piano books
- » Radio stations and sites that you rarely listen to
- » Audience members' suggestions
- » iTunes "Ping," Pandora stations, and other music genome search tools
- » Suggestions from the group's members

There are literally thousands of fantastic songs waiting to be arranged for the first time.

Despite everything we've said about what a song needs to be a good candidate, here's the truth:

» *Any song could make a fantastic arrangement, if done well.*

But keeping all these factors in mind will certainly make your job easier.

» *Deke says: When groups are looking for new repertoire, the number one suggestion I offer to them is this: "Go to a karaoke bar on a quiet night, like a Monday (so you'll have the place to yourselves). Have each member sing a song they choose that they think they will do well, and then have every member choose a song for one other member that stretches them a bit. Through this process you'll likely come up with at least a couple of songs that would be great, as well as a deeper understanding of everyone's solo voice."*

The Ten Steps in Action

What's the point of talking about these steps without demonstrating them? To this end, we've each chosen an arrangement in which we take you behind the scenes, explaining how we built the arrangement from scratch, using the ten steps to explain our process.

Traditional holiday music is universal, well-known, and best of all, royalty-free. Deke has chosen an arrangement of "We Three Kings," and Dylan will explain his version of "Go Tell It on the Mountain." Both charts are included, in full, in Appendix A.

"We Three Kings," Arranged by Deke Sharon

I received a call from Don Gooding (a former member of the Yale SOBs [Society of Orpheus and Bacchus, just in case you were thinking of something else] and founder of a-cappella.com, among many other a cappella organizations and projects) informing me that Atlantic Records was looking for a new arrangement for Straight No Chaser's second Christmas album. They were signed after their video of "The Twelve Days of Christmas" went viral and wanted a similarly unexpected, zany, playful arrangement for their next album.

I hadn't worked with the group before, nor had I worked with Atlantic, so I had little to go on beyond conjecture. What did I know? The group has ten members, all men, who graduated from the University of Indiana, where they had formed the collegiate group. Their sound was roughly mid-1990s collegiate, which is to say that they used complex textures but were still largely vocal in production and sound, with perhaps some light vocal percussion but not full-on extended vocal techniques.

More important, as zany as a clever idea might be, it would also have to be at least somewhat cool. If I know anything about male collegiate a cappella groups, it's that they do not have an unlimited willingness to look stupid. In short, I knew any idea would have to tread a fine line.

As for the label's needs, it would be best to choose a song that's in the public domain. Why? First and foremost, it means the label doesn't have to pay almost ten cents for every copy it sells. Secondly, it allows for greater flexibility, since a publisher can deny the right to release a song if it doesn't like a version and if that version strays too far from the original recording (and the whole point of this arrangement was to stray). That's almost never an option when searching for pop tunes, but when it comes to holiday music, there are a few dozen well-known songs that are completely free of royalties and hassle. Most of all, I'd heard that the CEO of Atlantic Records wanted a song that kept changing musically (like "The Twelve Days of Christmas"), making the listener constantly wonder what would happen next.

So I put my thinking cap on and tried to come up with a clever idea, one that would make thematic sense and at the same time have a clear, compelling musical direction. However, I'm not above building on someone else's proven idea, and Don suggested several ideas from existing albums, including a version of "We Three Kings" sung to the tune of the *Mission: Impossible* theme song (by a group called VoxBop). A clever idea, but a "one-note" joke that wore thin rather quickly, leaving the listener knowing exactly what to expect through the second verse, the third verse, and so on. However, I liked the idea for visual reasons, and I could imagine this song being turned into a music video as well, with the guys playing the "Kings," madly rushing to Bethlehem with the *Mission: Impossible* theme providing the humorous drama.

Moreover, the style of the music could change throughout. In fact, to keep it interesting, the style would *have* to change. And as goofy as the idea seems, the *Mission: Impossible* music is thematically cool (well, cooler than, say, a polka!) and musically interesting (the 5/4 time signature presents challenges but also brings with it a measure of credibility, as it's not that simple a musical idea to pull off).

Everyone liked the idea, and I was on the next plane to New York for a meeting. Now all I had to do was figure out how to actually make it work. . . .

"Go Tell It on the Mountain," Arranged by Dylan Bell

This arrangement was a commission from a professional a cappella group from the midwestern United States called Home Free (http://www.homefreeband.com). They had been fans of my performance and arranging work with the Canadian a cappella vocal band Cadence and wanted me to arrange a song for their new holiday album. What they wanted was a holiday song that would be roughly in the style of an arrangement I had written of Stevie Wonder's "I Wish," heard on the Cadence album *Frost Free*.

The song selection process for this one was relatively easy. First of all, we were looking at holiday music, a very specific subset of the millions of songs out there. Chris Rupp, the musical director, had some clear parameters regarding what he wanted the arrangement to be:

> I need something uptempo, R & B stylings . . . very groove centered. Possibly a show-opener kind of song, a bit showy, very commercial sounding, i.e., something you'd hear on Top 40, as opposed to something more esoteric like a true Take 6 tune. I definitely love the jazzy Take 6 stuff, though it still needs to be more toward the approachable end for our audience than the hardcore-musician end (roughly the level that you did with "I Wish" . . . it really struck that balance well).

This painted a nice, clear picture for me. I asked them to send me a short list of songs. They came back with "Santa Claus Is Coming to Town," "Joy to the World," and "Go Tell It on the Mountain." "Santa Claus" seemed too cutesy to make a good show opener, and "Joy to the World"—well, it could work, but my instincts told me that funkifying it might come across as a little contrived. Since "Go Tell It" has gospel/spiritual roots, I thought it might lend itself more naturally to an R & B feel. Plus, the lyrics are bright and declarative in nature, so it would make for a good opening statement on an album or onstage. "Go Tell It" it was!

CHAPTER 9

Step 2: Listening to the Original

Chances are, you're going to base your arrangement primarily on one recording, be it the original version, the best-known definitive version (Aretha Franklin's "Respect" wasn't the original, but it is the definitive version), or possibly a less well-known interpretation that you want to bring to light. Whichever you choose, the first and most obvious step is to learn the song.

If you're planning to write a translational arrangement, listening is of primary importance: you've chosen to represent *this* particular version of the song, and so you'll need to know it up and down, inside and out, in order to know exactly what you want to represent and how. If you're writing a transformational arrangement, listening is part of a larger process: learning the essence of a song in order to extract greater meaning and creativity from it. In that case, we actually encourage spending *less* time learning the original: you want to avoid getting too much of the original stuck in your head, which can sometimes block your own creativity. If you're not sure which way you want to go yet, the process of listening is where you'll likely start making decisions.

If you don't know or remember what we mean by "translational" and "transformational," glance back at chapter 3.

How to Listen

Think about the difference between hearing and listening. Hearing is mostly a passive exercise: you hear sounds, talking, and music all the time, whether you intend to or not. Listening is an active exercise, involving focus and intent. Think of the difference between saying "I hear you" (I'm receiving the words from you) and "I'm listening to you" (I'm paying attention to what you are saying). You could use similar analogies with seeing and looking.

Moreover, since listening is a focused exercise, that focus means that you can listen to the same thing in many different ways and therefore perceive it differently every time. Think about how different people might listen to a recording:

» An engineer might listen *sonically*, naturally observing the mixing choices, or the use of reverb and compression.

» A performer might listen to *execution*, noticing aspects of phrasing and tuning that the engineer wasn't listening for.

» An arranger, composer or music director might be listening *structurally*, focused on how the voices are used and what chords were chosen.

» The average listener might listen *emotionally*. He or she may not notice (or care) about any of the things that the previous three listeners did, just about how the song makes him or her feel.

When you get right down to it, the emotional aspect is probably the most important, with all the other sonic and musical aspects serving a listener's emotional experience.

Since music can be listened to in different ways with different perspectives, you'll need to listen to this piece several times. How many? Most likely more than three or four times, unless your musical memory is extremely acute. For a beginning arranger, you'd benefit from a dozen focused playbacks. Lest this appear to be overkill, here are some specifics about the elements to which you should be paying attention, and how to go about focused, attentive listening.

Holistic Listening

The first few times, just listen. Don't focus on anything; just let it wash over you. Believe it or not, your brain will absorb many aspects of the music subconsciously, and by the time you get to the more studious parts of listening, much of the basic information will be already be somewhere in your head.

This is a good time to observe the less mechanical aspects of the music: the feel, vibe, and emotions it creates. If you want to, write down a few free-association notes as you listen. When you start focusing on the musically specific aspects of the song, it can be very easy to fail to see the forest for the trees and forget what moves you (or others) about this song.

If you chose this song, remind yourself of what it was that drew you to the song. If it's new to you, make friends with it. If it's a song you don't like, do your best to approach it with a fresh mind, and imagine what it is that draws others to this song.

Surprisingly, it can be hard to listen to music this way, and sometimes the more training you have, the worse it can be. (If you have less training, you very well may have an advantage here!) Often we instinctively want to analyze and dissect things. Try to listen with the ears of a child—openly and without your mind getting in the way. Think about how easily and quickly children learn compared to adults: they don't analyze and synthesize information, they just absorb it. At this stage in the listening process, that's your goal.

If you need help to listen holistically like this, try listening while doing something else: put it on your stereo or MP3 player while you're driving, jogging, cooking, or doing laundry. The extra concentration required elsewhere will be just enough distraction to allow you to listen openly.

Everything at this point is pretty fuzzy and nonanalytical, and that's good. If you're making notes about feel, vibe, and so on, consider these a sort of "mission statement" for the arrangement: when you're stuck or need inspiration further down the road, these words may help guide you and get you back on the path.

Eventually, you might find yourself paying attention to the more musical aspects without planning to. This is usually a sign that you're ready to move on to . . .

Structural Listening

This is still big-picture listening, but now you're paying attention to actual musical things, such as . . .

Key center and key changes. The key center (or tonal center) is the "home" of the song, harmonically speaking, and all chords relate to it in fairly predictable ways. Figure out the song's key aurally (some songs avoid the tonic, so it can be tricky), any places where it temporarily shifts (say, from a major section to a minor section, or even to a new key center), and any modulations (a common device in pop music is to raise the energy near the end by raising the key a half step or more).

Musical form. This term refers to the general building blocks of the songs, such as verse, chorus, bridge, solos, interludes, intros and "outros," and the order in which they are strung together.

Harmonic rhythm. Harmonic rhythm refers to how rapidly the chords change—every few bars, every bar, several times per bar, whatever. Listen for whether the harmonic rhythm is different in verses from that in choruses and how it affects the energy of the song. You're not transcribing the chords yet, just observing how the song flows.

Basic "arrangement." This is just the general instrumentation—how and where the instruments are used. For example, perhaps there's a piano in the verse of this song, with guitars entering only at the chorus.

If you haven't been making notes yet, now's the time to start. We suggest doing it the old-fashioned, pencil-and-paper way. It's easier to doodle, scribble, and correct as you go, draw little diagrams, or however you like to work. We're not talking about ordered, taking-notes-at-a-lecture notes (it's not like there's going to be an exam on Monday), but more like sketches, point-form observations, notes in the margins, and so on.

You'll know you have gotten the most out of this stage of listening when you can:

» Make a simple road map of the song (for instance, "ABABCAB" or "verse-chorus") without having to check the recording
» Include general observations of flow and energy (first verse is soft, builds to chorus, gets really fast and big at the end)

» Know the basic instrumentation of the song
» Know the key center and any key changes

Learning the Song

If this is "learning," than what exactly have we been doing for the last several spins of the song? That's learning too, of course. But now we're talking about what is traditionally meant by "learning" the song: knowing and memorizing the melody, lyrics, and chords. We also mean learning the arrangement: knowing what the parts are and what they do.

By now, this phase will come pretty easily, since much of the information has already been absorbed. Remembering lyrics is easier when you already know that the chorus follows the verse, or that the second chorus is only half as long as the first before you get to the bridge, for example. Chord changes in contemporary music are usually fairly predictable, so if you know that you're heading into another verse and you know how fast the chords are moving, you'll be that much more likely to remember how to get there, harmonically speaking.

Up until now, you've likely been listening to the song as a whole unit, from beginning to end without stopping. Now that we're getting into the nitty-gritty, there will be plenty of play–pause–scroll back listening to small bits at a time. You'll be giving your fingers a good workout.

The Lyrics

Even though you could rely on lyric sheets or web sites, we recommend learning the lyrics. Why? Partly because they can be hard to remember and will save you time later. Also, the rhythm of the melody, and often the shape of the melody, is determined by the lyrics. Small, hard-to-remember variations in the melody are often the result of different words in verses or choruses: it's hard to remember them if you don't remember why they change. Sing them with the lyrics, and they'll probably just happen by themselves.

Need proof? Try this little exercise. Take a song you know quite well and hum the melody. Chances are the lyrics are floating around in your head. Now try consciously to block out the lyrics. Can you even do it? If you can, did you feel lost trying to remember the melody? Or, take a song you sort of know. Sing the melody. You might remember most of it, but there's a good chance that you missed a few melodic details, or variations, as you went. Why? Because they're tied to the lyrics.

» *Deke says: Although much of contemporary a cappella relies on unusual vocal sounds and extended techniques, some of the most effective moments in any arrangement are when the background parts sing lyrics. As you learn the lyrics, you'll find yourself drawn to the best phrases and most interesting words, which will help you later in your choices regarding background textures.*

If you haven't tried it, we recommend learning lyrics the old-fashioned way, by writing them out by hand. The reason is simple: it's a mnemonic device. The act of writing keeps the mind focused on the lyrics, on what you just wrote, and on what comes next. Writing by hand is a slower, more learning-friendly process than typing, and it just feels more physically connected. There's something about the pen on the paper, the shaping of each letter, the spelling of each word, that really helps commit the process to memory.

» *Dylan says: I often find that, in the time it took to write the lyrics by hand, I've pretty much memorized them. After copying them down section by section (or even line by line) as I listen to the original, I'll often test myself by writing them out from start to finish on a separate page. Do this, and you'll have them forever.*

The Melody

As you were writing down the lyrics, you also were absorbing the melody. The process of completing this learning is simple. Approach the melody in sections and follow these steps in order:

» Listen
» Sing it to yourself
» Verify, listen back, and see how close you were. Repeat these steps until you think you know what you're doing
» Then, to be really sure, sing along. Note the places you missed and do it all again

After you've nailed one section, move on to the next.

Although we're taking a fairly precise approach, it's important to note that the end goal is *not* to replicate the original performance. In many cases the melody is highly interpreted by the singer; sometimes, especially in R & B–influenced styles, the melody is so stylized that it's nearly impossible to determine what the composer really wrote. You may be listening to a highly personalized performance that is not only nearly impossible to notate, but very well might not be natural for another singer to execute. If this is the case, you'll have to use some intelligent guesswork to figure out how best to represent it. Just use your musical intuition. You'll also get some help when you hear other examples in step 3.

The point is, the melody you end up with should follow the lyrics, the melodic arc, and the basic pitches of the original. It should sound like something you could write down or play on an instrument and still recognize. If the melody on the recording is fairly simple, learn it exactly. If it sounds improvised, work out a consistent approximation.

Even if you're not an experienced arranger, if you have been a singer for a while and spent much of your life around music, you might find you have an excellent melodic memory. If so, you'll likely be able to move quickly through the process of listening to the melody, because it's already fully embedded in your inner ear.

The Chords

Since the chords move a lot more slowly than the melody and lyrics, learning them will be less time-consuming. By now you have a sense of how often the chords move and how they affect the flow of the song. Now it's just a matter of identification.

Key center. You've identified all the key centers by now, and in most Western music, the chord changes have a clear and predictable relationship to the key center. You'll mostly be dealing with I, IV, and V (the tonic, subdominant, and dominant), the classic three chords in a "three-chord wonder" pop song.

Bass line. Much of the time the bass note is the root: if the bass line is moving quickly, either as a riff-based line or as a walking bass, it probably hits the root on the strong beat of the bar and outlines the chord as it moves. Listening to root motion will tell you most of what you need to know about the chords.

Chord quality. Chords are major or minor, dominant, or augmented/diminished (much less common, but they stick out and are usually easy to spot).

Colors. This term refers to added notes, such as sevenths, ninths, elevenths, and thirteenths. These are usually only essential if the extra note is the melody and has to be "backed-up" by chords that match. But these colors are often an important part of the song's character, so it's good to know them.

It's helpful to understand the chord changes both in fixed terms (C, F, G) and in movable terms (I, IV, and V as related to the key center). You could also call these terms "letters" and "numbers." Knowing them in absolute or letter terms can be simpler overall to write ("C" rather than "the I of the new key center," which can hurt one's head after a while), but knowing the movable or number terms is great shorthand and a better way to understand the harmonic building blocks of the song. Number terms make it much easier to put a song in a new key if necessary.

» *Deke says: After memorizing countless melodies at the New England Conservatory, our next step was a rigorous ear-training regimen. We had to be able to identify intervals quickly all over the keyboard (one per second), then triads (major, minor, augmented, and diminished), and finally extended chords, from half-diminished through ♯11. It's not easy and it takes time, but the resulting increase in the strength of one's ear is worth the work. Find a professor, friend, or online program to create quizzes for you.*

The Instruments

You don't need to know what the instruments are doing to know the song, but you do if you want to know the arrangement.

Identification. What instruments are there? You probably caught all this in the structural-listening stage, and if there are some sounds you can't identify, they're probably heavily effected instruments or some form of synthesizer. It doesn't really matter what they are, so long as you are able to separate them out sonically.

Placement. Where are they? Songs often introduce variety by adding or subtracting instruments in different sections. You may also ask yourself why a particular instrument is there, which leads us to . . .

Function. What does the instrument do in musical terms—that is, what's its "job" in the song? Some instruments provide a solid harmonic backdrop, some are primarily rhythmic, while some add melodic material. Most instruments do all three to some extent, but you'll find that each one has a job to do. Learning this helps you understand how all the elements fit together into one cohesive whole.

Role. This aspect is similar to the idea of function, but it's fuzzier and more subjective. Instruments can establish mood, create dramatic tension, push the energy forward or pull it back, or provide splashes of color, humor, sunshine, or darkness. Understanding the role of the instrument is a great way to bridge the gap between the practical elements of a song or arrangement and how they are translated into emotional energy. And that can mean the difference between a good arrangement and a great one.

» *Dylan says: I often think of instruments as characters in a play. You can have a hero or heroine, a romantic lead, a sidekick, comic relief, a villain . . . the list is endless. You'll find that the instruments, like these characters, play off each other, complement each other, or stand in opposition to each other to create tension and drama. Knowing how to treat instruments (or vocal parts) like characters is possibly the greatest power of an arranger or producer, so pay close attention here!*

» *Deke says: When coaching groups, I sometimes suggest they consider their performance from the perspective of a movie director. It's a director's job to steer a moviegoer's focus to the important elements in each scene while creating a background that constantly supports and contextualizes the action. While listening, learn from the producer (who is essentially the song's director) how to similarly direct focus using sound, weaving what you learn into your arranging choices.*

This is the most exhaustive stage of the listening process. You'll know if you've made it when you can:

» Make a "lead sheet" of the song, with melody, chords, and lyrics. You don't have to do this . . . you just have to know that if someone asked you to, you could.
» Describe to someone how the instruments all fit together and roughly what they do.
» "Perform" the song with notes in front of you. If you play an instrument such as piano or guitar and can play it by ear, you could bang out a simple, round-the-campfire version.
» Play a recording of the song in your head. You may not hear every little bit, but there are no dropouts, skips, or blanks

Details and Ornamentation

Toward the end of your process of careful and focused listening, it's time to loosely catalog the specific details and "ear candy" that don't make up the fundamental parts of the song or recording, but that add spice to it and separate this version from others out there.

If you're planning a transformational arrangement, this step is less crucial, but paying attention to how little effects and sounds are used might add some insight to the overall character of your version. If your arrangement is more translational, however, it's essential that you understand how the small elements in a recording affect the overall sound and mood. These little elements are sometimes critical in fully representing the character of the original in your vocal version.

For some people, accurately replicating these little moments with voices is where much of the novelty of a cappella is found, and while music should never only be about novelty, neither should you shy away entirely from making the audience smile.

What do we mean by "little moments?"

Variations. This is a good time to notice such things as a subtle shift in an instrumental part from one section to another. You may not have noticed it in the first few listens; or maybe you did but just assumed it was intended to be the same every time. Sometimes these variations are random and possibly unimportant, just the result of what that player happened to play in that one moment. At other times they are very deliberate and give a really interesting shift to the song, one that you feel but don't necessary hear unless you're listening closely. Pay careful attention to these. More often than not, somebody put a lot of effort into creating these little changes. Noticing and using these variations (or adding your own—more on that later) will often contribute to the "repeat listenability" of an arrangement, continually offering something new to both the performer and the listener and giving your arrangement a long life.

Dynamics. Which sections are louder, softer, more energetic or less so? If you've unconsciously absorbed these already, take a moment and pull them into your conscious mind by writing them down. They'll help you make intelligent decisions later on in the arranging process.

Signature elements. These are the elements in a song that don't define the composition itself but that everybody knows and likes. This can include a particular instrumental riff, or drum groove, or horn line. Yes, the song is still the song without them, but take them away and you feel as though you cut a big piece out of the song that people might notice.

Effects and ear candy. These could include sound effects (record scratching, sampled things in hip-hop tracks, something like the jet-airplane noise in the Beatles' "Back in the USSR"), or interesting uses of studio effects such as delay, reverb, chorusing, or flanging. It can also include one-time musical things, such as an extra guitar phrase that shows up once in the second verse. It's those deliberate little choices that make you smile and appreciate a band's creativity.

Random bits. These may not be intentional, but they really put the stamp on a song. Maybe the lead singer cracks on the high note, or there's a bit of guitar feedback, or a wrong-sounding note was left in, or a there was a cymbal crash in an interesting but unexpected place. Most people don't remember them, but the real fans and nerds probably remember every single pop, click, and squeak.

At this point, you want to make notes of what these bits are and where they appear in the song. It's useful to keep track of everything for now, but you should also start mentally prioritizing them into "must-have" and "optional." By the time you get to notating on paper, you'll have a sense of how many of them you want to keep.

You don't have to have every squeak and wiggle committed to memory. But once you've gotten this far, there's a decent chance that you've done just that. By now, you can probably play a recording of the song in your head, more or less complete. Not only have you learned the song inside and out and internalized it, you have also developed the inner ear we talked about earlier. You're ready to move on to the next step.

» *Deke says: If you're an experienced arranger, let's be honest: you're not going to listen to a song a dozen times for every single commission. Truth be told, in a time crunch I've even arranged songs without ever having heard the original version, working directly from sheet music or a MIDI file. Sometimes as an arranger you're not cooking filet mignon, you're flipping burgers while people are impatiently waiting at the drive-thru window. That's OK—a really good burger is a wonderful thing. But when it's time to create something special and unique, don't forget the importance of listening.*

The Ten Steps in Action: "We Three Kings"

So I was on my way to New York to take a meeting, and needed to figure out how to make "We Three Kings" *à la* the *Mission: Impossible* theme work as a compelling musical piece, start to finish.

I started by listening to the VoxBop recording, which was clever but not in the ballpark musically, since they're a mixed quartet whose holiday album was themed as a 1940s radio hour. As such the arrangement was very vocal, with an Andrews Sisters quality that would not translate. Cute, not cool, and once the initial premise is laid out, it doesn't go anywhere else. Works well for them, but not for Straight No Chaser.

This arrangement would have to go many different places. It was time to look elsewhere for inspiration . . .

The Ten Steps in Action: "Go Tell It on the Mountain"

Since this is a traditional piece, there is no real "original version" to learn. I found a couple of standard sheet-music arrangements and made sure I knew and remembered the melody and lyrics.

But because this was to be an arrangement "in the style of" another arrangement (my own version of Stevie Wonder's "I Wish"), I went back and looked at and listened to my arrangement of "I Wish," treating it as an original version. This was an interesting exercise, since I clearly wasn't listening for the usual things: melody, bass line, form, and the like. Instead I was listening for "essence." What was it in this arrangement that the guys liked? What made them connect my arrangement to "Go Tell It"? What techniques would transfer well from one chart to another? I came up with the following commonalities:

» *Joy.* "Go Tell It" is a true gospel song: a "good news" song about spreading joy through the news of the birth of Jesus. "I Wish" is a joyful song where Stevie reminisces about his childhood days.
» *Feel and groove.* "I Wish" has a signature groove to it. "Go Tell It" is usually a bouncy gospel swing or shuffle. Not the same, but it's easy to superimpose the "I Wish" feel on to "Go Tell It," and this seemed to be what the guys wanted.
» *Voice allocation.* Cadence is four guys; the "I Wish" chart was written in six parts; Home Free is five voices. It was clear that they could hear how their own voices would work with the "I Wish" chart. I could probably use a similar voice allocation for this arrangement.

With that figured out, I could now check out other versions for some cool ideas.

CHAPTER 10

Step 3: Listening to Other Versions

If you've put so much work into learning and absorbing one version of the song, why check out others? There are plenty of good reasons.

Other Recordings

Thanks to the incredible availability of recordings online, you can easily obtain all sorts of different versions with a few clicks of the mouse. An easy way to find them is to check Wikipedia. Though not an absolutely authoritative source, Wikipedia song articles usually include information on other versions of the song, including the artists and the date of recording. iTunes is another great source: searching by song title will quickly give you sixty seconds' or so worth of a variety of versions at your fingertips. A third great source is YouTube. Some amateur musicians will upload videos of themselves performing the song. Many are unimpressive and/or uninspired, but occasionally you stumble upon a clever, effective take on a song.

Once you've found the versions you're most drawn to, download the songs and start listening. If you want to hear other a cappella arrangements, try doing a web search using the term "[song title] a cappella" and see what comes up.

What if there are twenty or more versions? A simple rule of thumb: try for at least three, preferably in contrasting styles, instrumentations, or eras.

Listening to other instrumental recordings gives you many different perspectives on the same song, like seeing different sides of a building or different characteristics of a person. As you listen to the different versions, ask yourself:

» What overarching choices have been made differently by each artist (mood, feel, etc), and how is this reflected in little decisions (instrumentation, form, and so on)?

» What do all of the versions have in common? If there are places where every artist made the same choices, it may indicate what the "soul" of the song is. (It may also indicate a lack of ingenuity, but that's another matter entirely.)

» What are you personally drawn to and why? Sometimes it's impossible to fully analyze why you prefer one musical choice or performance over another, but it is still valuable to search for the elements that likely affect your preference.

» Which musical choices reinforce the meaning of the song and which don't seem to fit? Professional musicians are not perfect, and at times they make nonsensical choices. Don't hesitate to criticize decisions that might have once made sense but have not aged well or otherwise strike your ear and/or sensibility as problematic.

Hearing a song in different ways like this also allows you to build a vocabulary of choices, opening your mind to different musical directions. If it can be done in many different ways and still sound good, it's a work of art that can transcend musical genre. That means it will probably work well as an a cappella arrangement. And after burning one version of that song into your brain, it's probably good to shake it up a little.

» *Dylan says: I once heard a band cover a Prince song in a hillbilly/bluegrass style. The classic crooners Paul Anka and Pat Boone both recorded albums of rock and heavy metal songs done in a Las Vegas big-band style. The results were crazy, unexpected . . . and fantastic.*

Listening to a cappella versions (or knowing that they're out there, even if you can't find recordings) helps as well. If a song has been covered by many other a cappella groups, there is a good chance that there's already a "translated" version out there. If you're not overly concerned about writing your own version, you could simply contact the group or arranger and ask if you can use their version. If you want to make your own arrangement, and you now know that there are many out there, they may influence your choices. If you're confident in your arranging skills, maybe you'll work extra hard to make sure that yours will become the best translation available. Or you may choose to go the other way and make sure your arrangement is creative, different, and original. Either way, it can help you raise the bar on your own work.

» *Deke says: Mouthoff, the excellent contemporary a cappella podcast produced by Dave Brown and Christopher Diaz, often features a segment called "Head to Head" where they play two groups' versions of the same song, then analyze which is more successful. Listen to their commentary for some excellent analytical insight, and then try doing it yourself.*

Sheet Music

While not as easy to obtain or to absorb, a published arrangement can provide you with immense insight. For composers, arrangers, and music directors alike, score study is an essential part of your training. It allows you to really look "under the hood" of an arrangement and see what's going on, and at your own pace. If it is published, it is also probably done reasonably well, and you can learn a few things about what works (as well as what doesn't) in arranging this piece yourself.

You also may learn a few things, both good and bad, about how the music can be notated (an issue we'll take up in the following chapter). And you'll be brushing up your score-study and reading chops, which are both useful skills for any arranger.

Take what you like; avoid what you don't. Remember, this isn't plagiarism. Chord changes aren't copyrightable, voicings are just ways of organizing notes, and you're already using someone else's work by covering an existing song! As long as you don't fully copy large sections of the arrangement, you can borrow a few techniques here and there, and it will end up as your work in the end.

MIDI Files

It's something of an outdated technology, but MIDI files are a useful time-saving tool. As an instrumental representation of melody and harmony, a MIDI file can provide an uncluttered, abstract view of the song. By just hearing notes and chords, without hearing words or specific production techniques, you can approach the song as a blank slate and imagine your own ideas overlaid on the file without being distracted by the definitive version you spent hours stuffing inside your head.

MIDI files can also be played freely at any tempo, allowing you to slow something down to get a better handle on a complicated part or to imagine the song in a wildly different tempo. You could try this with your audio recording, but it's far less useful: many of the ideas and instrumentations won't sound good at faster or slower tempi, which may unduly influence your decisions. Also, the further away you get from the original speed, the worse the sound quality gets. If it sounds bad, you're less likely to imagine good ideas on top of it.

One other nice bonus with MIDI files, if you notate by computer: if you import the file into your notation software, you'll have a rough version of some of the elements partially notated. Note entry is tedious; why do the work if it's done for you?

We'll repeat the caveat that in printed scores and MIDI, there's no guarantee that whoever created them has done so without making some mistakes. But if there are errors, by now you'll probably be able to spot them easily.

The Ten Steps in Action: "We Three Kings"

I listened to a few other versions of "We Three Kings" to get a sense of how the melody and chord structure work, but there was little value in further listening once I'd digested the song (which I already knew well), since the leap to 5/4 was going to require me to rework the melody pretty thoroughly.

I listened to the original *Mission: Impossible* theme as well as the 4/4 remake from the original movie. I made sure I had a sense of those—but in the back of my mind I knew that if the song more than hinted at *Mission: Impossible*, Atlantic would have to pay royalties on that song as well, so I needed to be able to represent the nature of the song without fully including it. Sometimes it's valuable to listen just so you know specifically what to avoid.

Once I'd focused on everything above, it was time to set aside the recordings so my brain could digest the various musical elements and clear some space so I could figure out what else to add to the song. New musical ideas were needed so that the listener would not know what was coming next.

The Ten Steps in Action: "Go Tell It on the Mountain"

I had sung this song in a number of contexts, from pickup caroling choirs to an Afrocentric classical chamber choir (Canada's excellent Nathaniel Dett Chorale). I looked through the various charts I had from these different ensembles. Most choral versions were very standard and didn't offer much in the way of interesting ideas.

The version I sang in the NDC, though very different from what I was doing, was more creative in that it had a "composed" introduction and ending and an active use of background vocals against a soprano solo. It also had a few more verses than the other versions, which was interesting to note. In traditional pieces, new verses may be added, subtracted, or sung in a different order. This is another very good reason to look at other versions: you want to make sure you know the whole story!

CHAPTER 11

Step 4: Form and Conceptualization

You've chosen a song and listened to it to the point that it's fully internalized. Now you've got some good ideas about your desired focus and direction for the song, and you're eager to dive into the notes. But before you start making decisions about chord voicings, you'd do well to create a blueprint.

Writing an arrangement is not unlike erecting a building. The melody line, bass line, and BGs are different building materials, and in the end they're all that will remain. However, without a blueprint in advance to determine the size and shape of the various sections of your building, you might find yourself with a chorus that's too heavy and not supported by the overall form, or too many verses and not enough structure to support them all.

Conceptualization

Just as great architecture is a careful balance of art and science, so conceptualization is a similar combination of creativity and logistics. Considering the overall form, shape, and direction your arrangement will take will help inform more specific decisions you'll make later in the process, such as those concerning harmonic complexity and texture. To extend the analogy, this is where you decide whether your building is going to be a beach house, a cathedral, or a bungalow. There are a number of factors to consider.

Translation or Transformation

Your arrangement will very likely have aspects of both translation and transformation, but in the conception stage, you'll likely be leaning more heavily toward one or the other. Are you striving for a roughly straightforward representation of the song as most listeners know it, a true and faithful (and hopefully very cool) rendition of the original? Or are you wanting to take the song in a different direction, crafting the melody and harmony into something new that will result in a fresh musical statement? Of course both of these goals are points on the same continuum, and you'll no doubt end up somewhere between the most extreme examples of each; but to start you'll probably benefit from having one or the other in mind as a general target.

Your Ensemble

Arrangement style can influence voice allocation; the reverse is also true. If you're writing for a specific group, the voices at your disposal may take your arrangement in specific directions before you decide on your first note. The number of voices you have to work with, each individual's stylistic fluency and comfort, their vocal ranges, and their general musical proficiency will all result in boundaries, loose and firm, generous and narrow, within which your choices must be made. You disregard a group's strengths and abilities at your own peril; occasionally stretching a group can result in some wonderful moments, but keeping them outside their comfort zone for too long is a recipe for failure.

If you're arranging as an exercise, for no one in particular, you may wish to go completely to town with the vocal orchestration. Or you may decide to be strategic, keeping the number of voices and ranges fairly standard, for a chart that can be performed effectively over time by a wide range of groups.

From That to This

There's a good chance that, over many listenings, you found yourself unconsciously grouping real instruments into voice parts, however undefined they might be. This procedure helps clarify the translation-versus-transformation question: if you found yourself doing this quite a bit, you may be leaning toward translation. If you glossed over some instrumental details and focused on mood and atmosphere, you may be leaning toward transformation.

» *Deke says: In remembering that all music is communication, you need to consider what is being said, who is saying it, and how it is being said. Analogy: if an arrangement is a speech, you should consider what the you want the speech to say, the audience for whom it is intended, your ability to believably convey the message, and so on. I urge you to think of the overall emotion and message and to make your musical choices with the larger purpose in mind.*

In a very general way, you may start equating sounds to voices; as you do, you may be getting a sense of what your voice allocation will be or how it's going to approach these sounds. If this is happening, then your conceptualization is becoming clear. You don't need to know all the answers yet, since your ideas may evolve and even change once you get to the notation stage.

Decide on the Form

It's possible you may choose to keep the song form as is. Pop songs are designed to grab your attention right away, hold it, and let it go when the song is over. With the advent of recording technology, the pop song evolved into a three- to three-and-a-half-minute masterpiece, simple on the surface but meticulously crafted underneath (though the roots of this development can be found even earlier, in nineteenth-century sheet music and even classical art song). Originally this time frame was determined by the medium: it was the perfect length for 78 rpm phonograph discs, and later for 45s. This remained the standard long after it was necessary: cultural norms (and dwindling attention spans) keep the three-minute hit alive today.

If the form works as is, fantastic. Your job is done. On to the next step!

But hold on. There are still some things to consider.

We also mentioned that a cappella music is an especially intense, heightened listening experience. The ear naturally gravitates to the sound of the human voice. In a band, there's likely one voice (or maybe a few) to grab your attention. In a cappella music, it's *all* voices: even if the vocal parts are passive and repetitive, you'll still be drawn to them.

This presents two important considerations for the a cappella arranger. First, if the listener's attention is more likely to be spread around when listening, then the arranger has to keep the vocal parts at least somewhat interesting. A passive, droning keyboard part fades into a background as a subconscious texture. A vocal part that does the same thing could end up being annoying. At the same time, the arranger has to keep the listener's focus on the main melody and words. A delicate balancing act, for sure.

All this means that a cappella music demands more of the listener, and the listener can get fatigued that much faster. A two-minute song can feel like four, our three-minute hit can feel like five, and a five-minute song can feel interminable.

» *Dylan says: It's embarrassing to admit, but I'm a terrible listener: I get bored far too easily. However, it certainly helps in the arranging and form-editing process. I never want the listener to get as bored as I do, so I make sure every moment counts!*

Compressing the Form

This is not to say that every song needs a hatchet job to work in the a cappella world. But it does mean that it's worth taking a good, hard listen to your song, imagining the balancing act and intense listener experience, and asking yourself if anything needs changing.

Here are a few examples of places where you might want to cut.

Instrumental solos. Some work when they're sung, while others sound silly or cheesy. Sometimes a solo is a signature part of the song (remember our notes from step 2)—you'll incite rebellion if you remove it. It's interesting that most pop music today rarely contains instrumental solos, since they used to be rather commonplace. Blame our dwindling attention span. Or maybe they're stuffing more lyrical and melodic material in those three and a half minutes.

Repeated sections. It's been said before. Maybe it needs to be said again, or maybe it needs to be said differently. Or maybe once is enough, and the repeat should be cut. Or maybe we should say it again: cut the repeat. A repeat isn't necessary. People get the point. Don't repeat yourself again. Because repetition often isn't necessary. Or maybe you're the kind of person who likes extra repeats, so we'll say it yet again: cut the extra repeat. Are we making sense?

That extra verse. If it's part of the story, chopping out a verse might be like chopping off a limb. But if the piece feels long and the verse doesn't really add much to the song (or if you don't like the lyrics for some reason), cut it loose.

Long endings and fadeouts. These can feel gratuitous or unnecessary, especially if the arrangement is intended for live use. Live fadeouts in particular are just about the single most awkward arranging choice possible.

Does it feel weird to put the knife to someone else's song? It's done all the time, often by the artists (or their production team) themselves. It's not uncommon to have an "album mix" (a longer version) and a "radio mix" (a shorter one). On radio, long endings and fadeouts are rarely heard to the end before the DJ comes on or the next song starts; sometimes the song is cut off as soon as the final chorus is done. You're the arranger here: don't be afraid to make bold choices.

A simple exercise is to sing through the song, omitting the sections you thought you wanted to remove. If you use recording software, you can try the "radio edit" method mentioned earlier. If unsure, arrange more and bring it all to your group, with an eye toward trimming sections if the arrangement feels long.

» *Deke says: With sometimes as little as ninety seconds in which to present an entire song, The Sing Off has taught me to wield a scalpel brutally. If you're not entirely sure how a song can be successful in less than three minutes, I suggest you visit YouTube or Hulu and view some of the performances. There is great value in leaving an audience wanting more, as they'll either watch/listen again or, better yet, look for more music by your group.*

Expanding the Form

Occasionally some songs, such as jazz standards, will feel too short on their own and need to be expanded to feel like a full song. In other cases the song may be a nice, compact little story, but you want to create a longer experience. If you listen to a song and find yourself saying, "But it's over before it starts! I want more!," it may be worth expanding. Here are some ways you can do so.

Extended introduction. If the song has a real sense of atmosphere about it, maybe you want to set the mood and invite the audience into an aural space you create for them. You could lengthen the introduction, perhaps by layering the voices in every few bars. The soloist could choose to improvise. Or an extended introduction could serve as a performance device over which someone can introduce the song, the soloist, or the group, or give a general message such as "This is our last song."

Added solo section or interlude. If the original song seems to barrel from section to section, you can work in some breathing room by adding a short interlude between sections, or possibly a vocal or group solo section. You can try this anywhere. The most common place is probably after the bridge (if your song has one); or it could come after a chorus, before another verse, or in between two back-to-back verses. It's unlikely that you'll insert one before a chorus: whatever section precedes the chorus is usually designed to set it up. Take that away and you risk losing the energy of the chorus, which is usually the heart of the song.

Here's another interesting take on the idea of adding an interlude: inserting a piece of another song. This works particularly well in a song with a relatively uninteresting form (say, verse and choruses but no bridge, or even a song that's only verses). Adding the new piece does what a bridge normally does in a song: takes you somewhere else for a breath of fresh air and brings you back.

This technique works best if there is a clear connection between the "inserted" piece and the rest of the song. The new piece might be from the same artist or the same style of music, but often the best connection comes from the lyrics. In this example below, we see the third verse of the Beatles' classic "Let It Be," with the lyrics "and when the night is cloudy, there is still a light that shines on me." The inserted piece comes from the spiritual "This Little Light of Mine (I'm Gonna Let It Shine)." The lyric and sentiment clearly match the Beatles' song, and it works well in the same key, tempo, and time feel.

Repeated verse or chorus. If there's an important message, it may be worth saying again, either with a repeated chorus or a reprise of a verse. Many songs do this already: if yours doesn't, you could always give it a try.

If you feel a strong urge to expand the form, follow your instincts. You'll get a feel for whether or not it works by the time you get to steps 9 and 10 (if not earlier, as you're writing the actual parts). If it doesn't work, go back to the original form (or shorten it).

Let It Be

Arrangement by
Deke Sharon

Words and Music by
John Lennon and Paul McCartney

Switching Things Around

Altering form can be a powerful tool. It can alter the message of the song or put more emphasis on a certain lyric. It can be an interesting change for the audience: they hear what they know, but in a different way. Putting the chorus first can make a bold "thesis statement" for a song, getting straight to the point instead of having a gradual lead-up. There are no real conventions here, so just experiment. Many choices will clearly not work, but some may make you say "Hmmmmm," or, better yet, "Aha!"

Exercises

» Analyze a dozen of your favorite songs, breaking them into intro, verse, chorus, bridge, and so on. How does the overall flow of the song affect your listening experience? Can you edit the song into a form that you prefer?

» Although most popular songs now are a variation on the verse–chorus–bridge structure, fifty years ago "song form" (AABA) was very common (think of "Somewhere Over the Rainbow"), and before that the blues and AAA (folk structure—heard in "Bridge over Troubled Water," for instance). When listening to the radio during the day, analyze each song's structure, searching for the most uncommon forms.

The Ten Steps in Action: "We Three Kings"

The form of "We Three Kings" is simple:

Verse 1 ("We three kings . . .")
Chorus ("star of wonder")
Verse 2 (gold)
Chorus
Verse 3 (frankincense)
Chorus
Verse 4 (myrrh)
Chorus
Verse 5 (behold, hallelujah)
Chorus

No bridge, no other musical elements. I knew that if I stuck to this form without variation, things would get boring. It might be fun to sing to while caroling, but if this was going to work as a compelling performance piece, I knew some trimming was needed, and perhaps some addition as well.

First of all, I needed an intro. Something short, to establish the *Mission: Impossible* feel (without exactly quoting the *Mission: Impossible* theme), and it would be great to start with the signature match lighting and violin tremolo. Two times through the bass figure should be sufficient before launching into the chorus—just enough to establish the sound and feel, and to give the upper voices a chance to build a tension-filled chord.

Verse 1 should be straightforward, establishing the core premise. I figured that since it's about three kings, the song should have three different soloists, singing the first verse together in three-part parallel harmony.

Verse 2 would be the first king, and we should come out of the gate swinging with a high tenor.

Verse 3 will need some variety at this point. How about having a bass sing this verse? Kings tend to be stately, and those roles often require a bass in operas and musicals, so it should work.

But wait—at this point it's clear that I'll have three verses in 5/4, which will build tension; but keeping the entire song in 5/4 will get old. How about a different feel in the choruses? Something to release the tension and allow the song to settle into a warm, approachable groove. The original is in 3, but a 3/4 feel would be too lilting. Perhaps a 6/8, finger-snapping, soul-pop, Boyz II Men feel for the chorus? Works comfortably with the melody, works with three-part harmony (Boyz II Men is all about parallel harmony in the choruses), and gives the guys a chance to sound cool so that not everything is zany and theatrical.

Verse 4: by this point I feel as though the 5/4 has done its job. We had a trio verse, a high tenor verse, and a low bass verse. There's nothing left to do here, and moreover, it would be nice to really go in a different direction.

There are many musical styles that could be pasted in here, telling the musical story of a king from somewhere exotic. But they had been silly long enough in this song, and we needed some more cool to balance it out. So what's the coolest style of music I could fit in here? Reggae! We've had tension from the other two kings, so let's go for a laid-back feel from the king that shows up last. When you see the three kings portrayed, one is usually African. If we're using reggae, why not have our third king come from Jamaica?

And the subsequent chorus? No need to go back to the 6/8 feel—let's keep the reggae feel, as if, once he enters the stable, everyone joins his party.

Verse 5? Don't need it, and another chorus would be too much. Wrap up with a couple of repetitions at the end, perhaps a IV–I plagal ("Amen") cadence with a gospel feel, and we're set with a form that jumps from feel to feel and takes a left turn at the end, leaving us with a smile on our face.

You might be wondering why I didn't use a different musical style for every verse and chorus. I considered it, but it struck me that all those changes could leave the audience with whiplash. I wanted this arrangement to be about the group, not about myself, and shifting styles constantly would draw too much attention to the arrangement, stealing focus from the performance. Their version of "The Twelve Days of Christmas" worked in part because even though the song jumps the rails and heads off in different directions, it returns to the song's core to reset periodically before going off on a final tangent from which it never returns. I figured going with a similar formula would work here as well.

I've settled on a core form, with lots of general ideas, but nothing's set in stone yet. Time to get to work.

The Ten Steps in Action: "Go Tell It on the Mountain"

The general form of "Go Tell It" is equally simple:

> Chorus ("Go tell it . . .")
> Verse 1
> Chorus
> Verse 2
> Chorus

. . . and so on, ending with the chorus. The big question mark is the number of verses: when I checked out other versions in the previous step, I discovered that there are at least five verses. Most versions used three or four and sang them in just about any order. How do you make sense of it?

The good news is that each of the verses is a four-line mini-story, more or less complete on its own—unlike many songs, which build their story verse by verse. This means you can freely add, switch, or subtract verses without ruining the song. (Try that with "We Three Kings" and you might end up snubbing one of the kings—not a great idea.)

My first decision was to choose the verses I wanted to use. Since this song was being done in a modern jazz/funk context, my instincts told me to use three verses—pretty average for a contemporary song. I then chose my favorites. The central theme of the song is basically "Jesus is born. Hooray! Tell everyone!," and I chose verses that I thought supported the story best.

The Verses I Kept

Verse 1. "While shepherds all were watching . . .": I like this one, and it sets up the basic story.

Verse 2. "In a lowly manger . . .": This is a logical progression from the shepherds watching and describes the "main event."

Verse 3. "When I was a seeker . . .": There are a couple of verses told from the perspective of the storyteller, and this is the one I liked best. It also makes a nice concluding statement to the song ("I asked the Lord to help me, and He showed me the way"), whereas many of the other verses leave the story feeling half finished.

The Verses I Cut

There's a second verse about the shepherds, but it didn't advance the story much, so I let it go.

There's another verse from the storyteller's perspective—"The Lord made me a watchman . . ."—which not only makes a similar point to "When I was a seeker," but also has a little too much of an "Onward, Christian Soldiers" feel to it. Though this song is clearly Christian in nature, as far as possible I like to keep holiday songs accessible to everyone. This verse didn't really add anything to the overall story.

I now have three verses and four choruses (one to start, one to end). Simply flip-flopping between verses and choruses felt uninteresting to me. So I decided to flesh out the form by:

1. *Adding an eight-bar intro.* The intro would set up the groove and allow the piece to jump out of the gate with some real energy.
2. *Adding a little buffer material between the choruses and the verses.* This could be four to eight bars, depending on how quickly we wanted to advance to the next verse. The song has no bridge or other sections, and I didn't feel like adding an instrumental solo or inserting a section from another song. Instead, I'd reprise the eight-bar intro groove and step up the energy with a half-step-up key change—a common device in pop music.
3. *Adding some funky extra jam material at the end.* The chorus never felt like a strong ending to me. Instead, we'd "go to church," stepping up one more level of energy to wrap up the song with a bang.
4. *Building up suspense before going to church.* I'd throw in a drum solo featurette over a bass line–vocal motif. This would act like the windup to a baseball pitch, building up tension until we let loose with the funk at the end.

I now had all the elements in place, sung them through in my head, and liked the rough form I had come up with. A chorus–verse–chorus hymn now had a real sense of flow and development—perfect for the "showstopping" vibe the guys wanted.

CHAPTER 12

Step 5: Preparing Your Materials

You've chosen a song and listened to several versions. You've got a general creative direction and you've settled on a form. Time to get writing, or recording, or singing.

The first step: getting your materials together and set up. This varies depending on the arrangement style you choose, as we described in chapter 2.

By Ear

If you're arranging by ear, getting your materials together is easy: get your singers in one room (sometimes easier said than done). Treat the session like a rehearsal: choose a suitably quiet location, ideally with a piano, keyboard, or other harmonic instrument. Give yourselves a reasonable amount of time, at least an hour.

When arranging by ear, it's best to start and finish in one session if possible: ideas are built on top of one another, and it can be hard to restart the creative process if you stop. Short breaks are fine, but if you find yourself picking up where you left off a week before, you'll likely spend half your time just remembering your parts and getting back into the creative groove.

"By ear" doesn't mean "with nothing written down." All the group members should bring writing materials and take notes as they go along. These notes may include actual notes on staves, letter names, road maps, or whatever squiggles work for each singer. In addition, everyone should bring a recording device to sing his or her own part to himself or herself (voice memo functions on cell phones work well); you'll also need to make sure someone brings a recording device for the whole group. You can use this to sing the song from beginning to end, to sing individual sections once they've been worked out, and to sing difficult passages slowly for easier remembering and learning down the road.

» *Deke says: When directing groups at Disneyworld (American Vybe) and Disneyland (Groove 66), the single item I insisted everyone have was some kind of recording device. New group members would often be responsible for twenty to thirty new songs a week, and no matter how experienced and talented they were, they needed those recordings to remember their parts and drill themselves while driving to work each day. It's easier to learn music via sheet music (if you're able), but nothing beats a recording when it's time for repetition.*

The process for small groups is somewhat different from the one for large groups; they require different levels of structure. If yours is a small group, with one or two singers on a part, and everyone's role is fairly well defined (say, a four-part SATB group), then the process can be more organic. There may be one "lead arranger" (although in a small group this isn't necessary) who gives ideas of who does what in general terms, such as, "You be the guitar, you sing lead, and I'll cover the piano," and the singers work out the details themselves. In a simple doo-wop style of arrangement, this can be as easy as one lead and one bass, with the other few singers covering triadic harmonies: this person high, that one middle, the other one low. In such a case, the notes will almost take care of themselves.

For a larger group such as a collegiate ensemble or community choir, arranging by ear is a little more difficult and requires more structure. You may want to come to the session more prepared, with general ideas of what roles each part will play. Work in partnership with the director to teach parts to the sections or to facilitate the sections' finding the parts themselves. It may be useful to have section leads who work out the part on behalf of the entire section. Rather than having everyone record his or her own part, you or the director can do it. Have the sections sing their parts individually as they learn them, and record the song in pieces. Or have them sing the song, or the various pieces, as an ensemble. If you walk over to the bass section and stick the recording device in their faces, you'll get a bass-heavy recording of the song section. Do the same with each part.

» *Deke says: People's time is precious. As much fun as it is to create an arrangement in a room with lots of people, it's usually far more efficient to get a small group together, one per part, and then, once you have an arrangement figured out, teach it to the entire group. The exception can be a Bobby McFerrin–style circle song, where parts are improvised and handed to groups in real time. There are some amazing videos of him doing this, including the season one finale of The Sing-Off, where he improvised on live television in front of 9 million people. Now that's gutsy arranging.*

When the arranging session is over, you should have some sort of record of the arrangement: nothing is more frustrating than coming back next week and hearing, "How does my part go?" and "Wait, you're singing my note!" If yours is a small group, your singers will have their individual notes plus your full-group recording. If it's a larger group, you'll have the various voice parts recorded. But this means nothing if the singers don't have access to them. So compile the recordings into one rehearsal package, include a page or two of notes and road-map information, and e-mail it to everyone. Make sure the notes and recordings are clear and easy to understand: imagine that someone has to come in and learn the song from the notes and recordings alone, without having been at the arranging session. After all, chances are someone missed the rehearsal.

One other option: find someone who can transcribe the arrangement and bring sheet music to the next rehearsal (provided your group reads music).

Arranging through Recording

If you're arranging through recording, "getting your materials together" means creating a song file, making sure your mic and hardware are up and running, and laying out tracks in your recording software. You could just make new tracks as you go, but laying them out in advance is a better way to go.

» Track layout helps you imagine part allocation, even if only vaguely and subconsciously.
» Once you really start singing, you'll want to lay stuff down immediately as you think of it. Having to stop to create new tracks not only can slow down your process, but you might forget an idea while you're hassling with mouse clicks and file management.
» If you want to change a part, you'll probably be changing the parts around it as well. You need to know where they are, and if everything is clearly laid out you can record seven parts in the second chorus and know where the second alto's line goes without a moment's thought.
» Trying to make sense of a million disorganized snippets and tracks after the fact can be a frustrating experience. This isn't a studio recording: eventually, you'll have real singers singing these parts in real time. You can spend a little time organizing in advance, or a bunch of time on the back end.

Flexible organization is the key here. The good news is that audio recording tracks are like staves on a score: they indicate what one singer is doing in real time. You can organize your "recording score" in a couple of different ways:

Score style: This follows the general rules of notation: the solo line on goes on top, any duet and/or trio parts and "ear candy" parts next, then the BGs, and last of all the bass.

Functionality/engineer style: Engineers tend to organize tracks from the bottom up. This is basically the reverse of score style: drums or bass first, next the lower parts, then the upper parts, and the solo last. In addition, if your chart is based on instrumental representation, you could arrange your tracks as "guitar 1/2/3" and then translate them into vocal parts once the arrangement is done—or even leave them as is.

A notated score allows for multiple parts on a staff and/or *divisi*, while a recording track only allows one voice at a time. Keep a number of spare tracks at the ready and in order (soprano 1, soprano 1a, soprano 2, soprano 2a, and so on) so that you're free to expand the number of parts should you desire.

Handwritten Notation

If you're writing by hand, you'll want to put more effort into organizing your score. The details of how to do this are found in chapter 1. Since it's harder to change a handwritten score as you go, you may want to be further along in your overall conception of the parts and their functions and allocations. If you are writing for a fixed number of voices or a standard format such as SATB, you can probably go ahead and lay out the number of staves. If your voice allocation is going to be determined by how the arrangement develops, you might want to have a separate pad of staff paper to jot down preliminary ideas or a few scraps of rough voicings before committing to a staff order. Or you can set some ground-rules for yourself—for instance, "a maximum of three voices for guitars"—and work within those parameters.

» *Dylan says: Surprisingly enough, working within parameters can be more liberating than constricting! When arranging for the last Nylons record I decided that, even though I could have an infinite number of parts for any arrangement, I would decide on a fixed number (usually from five to eight) and stay within it. It helped me to avoid getting drowned in options and choices, pointless divisi (see below), and other such issues, and I could focus on writing and moving forward—important when you're trying to write a dozen enduring, masterpiece-quality arrangements in a short time.*

Computer Notation

Preparation for computer notation follows most of the same process as that for notating by hand, with the following exceptions:

» Staves can be added or subtracted at will, so you don't need to lock in to a particular number of staves right away. As with track layout when arranging by recording, you don't want to spend much time with logistics in the midst of the creative process, so you'd do well to create more than you need, then delete the extra ones later.

» Most notation programs have a continuous scroll view of some sort. You'll probably want to do much of your work in this view and format your pages when the writing is done.

» Even with computer notation, it's often helpful to keep some good old staff paper nearby to scribble out ideas. You could keep the computer notation as your working copy and make rough notes on paper.

» *Deke says: While Ed Boyer and I were producing the Committed album, I noticed he was scribbling a series of letters on a piece of paper. When asked he showed me a series of note names in a large grid (6 × 6, for example) that indicated which chord factors he was looking to have each member of Committed sing during the next six chords. Ed has two college degrees, directed the Tufts Beelzebubs for several years, and has multiple gold records for his arrangements on Glee. Nonetheless, he relies on a simple nonstandard notational system when figuring out a short chord progression.*

While we're on the subject of notation, let's talk about . . .

The Great Commandments of Music Notation

This is not a crash course in notation theory or how to write key signatures and rhythms properly. We're assuming you know how to do that, and if you need some brushing up, the resources at the back will help. We're talking about practical considerations, based on thousands of hours reading well-notated (and awfully notated) charts.

Put another way, this section is about "notation etiquette," which you should follow in order to make sure your singers don't suffer brain damage from trying to read your chart. Remember, the harder your arrangement is to figure out, the longer it will take to learn and, consequently, the less time they'll have to perfect it.

We're going into some specifics here, and since we haven't written a note yet, it may at first feel like we're putting the cart before the horse. But forewarned is forearmed. Considering these now, instead of being forced to consider them at the refinement stage, will save you a lot of headaches and earn you better karma in the end.

Thou Shalt Avoid the Road Map

We arrangers spend a lot of time in our own heads, and much of that time is spent deep inside one song at a time. By the time you've spent dozens of hours with this one song, you know it backward and forward. Many of the sections (for example, the choruses) are the same, maybe with a few small variations. So you hand your singers a two-page chart with a few well-notated musical sections and a list of instructions like this:

» *Verse–Chorus–Bridge (with a variation)–Chorus (only half)–Verse–Verse(basses only)– Solo–Interlude–Verse (in the new key)*

Should be easy, right?

Wrong.

It's not that you're lazy; it's just that you figure that fewer dots on paper equals a more practical way of expressing a chart. But that's only true if you know the chart itself backward and forward, when in fact these folks have never seen it before. A road map seems like a convenience to you, but it's a headache for those who don't know the song. Even if one section is the same as another, you may want to write it out again.

This goes back to step 4. Choosing your form and how to express that form in music notation can be more of an art than a science. Traditional music notation uses three ways of jumping back to a section: repeat dots (do the same section again), *da capo* (from the beginning), and *dal segno* (from the sign). There are also two ways to jump forward or end: mark a section as *Fine* (meaning "end here") or "to Coda" (which indicates that the singer should jump to the end section). Old as this system is, it represents a good limitation for how many times you can jump around inside a chart. If you can't express it clearly with these, rewrite (or, if using computer notation, copy and paste) a section if necessary. A good rule of thumb is: could the group read this without me there? Do I have to explain it? If the answers are "no" and "yes," respectively, write it differently.

But no rule is without an exception. If your arrangement is something simple that can be taught by rote and has a small number of repeating sections (say, two or three), a road map can work well, especially in conjunction with a director's hand signals or cues for each section.

» *Deke says: When directing the Bubs, I would sometimes bring the group what became known as a "one-pager"—an entire arrangement on a single page of notation paper (handwritten, since back then computer notation programs were not yet very useful): no solo, eight measures of verse, eight measures of chorus, BGs written three to a staff. Not pretty, but not unlike Twitter in that there's a subtle science in saying a lot in a small space. Moreover, there is great satisfaction in learning an arrangement in thirty minutes, and in having, after a few tweaks, something for your next show within an hour. Yes, I know, I was breaking all the commandments. Sometimes college is all about rebellion.*

Thou Shalt Not Cluster

You've got three parts that always do the same thing together (say, homophonic vocal BGs or an instrumental part). Naturally, you put them on the same staff with one beam, and it looks easy and clean as a whole. Take a look at this example:

You can see the triads and chords clearly, and even play them on the piano. That's good, right?

Now try to read the middle part. Are your eyes crossed yet?

» *Dylan says: I've spent more time than I care to recall reading badly written arrangements, connecting the dots with a pencil on my score, never sure if I'm singing the right part or not. You've just made your middle singers feel like middle children in a family: neither here nor there, unsure of their place in the scheme of things.*

Fortunately, this is easy to fix: use two sets of beams, and always attach the middle notes to either the top or bottom. If you have more than three parts, use two staves.

No, your chart isn't as simple-looking with the two sets of beams, but everyone knows what they're doing—and that's more important. You can also see the individual voice movement a little better.

Thou Shalt Not Staff Jump

OK, we'll modify this: "Thou shalt minimize thy staff jumping." In a chart with multiple textures but a fixed number of voice parts, it may very well happen. You may wish to "borrow" a part for a section; for example, you may want the first altos (who were singing the top line of a guitar part) to join the sopranos in the chorus to sing a "fly-honey" vocal part. You *could* give the first altos a separate staff, but maybe in this case they'll have an easier time of reading and learning the piece if they can see how their parts function relative to each other on the page:

If that's the case, go for it. If you are going to have a part jump staves, consider the following:

» *Do it by song section or by phrase.* You're asking your singers to abruptly switch gears, both visually on the page and musically with their phrasing. Doing this for a bar or two can feel and sound awkward and jumpy—and furthermore, it can look ugly on the page. Go section by section and the result will look, feel, and sound smooth and logical. In the case above, it makes sense. When the sopranos sing the real words instead of "oo"s, the altos join in.

» *Make it easy and consistent.* In our example, the altos were guitars in one section, fly-honeys in the next, then guitars again—nice and easy to remember and to sing. If you have them singing guitars, then singing fly-honeys with the sopranos, then doubling tuba with the basses, the result will sound jumpy.

The altos will not have any sonic identity and will spend the rest of the concert in a daze, not knowing who they really are.

» *Don't ask everyone to staff jump.* If it looks weird on the page, it may sound weird in real life. Try to limit any staff jumping to one part, or at least one part at a time.

If you really want this sort of jumping around, consider adding a separate "floater" part that catches everything . . . *and give them their own staff.*

Thou Shalt Avoid Pointless Divisi

This one's up for debate, but it's a personal pet peeve of ours: one-note *divisi* parts that come and go. This is usually the result of an arranger working through the music, writing down the sounds he or she hears in his or her head, instead of working though the voices, imagining the music being sung by a group. The former is not wrong, but the latter is invariably more practical.

Think about the textures you want as sung by a smallish ensemble with only one or two voices per part. Voice additions and subtractions in a small group are the most obvious, and the popping in and out of extra voices can disturb the texture. There's a good chance that in the chord with the *divisi*, there's a note (or two) doubled. If it's the *divisi* note, it's probably unnecessary. If the *divisi* is adding a color that you really want to keep, try revoicing the chord with the existing parts to include that color, even it means a little tweaking of the parts before and after to accommodate. On the other hand, you may want a little spot where the texture thickens for just a moment, then goes back. If that's your intention, go for it.

The upper *divisi* in the third bar of the alto just doubles the soprano, and the second *divisi*, the A on the last bar, while it isn't hurting anyone, just doubles the root in an otherwise nicely balanced chord. Pointless!

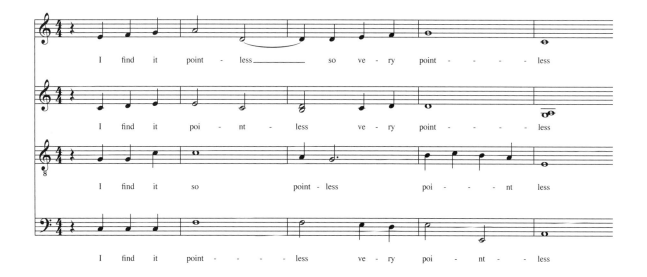

A good rule of thumb with *divisi* that occur only occasionally is that they should add something nice but still remain optional: the chord should sound functional without it. If you have a four-part chart where the two *divisi* in ten pages are absolutely crucial, then it's not a four-part chart: it's five parts, with a lot of redundant doubling. Either revoice those two chords so that they can be sung without the *divisi* if necessary, or go ahead and use that "necessary" fifth voice to full advantage and fill out your chart a bit more.

This all points to the larger concept of vocal efficiency—of making the most out of the voices you have. Vocal efficiency isn't always necessary, but it's a great skill to have, and an essential one when writing for smaller ensembles (more on that later in the book). Vocal efficiency often translates into better and more universally singable charts. So if you have *divisi* showing up here and there, make sure they count.

» *Deke says: When I took over as music director of the Beelzebubs, divisi in arrangements made me crazy. One guy has to miss a concert because he has an exam the next day, and you can't remember if you have a third in the chord in m. 23. As a result, I found myself avoiding divisi like the plague, so I always knew that in a eight-part arrangement, if I had each of the parts covered, we'd be safe from start to finish.*

Thou Shalt Avoid Pointless Variation

Little frustrates singers more than a lack of logic within an arrangement. Variations are essential, but make them for a reason. We've seen and worked with too many arrangements that never repeat so much as a measure, with insignificant differences from verse to verse, rendering the chart almost impossible to memorize. If you're going to have a section be different, make it different for a reason in a way that's easy to remember. And if there's no need to change something, don't! You can have ten logical arrangements in your repertoire or five illogical ones; they take the same amount of time to learn and memorize.

Put it this way: your singers (not you—they!) should be able to understand a variation and explain it in a sentence. If they don't seem to get it, explain why you included that variation. If you don't know or remember why, scrap it: it clearly wasn't important. If you explain it and it still doesn't stick, consider the possibility that what seems important to you, the arranger, doesn't have as much significance to the performer—and therefore even less to the listener. This may be a place where the arranger needs to get out of the way and let the music do the work.

Thou Shalt Mark Thy Sections Such That They May Be Easily Read

Pop music is, more often than not, very predictable in form. Verses and choruses are usually eight, sixteen, or thirty-two bars long; vocal phrases are usually two to four bars long. This makes it easy to be considerate when notating sections. Wherever possible, start verses, choruses, or other sections on a new page, especially if you have to flip back to them. Try to notate your bar lines as they are phrased. If your song is in two- or four-bar phrases, go for four bars per line. If it's in three-bar phrases, try three bars per line. If the phrases are an odd number of measures (say, five), try five bars per line, or two plus three. Think of the phrases as musical paragraphs: if you start a new idea at the beginning of the line or page, it's much easier not only to read, but also to find a specific bar or section when rehearsing. Those little bits of time the singers spend hunting for the start of a phrase or section can really add up, and the easier you make it for them, the better.

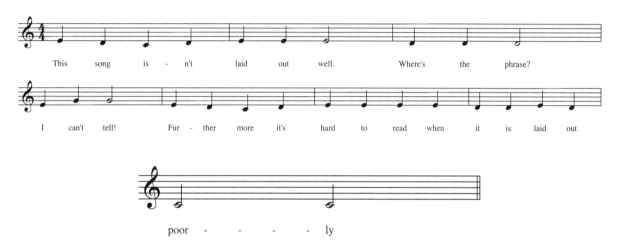

When in Doubt, Write It Out

This general suggestion guides many of the others. It is natural to imagine that fewer notes and pages would make a chart look easier, and that handing your choir a long chart might seem intimidating. However, reading through a chart involves three simultaneous processes: singing the notes and words on the page, interpreting expressive information such as dynamics and articulation, and decoding nonmusical information, such as navigating the form or reading such instructions as "1st time only." Jamming your chart with a lot of simultaneous instructions can make it very hard for the singer to read.

This is a place for judgment calls. A classic example: a second verse that is a variation of the first. In a general sense, it's the same: same melody, same chord changes. Now think again, concentrating on the differences rather than the similarities. You discover that:

» The words are different, so the rhythms and maybe a couple of the notes of melody have changed slightly.
» You've decided to add a rhythmic variation to the BGs.
» Verse 1 went to the chorus, but verse 2 goes somewhere else.

On their own, any of these changes might be explained with a repeat sign and a couple of written instructions. Add them up, and it's just too confusing. It may feel the same musically, but it's different enough to warrant being written out.

Another example: a chorus that's sung the same way each time but goes somewhere new each time. If you sing this chorus twice, you can use the standard "D.S. al Coda" to get you coming back to the chorus and then jumping ahead to the next section on the second go-round. If it happens more often than that, you could use written instructions: instead of "D.S. al Coda," you write "back to m. X" (the chorus); then, at the end of the chorus, write "first time: go to m. Y; second time: go to m. Z." If you've laid out your chart nicely and your sections start on new pages, you can use page numbers, which are easier to find, instead of bar numbers. But more often than not, it's just easier to read the chart through, rewriting the chorus. Bottom line: if you're not sure, go ahead and write it out. Your singers will thank you in the end.

The Ten Steps in Action: "We Three Kings"

I work in Finale, so I cracked open my computer and started making decisions.

I knew these guys had mixed feelings about vocal percussion, and it's essentially absent from their first album, so no need to try to convince them to use it here. Go with their core sound of ten guys singing.

However, I did decide to push them beyond what I'd heard them do before, as I really wanted to write a ten-part arrangement for them. Three soloists, singing in three-part harmony during the first verse and all choruses, plus a bass line and three-part BGs . . . that's seven parts already. I could have the upper three BGs double when needed or desired and go with a pair of background trios, making two layers of sound. It would be impressive live and would sound full when recorded.

The top three parts would be the three soloists. Then there would be a background trio, then another background trio, then the bass. Since I was planning to use arpeggiations through some passages, I decided to give each singer his own line, making it easier to follow the sheet music and to generate learning parts (see chapter 17, "Step 10: Record/Rehearse," for details).

This ten-line staff system would mean that the sheet music would be several pages long, but length was less of an issue than ease of learning. I wasn't expecting to have a great deal of repetition throughout. These are professional singers, and this arrangement needs to tell a story and develop, so there would be far more variety than the original traditional holiday singalong version.

All straightforward, except for the key. I'm looking for a first tenor solo, a bass solo, a reggae verse, and a chorus. This is going to take some consideration, so I'd better start by playing with the melody.

The Ten Steps in Action: "Go Tell It on the Mountain"

I also work in Finale, and it's at this point that I make more detailed decisions about number of parts and such. Here's how it went down.

Home Free is a five-part group: two tenors, baritone, and bass (TTBarB), plus a dedicated vocal percussionist (VP) who sometimes sings a BG part when there are no drums. This was to be a studio arrangement, meaning I could theoretically write an unlimited number of parts. But the guys wanted it to have the potential to be sung live. So I decided to write a chart using what I like to call "trap doors": built-in places where the number of parts could be reduced for live use. The guys are fans of Take 6, and the model arrangement of "I Wish" was written for six parts. However, it's hard to reduce six parts to four, and this arrangement was to be more R & B-ish than jazzy, which meant I wouldn't need to write a lot of dense chords. I decided to compromise and write a mostly five-part chart. This could then be easily reduced for live use by mixing and matching three strategies:

» The bass singer could "beat-bass," that is, sing the bass line and snare back-beats at the same time. The syncopated bass line easily allows for this. This frees up the VP to sing notes instead.
» Any *divisis* are optional and are placed in the baritone part. Also, many of them occur when the lead isn't doing anything important, meaning he could sneak them in while singing the lead if he wished.
» I included some "gang vocals" to add another texture layer in the recording, over which the lead singer would do R & B styling. These parts are optional in live performance; alternatively, the lead singer could sing them instead of styling.

I organized the staves by person: lead, "extras" (primarily the gang vocals), the 3 BGs on separate staves, and bass. Since the VP would be a straightforward backbeat groove, I didn't bother notating it (see chapter 20, "Vocal Percussion," for some tips and conventions). Nice and easy!

When I'm commissioned to write an arrangement, especially for a smaller group, I always ask for a detailed profile of the individual voices: not just ranges, but details on timbre, vocal breaks (particularly for male groups), strengths (which I try to highlight), and weaknesses (which I try to avoid).

With all this information, I decided on the key of B♭, modulating to B. This would allow the tenor soloist a medium-high **tessitura** (mostly B♭3–F4), with opportunities to belt into his upper chest notes of B♭4–B4. Also, I'm something of a key-signature geek, and I hear different key signatures as having different characters. Some of these are probably a result of convention: horn-based jazz and soul tend to happen in flat keys, guitar- and string-based rock and folk tend to be in sharp keys. So, B♭ it was. On to the melody!

CHAPTER 13

Step 6: Melody and Lyrics

Step 6 is writing out the melody. The melody is the single most identifiable and important element of any song, so it's best to start here.

It's important to remember that for almost every song, the melody is the core, the spine, the central river of each song. Never forget to treat the melody of your arrangement as the most important part. Don't let the other voices pull focus away from it unless you have a specific reason to do so, and even then don't let it happen for long, since they only exist to support and develop the melody.

This is obvious, but it still needs to be said and remembered, to avoid the risk that the melody is no longer your highest priority when you get excited about a cool harmonic pattern or polyrhythmic texture.

Altering the Melody: Where and When

Although we say that the melody is the heart of the song, that doesn't mean that it is absolutely sacrosanct and unchangeable. A melody can be altered, by the arranger or the lead singer, but it needs to be done with grace and careful intention. For example, if you reharmonize a passage and need to alter a single melodic note or rhythm to fit the new chord changes, make sure that the new note makes sense "horizontally" as well. It should sound just as melodic as the original, so that if you didn't know the melody well, you wouldn't know that anything had been changed. If the melodic change is out of character, it may take an audience member out of the experience of the song and force him or her to think about the mechanics of the arrangement. An average listener might just be jolted into thinking, "What was that?!"

There is always room for a soloist to ad lib and improvise, reshaping the melody, but that too is a choice that requires care and taste. As a general rule, you should instruct soloists to remain true to the melody early in the song, changing only after each section has been sung in its pure form. This will set up a sonic experience not unlike a theme and variations. But for the audience to hear changes in this way, it first needs the theme, which is the original melodic form, rhythm, and shape. And although it might appear too obvious to state, make sure a solo line doesn't include improvisation for improvisation's sake. Little is more powerful than a lead vocalist "going to church" when the inspiration arises; at the same time, little is more distracting than unfocused riffing that's more the result of showing off than of having arisen organically.

You can sometimes alter the melody, but remember that your audience will focus on the melody above all else—so make sure any changes are made for a reason and handled with care.

How to Treat Melody

How you decide to build your arrangement around the melody will be based on the style of the song and the extent to which you're planning to have the melody sung by an individual as opposed to a group.

One important consideration is the extent to which there is flexibility in the melodic notes and rhythms, which will be in part determined by the role your other singers are playing. In the case of a four-part arrangement in close harmony, not only will it specify how the melody is to be sung (by means of precise notation indicating the rhythm and length of each note), but each note in the other voices will be chosen in relation to and as a result of each melodic note.

By contrast, in the case of an R & B arrangement, you might not ever write out the melody at all (or you might write a simplified, symbolic version that is never sung as it appears on the page). The emphasis in this case is on performance, and the assumption is that that the soloist's delivery will be improvised and vary drastically in each performance. The backgrounds will be arranged with this in mind: their rhythms will complement but not crowd the melodic rhythm, and the important harmonies will be written in such a way that the melody's pitches are not relied on to complete the chords.

To this end, it's important to notate your expectations into an arrangement. Usually, if the melody is written on the top line and is to be sung by a soloist, you'll need to write "sing as written" if you want every note and rhythm to be exactly as you indicate. Without that note, some soloists will naturally take liberties. If you're worried that the soloist will adhere too closely to what's written, you can write "sing freely" or perhaps "phrase like the original recording" if the recorded lead (such as those sung by Billie Holliday or Ray Charles) spends lots of time "in the cracks" and is pretty much impossible to capture in conventional Western notation.

Regarding ad libs, if there's a passage that is meant to be freely improvised (for example, a chorus in which the ensemble sings the melody while the lead singer "styles" over top), write "ad lib" and do not include any notes or rhythms. If you'd like an ad lib that sounds similar to a recording, or if you have a specific shape in your head, you can notate what you'd like with "ad lib" written underneath.

Finally, you don't want to overburden a singer with directions, but a few words here and there will help clarify your intentions. For example, "ad lib, rising in pitch to a high F♯ by the final two beats" is clear and helpful. Many amateur singers are less comfortable improvising, and little tips can help. The less interaction you'll have with the group singing your arrangement, the more you will have to rely on notes in the arrangement (this is true for all aspects of your arrangement in addition to the melody).

The Role of Lyrics

Unless you are writing a vocal arrangement of an instrumental piece, you'll also be dealing with lyrics. A song is commonly defined as "the melody and the lyrics": these are only parts of a song that are always protected by copyright. Bass lines, chord progressions, guitar riffs, and the like can be changed, added, or removed, and while doing so may also drastically change the feel of the song, it doesn't change the song itself. If you change the lyrics and melody significantly, the result can hardly be considered the same song.

Lyrics as an Inspiration for the Arrangement

Melodies can be evocative and can often influence arrangement choices. Lyrics can do the same, sometimes even more so. Melodies speak to us in the abstract: a beautiful melody may make you laugh or cry, but you probably wouldn't be able to articulate exactly why other than to say that it was beautiful or that it moved you.

Lyrics, on the other hand, tell a story. They may tell a very specific story, or they may tell many stories and be wide open to interpretation. This can be a powerful source of inspiration in the arrangement, and the relationship of lyrics to arrangement can be an amazing study in artistic symbiosis. A happy set of lyrics may lead to a bright, bouncing arrangement. Or you may choose to reread the lyrics in another light, taking a seemingly breezy set of lyrics and exposing a darker underside to the story by framing the lyrics in a moody arrangement.

» *Dylan says: A great example of the way lyrics influence an arrangement is Clare Wheeler's arrangement and vocal delivery on the Swingle Singers' version of the classic Beach Boys song "God Only Knows," from their album Ferris Wheels. The song is usually interpreted as a sweet, tender love song. But when we got Clare in the booth, after laying down her evocative arrangement, we explored the darker side of the song, evoking feelings of dependence, longing, and desperation.*

Lyrics can also be a source of much of the arrangement's material. Background parts can be made from slices of the lyric, or they can be built on wordplay or free association with the lyrics (more on this later).

While notating the melody in your arrangement, you might want to jot down a couple of notes to yourself about key words or short phrases that will bear repeating in the background voices, that deserve to get additional focus by making them duets or trios with the melody, and so on. If there's a particularly important lyrical moment and you'd like it to get a very intense focus, there are few more arresting choices than having everyone sing the same words at the same time, especially if the entire group has been weaving a more instrumental texture.

If you're looking for more subtle ideas that involve lyrics, some words, such as "no" and "you," are very effective when woven into a textured tapestry. When you slow down the word "no," you're left with a light initial syllable (the "n") followed by an "oh" vowel, and then an "oo" (in an American pronunciation). Sung repeatedly on quarter notes, "no, no, no" in essence becomes a vocal filter sweep, a modulating "oh-oo-oh-oo-oh-oo" that's gently restruck. If you want to hint at the word "no" but control the rate of the diphthong, you should write out "noh" and "oo" alternating on successive eighth notes.

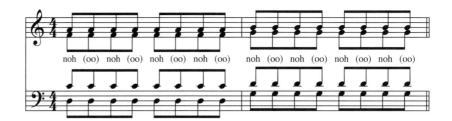

The repetition of a lyric in this way creates a somewhat trancelike texture, somewhere between instrumental and vocal, a sound that exists essentially only in contemporary a cappella.

We spend more time discussing these kinds of textures later in the book, but we mention this one now for the express purpose of having you, as an arranger, consider lyrics not only as words with meanings, but also as complex combinations of sounds that can be elongated, dissected, and so on. Through repeating and repurposing you can create sounds and textures never heard before while simultaneously emphasizing key lyrics, reinforcing a song's message and effect.

Imitating instruments is fun and impressive sometimes, but creating sounds and textures that don't exist anywhere else is extremely powerful. It's in these choices as arrangers that we show that a cappella is not just a parlor trick—that it is, in fact, a legitimate and unique musical genre.

What If I Want to Change the Melody or Lyrics?

Before you change the core elements of a song, be sure you have a good reason to do so.*

If you've chosen to arrange a particular piece (as opposed to writing your own song), it's probably in part because the piece is well-known and liked by yourself and/or your group and audience. And remember: melody reigns supreme, and that's what people recognize when they say they "know" a song. If you change this, you may erode people's ability to understand and appreciate the song.

That said, it's not uncommon to alter the melody in particular types of music. Jazz singers very often play with rhythm of a standard melody, embellishing or improvising a phrase here and there. You'll notice that in most of these cases the basic sense of the melody hasn't changed much: you could hum the melody on top and it wouldn't sound all that different.

When you listened to various versions of your song, you also probably heard many different versions of the melody. You may have observed that certain phrases were sung differently by each artist, and that some were sung virtually the same no matter who sang them. This is an important clue: it tells you which parts of the melody might be considered essential and which are open to interpretation.

If lyrics tell a story, then when you change them, you also change the story. Some lyric changes are simple and don't change much—for example, changing "he" to "she" when changing the gender of the soloist, or substituting your hometown or group name for another town or band name reference in the song. The story of a song can be artfully and powerfully turned around by switching "you" and "me": an angry song accusing a loved one of cheating may suddenly become a tearful confession from the unfaithful lover. Lyrics may be cut if they are offensive or uninspiring, or if the song is too long.

The big change comes if you write your own alternate lyrics: change enough of them, and you may no longer be singing the original song anymore. An extreme (and hilarious) example is the parodies of Weird Al Yankovic, who spoofs popular songs by completely rewriting the lyrics.

---

*American copyright law does grant the original songwriter and his or her publishing company the right to deny a group permission to record a version of a song if it is not in keeping with the original intent or up to the songwriter's standards. This right is very rarely exercised, but you should know that a few artists—Jay-Z, for instance—have withdrawn a compulsory mechanical license if a song is too far from the original. Moreover, while still alive Irving Berlin would not allow a song of his to be published or recorded if it was not in the original form. Example: "White Christmas" needed to start with the verse—"The snow is snowing . . ."—before getting to the chorus, the "I'm dreaming of a White Christmas" part. His estate is more lenient. All this doesn't much matter if you're arranging primarily for casual live performance, but if you're planning on publishing a piece of music, you should be careful not to play fast and loose with the melody and lyrics unless you have obtained the necessary permission from the author or his or her representatives.

» *Deke says: Back in my college days, a member of the mixed group on campus (the Tufts Amalgamates) came up with a cool, slow groove for the Beatles' "Daytripper" and proceeded to arrange the song in this style. After completing about two-thirds of the arrangement, he felt he really needed a bridge. The song didn't have one, so he wrote one. Did it work? Some people thought so, others didn't . . . but the bigger question is: would you want a passage in one of your arrangements that will immediately draw attention to itself? And do you have the requisite hubris to add a bridge to a song by one the greatest songwriting teams of the last century? When changing a song in a significant way, the considerations are not purely musical.*

Melody and lyrics are the heart and soul of the song, and of your arrangement. Giving them careful and creative consideration can be a great source of inspiration, and if you keep them first and foremost in mind as you arrange, your arrangement will be all the better for it.

Exercises

» Write an arrangement for only two voices—melody and countermelody. What choices do you have to make for the arrangement to work?
» Take two melodies and try to weave them together. Example: Simon and Garfunkel's "Scarborough Fair/Canticle."
» Write an arrangement for three voices. Pay close attention to the ways that counterpoint becomes harmony when all three voices line up into triads.
» Take a well-known song, change the pronouns ("he" to "she," "I" to "we," and so on), and consider how you'd arrange it now that it has a new perspective.

The Ten Steps in Action: "We Three Kings"

The melodic shape of the song in the verses is pretty straightforward, and since I was changing the feel and the meter, I knew I needed to stay very close to the specific melodic shape and notes. The first half of the verse melody outlines a descending fifth twice. No surprises there. The third line starts in the middle of the first two melodic lines and ascends to a third above the previous high note, leaving us with the outline of a major seventh. Not too rangey, so we have some flexibility.

The chorus outlines a sixth, never quite reaching the verse's high note, so for the purposes of range, the verse was where I focused my energies.

Not having worked with these guys before, I was sure they had tenors, but did they have screaming high tenors? To further the song's tension and keep it cool, I wanted the highest note to be in a powerful chest register, rather than popping into **falsetto**, which would have less impact. Rather than assuming they could chest out high Bs, I thought a high A to be a safe choice. They had to have someone with an A. That would have the verse lines starting on an F♯, which has some edge but isn't too high. And that would put the song in B minor, which would allow the bass singer to drop to the low fifth (an F♯) and even the fourth (E) if needed. Plus, if they have a real bass in the group (turns out they have two), a low B at the end should be no problem if it's tracked first thing in the morning. All workable.

What about taking the bass solo an octave lower? Perfect. Low enough to be rich, but not in the bottom fifth of most basses' ranges, so it won't get too quiet or muddy the harmonies.

As for the rhythm, it was necessary to recast the melody with a different rhythm, as we've shifted from 3/4 to 5/4. Rather than stick with the strong-weak-strong-weak emphasis of the original melody, I decided to keep the *Mission: Impossible* feel and have the melody land with a strong-strong-weak-weak emphasis: a dotted eighth–dotted eighth–eighth–eighth pattern, like the bass line (see m. 6).

As for the second line (m. 7), after singing it a few different ways, the eighth–quarter–dotted quarter–half note rhythm felt best. Once I'd figured out those two measures, the rest of the melodic rhythm flowed rather obviously.

One more consideration: the three-part harmony I was planning. The verses would have the melody on top, with the second and third soloists singing parallel harmonies below, following the same melodic shape, and outlining the diatonic scale; but since the song is in a minor key, when the second measure lands on a V chord, we need an A♯, which makes the most sense in the middle voice. This results in a melody and harmony with a Middle Eastern flavor, which I liked, and to further emphasize that I decided on a little sixteenth-note flip in the lowest voice (the "L3" staff, m. 6). The leap from the tonic note down to the sixth degree of the scale, which is flatted here, is one of the most recognizable elements of a Middle Eastern scale, so I chose to have that voice, and only that voice, flip.

When the chorus arrives in the relative major (mm. 14–21), the melody is lower, starting on the third of the chord. Continuing a parallel harmony with the other two notes below the melody would be too muddy, so I decided to keep the melody in the top voice (for sonic continuity) and have the middle voice leap above. This happens frequently in Boyz II Men and other R & B pop songs, and the revoicing will be one sonic clue that the song has shifted style here. This puts the middle voice on a high B, but falsetto here is not a problem; in fact it would be welcome as another sonic and stylistic shift. The chorus is more laid back, so a little falsetto is preferable to a high belted-out chest note.

So far so good, until the Jamaican verse (mm. 54–61). Time to shift gears into a swung 4/4 feel, once again requiring that the melody be recast in a new time signature against a new groove.

I didn't want to take any time establishing this new groove, so the melody had to clearly delineate the feel immediately, which I felt was best served by a quarter–quarter–quarter followed by a short break and a chain of eighth notes. This is reminiscent of Bob Marley's classic "Jammin'," where the first two measures alternate between straight, square quarters and swung eighths. Can't get more reggae than Bob! Throw in a couple of triplets late in the verse, and the melodic rhythm is set.

I kept the "Jammin'" interplay between quarters and swung eighths in the chorus as well (mm. 62–end): four quarters in the first measure ("Star. Of. Won. Der.") followed by an eighth rest on the downbeat (just like Bob), followed by three eighth notes ("star-of-night").

To break up the monotony, I thought a triplet would work well in the sixth measure of the chorus. As for the harmonic spacing, it's essentially the same as in the previous choruses. Same notes, same voicing—only the rhythm needed to be changed. Different, but not too different.

The melody's all set, but it's hardly enough to establish the different feels. From Lalo Schifrin to Boyz II Men to Bob Marley, nothing will be more important in establishing the different feels than the bass line.

The Ten Steps in Action: "Go Tell It on the Mountain"

Boy, Deke sure had his work cut out for him! Between singers he hadn't yet worked with and a mishmash of different time signatures, vocal textures, and styles, he had a lot to think about. My melody work was comparatively simple.

With a detailed voice profile and a few recordings of the group, I had a pretty good idea of what my soloist and ensemble could do. The key of B♭ (modulating later to B), chosen in the previous step, would do just nicely. The chorus melody covers about an octave, from F3 to G4—right in the zone for a tenor. The verse melody is actually a little higher but with less range: B♭3 to G4. This leaves a little room at the top for some extra-high improvising.

Since the melody was being sung primarily by a soloist and wasn't being changed up, I didn't have much to consider for specific melodic rhythms for much of the piece. But the melody isn't all that interesting, and the piece has a basic chorus–verse–chorus structure (plus my changes and additions), so simply repeating the melody each time would get boring awfully fast. I chose a couple of techniques to switch things up and create some development:

Chorus 1 (mm. 5–12): Sung straight up except by the soloist. The BGs harmonize the melody with him on the words "ev'rywhere" and "Jesus Christ."

Slight melody/form change (mm. 12–15): Earlier, in the section on form, I mentioned that I added four bars of buffer material, basically some groove between choruses and verses. In addition, I snipped one bar out of the chorus. Instead of an eight-bar chorus, we have a seven-bar chorus leading into a four-bar groove section, where the last note of the chorus, on "born," is the first beat of the groove. Put another way, the last bar of the chorus overlaps the first bar of the groove, which gives a sense of propelling the piece forward.

Verse 1 (mm. 16–23): Sung more or less straight up. The melody has a few rhythmic syncopations or "pushes" to keep it in the style of the rest of the piece; a super-straight melody would feel out of place. To come up with this melodic rhythm, I simply sang the melody to myself while "body drumming"—playing the drum groove with my hands on my lap. This is what came out. Nothing complicated or clever . . . just enough rhythmic feel to make it fit.

Chorus 2 (mm. 24–33): More or less like chorus 1, with one little melodic and rhythmic variation particularly at m. 27 for some extra style.

Verse 2 (mm. 34–41): Mostly straight up, with a little variation at the end (mm. 40–41).

Chorus 3 (mm. 42–52): Now we jump into higher gear. Instead of the soloist singing the melody, we add in a layer of gang vocals (on the "Extras" staff), singing the melody simply, while the soloist riffs and improvises on top.

Verse 3 (mm. 53–60): By now we've added a key change and ramped up the energy. I decided to start the melody high up for "when I was a seeker" (m. 53) in a Stevie Wonder kind of way. The second half of the melody (mm. 57–60) adds some blues flavor, and the last line jumps up an octave for an extra kick. This last verse was composed but meant to sound somewhat improvised.

Chorus 4 (mm. 61–67): Same techniques as chorus 3.

Going to church (mm. 72–end): By the time we get to the party at the end, the original melody's long gone. The soloist is all about improvising and styling. But I had two basic countermelodies happening. One happens in the BGs: "Go tell it! Get on up and . . . go tell it! Get on up and tell it on the mountain," done in a more bluesy/James Brown style. On top of that, the gang vocals have mostly static notes, singing "Jesus Christ is born."

Overall, working with the melody was about sharing it between the soloist and the BGs, adding variations to keep it interesting. But it ain't gonna groove without a good bass line. On to the next step!

CHAPTER 14

Step 7: The Bass Line

In eighteenth- and nineteenth-century four-part harmonic writing, the bass voice was considered the second-most important element of a composition, after the melody: it declares the roots of chords, maps the tonal structure of the piece, and casts the fundamental to which all of the other parts tune. The lowest voice also serves as an aural grounding point: the ear gravitates to it just as it does the highest voice, meaning it is often perceived as a countermelody. In short, the bass line is both the harmonic foundation and a melody at the same time. As arrangers, we usually remember the former principle but often forget the latter.

Basses Are People Too

Not everyone in the world is blessed (or cursed) with large quantities of testosterone, but luckily there are just enough of them to keep a cappella alive (and often kicking). Typecast more than any other voice part, basses are rarely given solos and are forced to spend over 95 percent of their time singing silly syllables. Too often they're relied upon to bellow yet another monotonous, poorly phrased bass line. Unfortunately, many arrangers can't see beyond writing a sometimes difficult-to-sing, sometimes boring, transcribed-off-the-original-recording, ridiculous-interval-leaping, electric-bass-mimicking line. Basses are the foundation of a rich and resonant group sound, and we need to take the extra time to make their part both interesting and fun while the rest of the group is busy singing interesting background syllables and melodic lines.

Know Thy Bass

Of course the occasional ballad demands pages of bass-clef whole notes, but even long, slow bass lines should have a melodic shape. If you're not convinced, ask your local bass to sing you a couple of his or her favorite lines. You'll hear not only how the line was intended to work on paper, but also that it has been brought to life—usually customized with slight rephrasings and vowel adjustments, not unlike when you individualize a solo to fit your voice and the specifics of the arrangement. Strive to ensure that your bass lines receive this kind of affection and attention from your singers, and they'll be sure to turn the bunch of dots on the bottom of the page into a tune.

More than with any other voice part, arrangers have to know exactly what their bass(es) can and cannot do, since basses are required to sing in the extreme parts of their range the majority of the time. Forcing a bass to sing too low or too loudly is a recipe for an unstable group sound and at worst can lead to permanent vocal damage for the singer. The first step in keeping your group in tune and your bass productive and healthy is identifying his vocal range. As many of us know, on New Year's morning just about anyone can hit a low C2. What separates the men from the boys is if they can occasionally be counted on to sing a low C, and what separates the *real* men from the rest is whether they can consistently sing low Cs. Right?

Wrong.

Knowing exactly who and what you're working with allows you to make *everyone* sound like they're singing low Cs. Audiences ooh and ahh when they distinguish the warm, low rumblings of a voice, but they can't tell if they're hearing a C or the G a fifth above. The most important job you have as an arranger is to make your group sound the best it can. This means writing to your singer's (or section's) strengths and avoiding his weaknesses, which you can only do if you are aware of, and understand, his idiosyncrasies. Yes, it's good to push his limits occasionally, but to do this, you have to know what they are. If you don't know who you are writing for, the range suggestions in chapter 7 are a good starting point.

When dealing with an entire bass section, consider its "critical mass": the lowest realistic projectable note. We caution you against relying too heavily on your lowest bass and his lowest notes, because the group sound will be uneven and will vary considerably in volume and timbre. Be sure that your lowest note is being sung cleanly and clearly by at least half the section. Before you do your next arrangement, take at least a few minutes to confirm what they can and cannot do. Have them sing down scales and land on low notes approached from the octave above. Try a variety of vowel sounds and note the lower limit of each so you'll never again have to hear the words, "I just can't sing this."

One other approach to maximizing a section's sound is the judicious use of octave splits. Low Cs, low Ds, perhaps even low Es can be written as alternate notes, or you can just indicate a split in the bass line. It's also possible to split your bass into the low octave and fifth above, but be careful: a low G2 will likely overwhelm a C2 when each is sung by half of your bass section, resulting in an apparent 6/4 (second inversion) chord, which is far less sonically stable. An octave will give you the effect you want most of the time.

» *Deke says: You usually want to keep the spacing between your singers akin to the harmonic series (an octave at the bottom, more and more closely voiced in the upper parts), but there is one place where a low fifth is just what the doctor ordered: rock guitar power chords. Split your bass section or have the baritones sing the same notes and rhythms as your bass a fifth above, usually on quarter or eighth notes, ideally with a guitar-sounding syllable ("jm," "zhum," and so on). We use this in the House Jacks frequently, and the end result, when amplified, is very powerful.*

jun jig-ga jun jig-ga jun jig-ga jun jig-ga jun jig-ga jun jig-ga jun jig-ga JAH JAH

The Bass Section: It's Not Just for Bass Lines Any More

Now that you've compiled all of your bass section's limitations, consider the freedom you have with an entire section. From deep, resonant bass drums and other nontraditional vocal sounds to combined textures, having more than one bass is a blessing if you take the time to consider how to take full advantage of each voice. It is indeed rare for an arrangement to take advantage of more than one bass voice. Yes, it's impossible to have a two-measure improvised bass-section break, but what you lose in individual interpretive freedom you gain in texture. The possibilities are almost limitless, so don't unconsciously constrain yourself to one note and sound at a time.

Ideas? In a slow song, consider having the basses restrike the same low note at different times. For example, if you have four basses and your bass line is a chain of four quarter notes, you could have each one of them sing one of the four beats.

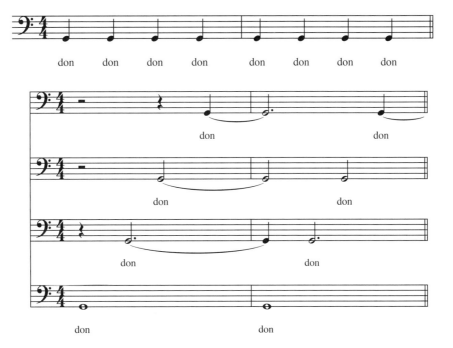

For an ethereal quality, give them long held notes and have them restrike at will, out of time, or have your bass section hold a long note and modulate their vowel sound out of time, creating a flanged overtone effect. How does one flange a vowel sound? Have them start on one vowel, such as "oo," then change to "oh," "ah," "ee," "eh," and so on. Once they understand that they are free to move between vowel sounds, they'll move away from the specific vowels used in language and start to completely morph the sound, using all of the range of their tongue and palate, emphasizing more overtones. Were this written, it would look something like "oooorreeeaayyiiiiiooo" (and so on). This effect can give a sound like anything from a synthesizer to a didgeridoo to a roomful of Tibetan monks.

Don't think it's impossible to use large intervals or blindingly rapid rhythms, because you can divide the section and have them sing half each. This is particularly useful for rhythmically complex funk bass or octave-leaping disco lines. For a seamless quality, write a seemingly relentless line and have the singers stagger their breathing—that is, each bass breathes on a different beat of the measure, so that there's a constant flow of sound.

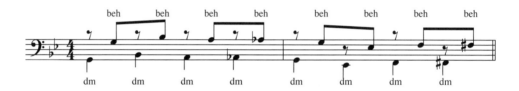

Also consider having the entire section sing the line, except for one who repeats the line a beat later—instant studio delay.

The Single Bass Singer

Just as there are advantages to arranging for a group, there are benefits to having only one bass voice. As you're probably aware, basses accustomed to singing alone usually develop their own sound and style. They often change notated rhythm, phrasing, and even text to get the best sound for themselves. Don't fight it; take advantage of it by to learning what he can do and then staying one step ahead. If more percussive vowels seem to be his forte, do enough research to develop a couple of sounds that haven't been considered. Also, when arranging for an individual, you have the freedom to leave certain passages unarranged, allowing for improvisation. I've found that basses are the only voice part who think they have a right to change their part however they please. Consider it payback for so often being forced to sing boring or silly parts! Leaving some sections undecided gives you a greater chance of preserving other, more important passages.

» *Deke says: Unless I'm publishing an arrangement or writing for an entire section of voices, I don't write in the syllables for the bass, knowing that what I write will likely just be changed by an individual bass who has his own sound and style. And when it comes to writing for the House Jacks, not only do I not write in syllables, I often don't even put in more than the most rudimentary core rhythms, with entire sections of whole notes, and empty measures for bass fills. In essence, a professional bass singer needs the same thing a bass guitarist does: a lead sheet with chord symbols, with specific notes written only when they're absolutely necessary. This is not to say that as an arranger you should relinquish all decisions to a bass singer; rather, you should make clear what is necessary, and where there is freedom: freedom to choose a rhythm, freedom to improvise a fill, freedom to sing the way a bass player would play.*

Although most bass vocalists sing an octave above a string or electric bass, there is a way to gain an extra octave on the low end: a lip buzz. Similar to the way a tuba player buzzes into his mouthpiece to create the bass notes, lip buzzing can create a pitch more than an octave lower than a bass can sing. Even better, women can do this too, giving them bass notes way beyond their normal range. And as if the subharmonic pitch weren't cool enough, it's possible to sing a second note at the same time, either an octave, an octave and a fifth, or an octave and a third higher, resulting in two notes from one person. Unbeatable. Caveat: unamplified, the sound is essentially inaudible ("pppppppp," like a faint "raspberry"), so you need a microphone and sound system to hear the full effect.

The Female Bass

Shaping the line before actually writing a note for the upper background voices is usually important for male voices; it's even more so for female bass and second alto lines, as there is less space between the bottom of the female range and first alto territory. You'll rarely encounter problems if you're completely free to write a line that adheres to the low female vocal range, but occasionally a certain melodic shape has to be preserved or the arrangement will lose the flavor of the original. This is most frustrating when the original relies on a repeated pattern or motif that lies just a little too low at its lowest point.

When you recognize this problem, choose one of these solutions:

1. Invert part of the pattern so that it retains its rhythmic and functional properties but some of the notes are displaced by an octave. This is best when the shape of the bass part is particularly important. No one will care if a few notes are sung up the octave.
2. Have them sing the entire line an octave higher. If you still want a bassy sound, have one of the singers sing with an **octaver**.
3. If the song isn't written around the bass line, rewrite the line entirely.
4. Transpose the whole song.

5. If you feel the song is reliant upon a low bass line *and* you don't think the above choices will cut it, it simply may not be a good choice for an all-female group. Cut your losses and choose a more appropriate song.

Whatever you choose to do, it's going to affect the rest of the vocal parts, making it important to consider the shape of your bass line before you put pencil to paper.

Sounds, Syllables, and Phrasing

From "dm dm dm" to "bowmp bank bank," most vocal bass lines are based on instrumental equivalents, be they an upright bass, electric bass, synthesizer, or tuba. Recognizing this as common practice can help expand your creativity, either in writing a bass line that's more like its instrumental equivalent, or in creating one that is decidedly dissimilar to anything you've ever heard an instrumentalist play.

Walking bass, funk bass, string bass pizzicato: all have been loosely translated into easily notatable syllables, such as "bm," "doom," and so on. You might choose to strive for a tighter, more exacting translation. To do this, listen not only to the recording of the song you're arranging, but also to a number of other tracks on the same album or to similar songs by different artists. This will help you define a wider range of potential sounds that you can translate to your vocal bass line. If you know someone who plays bass, have him or her play your bass part, record it, and take what you like from it. In doing so you may build a whole new vocabulary of sounds and phrasings.

» *Dylan says: I play electric bass, and on a number of occasions bass singers have asked me to play the bass lines to vocal arrangements. I'd play the bass line as written and also how I felt it as a bass player, which often included adding a few fills, skip notes, and other bass-type phrasing things I never even thought of as a vocal arranger. When I produced the last Swingle Singers album, the bass singer, Tobi Hug, asked me to do this. He recorded me playing the part on bass as written and then as felt, transcribed the part, and learned it as I played it. The result: a bass line that had life, energy, and a hard-to-define, yet vocally true, quality to it.*

These stock syllables and phrasings are well established and will get you where you want to go most of the time. However, you do yourself and your basses a disservice if you never think outside the box or never consider the sounds that may come naturally from your own singers. Never forget that your arrangement needs to inspire your singers to perform to the best of their ability, which usually means vocal lines that engage your singers' talents and emotions.

There's no single correct method for deciding on syllables; in fact, there's no authority besides you, your group, and the audience. This means it's up to you to develop your own vocabulary of bass sounds, which come from listening, exploration, and cataloging your successes. Always keep track of your discoveries, so that you won't find yourself constantly having to search for a new sound from scratch.

Learn by Doing

The best way to start creating new bass syllables and words, either imitative or unique, is to sing along with the recording. Often you'll be singing an octave above the recorded bass line, but don't let that distract you from following the exact phrasing and color. Let yourself go—once you know the part pretty well, you won't have to concentrate on the notes, leaving your imagination free to play. Experiment with your lips. Try vowel sounds that aren't used in English, diphthongs, and a variety of consonants. Eventually you'll be able to narrow your palette of sounds down to a couple of choices. Now you'll need to chase down your bass and have him or her repeat your new discoveries. You'll probably get some raised eyebrows at first, but, when sung with conviction, interesting new sounds can change an entire arrangement for the better.

Of course, once you've created a new sound, it's quite possible that there isn't an easy way to write it down. We recommend recording and sharing your vocal version, as well as writing down some combination of consonants and vowels, avoiding anything that looks like an easily pronounceable word, as singers will end up pronouncing what they read as opposed to trying to mimic your tone.

Another option is to draw sounds out of words. You can lean toward vocal-sounding scat syllables (like "bah-doot'n-doobie") or transfer pieces of the lyrics from the solo or background parts. For a challenge, arrange a song that has the basses singing words throughout. Writing a low countermelody is the easy part; making it work in the context of the arrangement is the challenge. Don't be afraid to try your strangest ideas: Richard "Bob" Greene went out on a limb with "yiddish bow dip" in the Bobs' version of "Helter Skelter" and was rewarded with a Grammy nomination for best arrangement.

Connect the Dots

Once you've got a shape and a sound, it's time to work your magic. There's no single correct way to fill in notes between downbeats or melodic fragments; that's up to your taste and your group's sound. If you find yourself stuck, you can try listening to the recording again; it's often not until the third verse or chorus that the interesting variations surface. If that doesn't help, go check out the different versions of the song you found back in step 3. If you're still not satisfied, you may not have fully internalized the song. Listen to it some more, focusing on the bass line until you can hear it in your head without the recording. Then put away the recording and focus on your arrangement. You should imagine what you have so far on paper in your head, as it will eventually be performed by your group. Once you've locked into the tempo and general feel you're striving for, the bass line on the recording should begin to conform to the new specifics of your arrangement. Some passages will translate well, others poorly. Keep what you like and consider what it is you like about it—rhythm? intervals? shape? Also consider what didn't work in the other passages. This should help you define certain parameters that will help you through the difficult sections.

If none of that works, walk away. Sleep on it. The next day in the shower, sing the song to yourself, focusing on the bass line. Don't get technical, and don't let your Editor overwhelm you. Just relax, sing, and have fun. Something workable should find its way to your vocal chords, and from there you can refine and notate.

If you're still stuck, call a friend who is a bass singer. Chances are he'll have some ideas when he hears how the rest of the song unfolds.

Make It Interesting

Once all is said and done, sing through your bass line from start to finish. After considering everything above, don't forget the most important consideration: how engaging is it to sing? Yes, there will be bass lines that aren't all that much fun, but there had better be a good reason, and a strong emotional content that will keep your bass from drifting into boredom.

For some reason, most arrangers aren't basses, and most basses don't arrange. Put yourself in their shoes and imagine having to sing your bass line over and over again. If you're less than excited, it's time to start over. Think of it this way: basses tend to be big and strong, and to speak in actions as often as in words. You wouldn't want a boring bass line to give them something negative to say, now would you?

》 *Dylan says: As a bass player and vocalist, I have a particular love of a cappella bass lines. Since I hear the bass lines as an instrumentalist would, I don't always come up with wild syllable choices: I'm interested in a solid tone and groove. As I write my bass lines, I sing them out loud, and little syllable choices will pop up here and there to reflect basslike phrasing that's voice-friendly. Below are a couple of bass lines that reflect this.*

The first bass line is simple but fun to sing. While it's based on a simple four-beats-to-the-bar pattern, two things are added to make it more interesting. First, there are a couple of passing bits to connect the chord changes. Second, the basses get to sing a few words—always a good way to make your basses happy. Notice that chord symbols are added to allow the bass singer to sing "off the page" if they want.

step out the back! dm dm dm dm dm dm dm dm dm dm dm dm dm dm dm dm ba-dm Get on that

bus! Dm Dm Dm Dm Dm dm ba dm-be-dm dm dm dm dm dm dm beh dm

» *The next one is a little more complicated, from a jazz-blues piece. Rather than swung, it's a shuffle-funk, conceptually based on the original bass style of the late, great Jaco Pastorius. Again, chord symbols are added in case the bass singer wants to work around the existing bass line.*

doo-dn bop n doo bay-oo-dn doo dit "I run a clean-ing plant"___ dm dm

doo-dit ba doo 'dn doo ba doo-dit dm dm doo 'dn doo ba doo ba doo

doo-dit ba doo-dit ba-dm dm dm ba doo-dit dm dm doo ba doo ba dm dm

Exercises

» Next time you're listening to music, focus on the bass line throughout. Is it melodic or merely the root of each chord? How could the line be made more interesting?

» Take an arrangement you've already completed and rewrite the bass line to make it more interesting and enjoyable.

The Ten Steps in Action: "We Three Kings"

The bass line presents us with a problem in the very first measure, since I need to figure out a way to keep it reminiscent of the *Mission: Impossible* theme without being close enough to require a mechanical license. After some experimentation I arrived at a bass line (mm. 2–3) that follows the first three notes (B–B–D–E), then takes a left turn in the second half (B–B–D–C♯).

For the verse, when on the tonic chord, I decided to keep the signature initial measure, then maintain the same rhythm and shape when dropping down to the V (dominant) chord, but because the latter half of the measure returns to the tonic, the third note is a B, with a C♯ to continue the shape, which resolves down to the B at the top of the subsequent measure (mm. 6–9). In m. 10, when the harmonic rhythm accelerates and we have two chords in each measure, I decided to stick with the tonic of each chord per the original, so that the progression was very clear.

When the chorus lands (mm. 14–21), the 6/8 feel has swung sixteenth notes. I needed to make sure that was clearly indicated via the bass line, since I was planning to have the upper voices all on lyrics, and in the absence of vocal percussion, it falls to the bass to clearly establish the new feel. The first measure of the chorus is intentionally reminiscent of "End of the Road" with the second half leading down to the IV (subdominant) chord—in this case G—and the second measure returns, ending with a common 5–6–1–6 figure in sixteenth notes. Because the song is shifting gears quickly, I wanted familiar, easily digestible musical figures to comfortably establish the new feel.

Halfway through the chorus (m. 18), when the descending bass line begins, the upper voices were clearly establishing the quarter–eighth, quarter–eighth figure, so I decided to have the bass restrike only on the second sixteenth, with each quarter note tied to the first sixteenth. I prefer the space that the held note creates, giving the melodic trio focus and propelling the measure only after they've sung their eighth notes.

As for the reggae section (mm. 54–end), again I wanted a simple bass line to establish the feel, so until the harmony demands, it's all tonic, dominant, and subdominant (I, V, and IV). Before writing a note of the background vocals, I knew I wanted swung eighths on the second and fourth beats, loosely replicating a reggae-style "skank" guitar, so I crafted the bass line to play against that rhythm. It's unusual to have a bass line avoid the downbeat of the measure, but at this point I wanted to signal a clear break from the rhythms of the past by creating a little interplay between the melodic break on the fourth beat and a break in the bass line a beat later. As for the reggae chorus, the bass line loosely maintains the melodic shape from before, this time in 4/4 with eighth notes.

And, as promised, a low D in the last measure.

Four voices down, six to go . . .

The Ten Steps in Action: "Go Tell It on the Mountain"

As a bass player, nothing makes me happier than writing a good R & B/funk bass line. This was a fun step for me.

I knew that my tune, unlike "We Three Kings," would have a VP giving the basic backbeat groove, which frees up the bass to be a little more bouncy and syncopated. A good R & B/funk song is about the rhythmic interplay between drums, bass, and BGs: each has a role to play, and these roles can switch section to section.

I started with the opening vamp (mm. 1–8). The first bar basically sets the bass line's rhythmic template for most of the song. As you'll see, it's a syncopated, energetic line that plays *around* the backbeat rather than outlining it. This not only makes for a nice interplay with the drums; it also means that the bass singer can "beatbass" and still sing snares on the backbeat if there's no VP, in keeping with my mandate of making this arrangement reducible to fewer parts. Also, with a good bass line, the energy in the line is sometimes defined by where the bass doesn't sing; these holes, these little bits of sonic space, provide great energy and movement.

As for the melodic bass fills, usually in the second half of the bar, these are very conventional with R & B/funk bass lines. I found them in one of two ways: by singing the basic bass groove over and over, improvising little bass embellishments, and writing down the ones I liked; and by picking up my electric bass and doing the same thing. Sometimes a bass line feels different in the fingers than it does in the voice, and new ideas arise that I might not find just by singing the line. I added a few of these in as well.

In the chorus (mm. 5–15), the bass line pretty much follows the chord changes using the basic groove set up in m. 1. The bass breaks from the pattern in m. 8, where the whole ensemble sings the same simple rhythm of four quarter notes on "ev'ry-whe-re." This gives a nice change in texture, going from multirhythmic interplay to a single unifying power-chord feeling. At m. 11 the bass sings repeated eighth notes on the dominant (F). This is a nice technique that builds energy into the next groove section.

The verse (mm. 16–23) follows the same formula of keeping the basic bass groove while following the chord changes. Another change in texture happens with the driving eighth-note passage at mm. 22–23. The opposite technique of energy-through-spaces, now the bass line drives the ensemble forward while the BGs sing rhythmically static block chords in half notes on top. This propels us forward into the next chorus.

The next verses and choruses basically follow the same formula. Things change at mm. 49–51. Here the bass sings driving eighth notes in **pedal tone** fashion on a single pitch: this creates tension, a sign that something new is about to happen. In this case, it's a key change. The driving eighths appear again at mm. 68–71, where there is a sense of expectation as the BGs leave more space and the drum solo happens. The bass continues the driving eighths in the going-to-church section at mm. 72–end. As the BGs get more complex, the bass holds the fort by hammering away on the pedal tone, finally ending in rhythmic unison with the ensemble. When written well, a bass line is a powerful tool for creating and directing energy within an arrangement.

CHAPTER 15

Step 8: Background Voices

Thus far, we've considered the two most important parts of any arrangement, the main melody and bass line, from the perspective that they're *both* melody lines—one is the primary melody, and the other serves as a secondary melody that connects the tonic and other primary notes.

What's left over? Your remaining singers, missing chord members, and any rhythms you haven't included. In other words, you've painted your foreground; now you need to nestle it snugly within a background that gives it momentum and context, musically and emotionally.

Since your melody was largely written for you and the bass line (whether altered or not) is usually a single, constant texture, it's likely that your arranging skills will be tested most rigorously in the writing of the BGs, and it's in this step that you'll likely spend more time than any other.

We can't write your BGs for you, but we can offer a number of considerations as you write yours. First we'll lay out some guidelines for voicing and voice leading. If you've taken traditional harmony courses or for other reasons feel pretty comfortable with this part, feel free to skip ahead a few pages, or scan for a brief refresher course.

Voicing and Voice Leading

We started this book with the statement "no rules, only contexts"—and we meant it. However, over the course of several hundred years spent figuring out what has worked well and what hasn't when writing vocal harmony, musicians have derived a number of pretty sensible, foolproof guidelines, and it would be crazy of us to simply ignore them. Not all of them always work in contemporary music (more important, many of the "don't"s in traditional choral music can be "do"s in contemporary writing), but they're a great place to start. They provide an excellent, sensible set of rules to follow—until you have a good reason to break them.

Voicing

You've probably heard of the "harmonic series," right? Every note we hear isn't just one pitch, but rather a series of pitches extending above the note in a mathematical progression. Consider a low C2. You think you're hearing a single note, but here's what's actually *inside* that note:

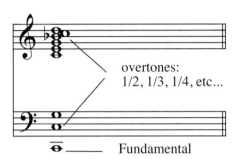

What do you notice about the first several harmonics above the main note (called the fundamental)? C, G, C, E, G. That's right—a C major chord. The harmonic series is the foundation of the Western musical scale, from which we get our intervals and pitches.

What does this mean for vocal arranging? It means that if you want a nice, full, balanced, easy-to-tune chord the way that Mother Nature intended, you should space your voices like the harmonic series above, with lower voices spread widely and close voicing in your upper parts.

Considering an SATB arrangement, if the tenor happens to be on the low fifth of the chord, that's okay and will result in a rich sound, but if you let the tenor line get down to the third of the chord (unless the bass line is remarkably high), you'll find the chord will sound muddy and be more difficult to tune.

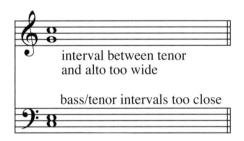

The opposite principle applies up above. If you separate your alto and soprano lines by any more than an octave, they'll find it hard to tune, and even if they manage to do so, it will sound as though there's a large hole in the chord.

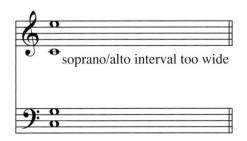

Luckily, the natural ranges of the human voice prohibit most bad decisions. In general, beginning arrangers should consider the upper three parts as a unit, with each voice as one of the three chord factors of a triad and the bass line an average of an octave or so below on the root of the chord. If you follow this principle, there's very little that can go wrong, and eventually you'll see for yourself what works and what doesn't.

While this holds for SATB writing, where the vocal ranges are evenly spaced, it doesn't always make sense for same-sex groups. For more information on writing for TTBB or SSAA, take a look at chapter 19, "Other Vocal Formats."

So now we have four voices, but only three notes in a triad. Which note should you double? With occasional exception, the root is the most sensible. The "three and one" model relies on this largely because 95 percent of all chords in popular music have the root on the bottom. Exceptions to watch out for include bass line patterns that occasionally stress a different chord factor or hold one note underneath a progression (this is called a pedal tone, or simply "pedal"). If the recording of a song or the sheet music indicates a bass note that's different from the root, you should follow suit, but otherwise, until you know what you're doing, keep the bass on the root of the chord.

If you happen to be in a situation where you have a more complicated five-note chord, and have more notes to sing in the chord than voices, drop the fifth of the chord. The root (if it's on the bottom) stresses the fifth more than any other note in its harmonic series (besides itself), so chances are the ear will miss it the least. Don't forget that the melody is often singing a note that can stand on its own as a chord factor, especially in groups with one vocalist per part. If you constantly find yourself needing to drop more than one note, chances are your chords are too dense, or perhaps it's time to recruit more singers.

Doubling the root reflects the fact that the primary note is repeated more than any other in the harmonic series (as you can see in the example above). More than one C in a C chord helps lock in the tuning with surrounding notes and also creates its own harmonics, which reinforce those of the root. Notes other than the root of the chord create harmonic tension, often intentionally, and need to be approached and resolved with the same sensitivity that all dissonance does.

Resolving Dissonance

Western harmonies are based around the idea of resolving dissonance, also sometimes called "motion and rest" or "tension and release." The most common example is the good old perfect cadence, in which the dominant chord resolves to the tonic chord (expressed in roman numerals as V–I)—the bedrock of harmonic development in classical music. Put simply, you have notes moving like this:

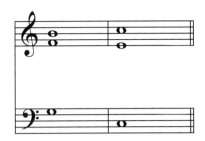

The B (the third of the G⁷ chord) naturally wants to go to the C (the root of the C chord). The F (the seventh of the G chord) naturally wants to resolve down to the E (the third of the C chord) The tritone (F–B in this case; also known as an augmented fourth), a buzzing, unfinished sound, resolves to the nice, consonant interval of a sixth (E–C). And now we're home.

Go ahead and try resolving the chords differently—say, like this:

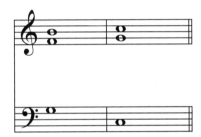

Without the third, the chord sounds empty. Or try this:

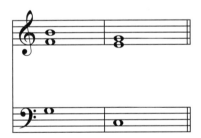

The upside: a nice-sounding resolution of F–E, and a three-note chord (with the fifth in it) to end. But somehow, it's just not as complete sounding as the first one. This has to do with two basic principles: voice leading and contrary motion.

Voice Leading

We mentioned earlier that harmony developed from sung lines, and as a result, the voices were never forced to make too big a leap in moving from one note to the next. In fact, the original rules of counterpoint suggested that no vocal line jump more than a fifth unless necessary; if it does, the following notes should fall back toward the original pitch. Remember that an octave is much easier to sing than a seventh or a ninth, and that intervals larger than a ninth are almost unsingable by most mere mortals (which is further proof that Bobby McFerrin is indeed not mortal). In addition to not making them jump too far, you need to remember where your singers' breaks lie, adjusting leaps so that they are more easily and pleasantly achieved.

In general, it's best to have the voices cover little vertical territory when moving from one note to the next. If one or more of the chord factors are present in the next chord, hold them over or repeat them in the same voice and have the other voices take the closest remaining pitches. If all three pitches are different, have each voice take one that's close. There will be times when you'll want the entire chord to leap up or down for effect, but remember that more than an occasional shifting will make the song difficult to sing and to tune.

Contrary Motion

The principle of voice leading we just described may lead you to believe that the best route is often parallel motion. For example, when moving from a C major to a D minor triad, the simplest thing to do would be to have all the voices move up a note, like this:

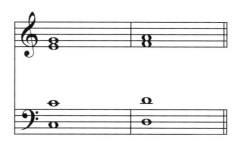

In other words, the higher voice that is doubling the voice at the octave (in this case, the tenor) gets "lost" in the harmonics. If chords are parallel in succession, that voice reinforces the lower one, and the result is a vocal line that overpowers the others. Parallel octaves or fifths sound great in some places, such as rock power chords, but they don't always work as well in the background of a four-part a cappella arrangement.

Too much parallel motion will result in an empty, street-corner sound, or in something that just sounds and feels too jumpy.

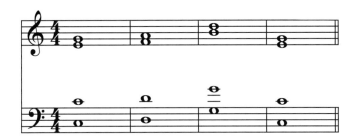

The way around this trap is to stress contrary motion between the outermost parts. In our three-and-one model, if any one of the upper voices moves in the opposite direction of the bass line, the other two usually follow. The result is a succession of voicings that sound distinct and full.

Note here that the tenor in m. 2 has an extra note. By landing on a A in beat 2, the tenor avoids parallel motion with the bass—but ends up doubling the fifth, the least favorite choice. This dilemma is solved by having the tenor then move to the D, doubling the octave without the parallel motion. The extra motion is an added bonus, adding momentum to keep the whole thing flowing. Good voice leading is often the process of figuring out how to solve little problems like this, and if you have an obsessive mentality, you can really get hooked on it.

The above was only a brief overview of harmonic writing. If this any of this wasn't clear, or you'd like more insight into these topics, consider spending some time studying traditional counterpoint and four-part harmonic writing. Even if you're not currently enrolled in a college with a music department that offers classes in these timeless subjects, there are many excellent books on the topic and several web resources as well.

Different Textures: Building a Vocabulary

There are almost limitless options available to an arranger who is having difficulty deciding on a texture for the background voices. What follows is in no way an exhaustive list, but rather a few core ideas to help you begin to think about possible directions for your BGs.

Obviously each group and arranger will have a different interpretation of the textural patterns described below. This is a good thing: we have no desire to steer future a cappella arrangers toward one specific sound or style. Contemporary a cappella developed over time at the hands of many musicians with different backgrounds who found a wide variety of solutions to some of the same problems. A standardized contemporary a cappella sound would be anathema and could result in its decline, even possibly its demise. We want arrangers to continually explore new textures, find new sounds, and keep apace of current popular music, which will keep contemporary a cappella fresh and relevant far into the foreseeable future.

Some of the ideas below specifically involve the bass line and others are independent. In the latter case, feel free to either follow the bass line of the original song or write your own.

Block Chords

These are cornerstone of doo-wop—triads, whole notes, and "oos" and "ahs." More than any other, this texture features (and consequently relies on) a strong solo. For those of you who scoff at this level of simplicity, remember that almost all successful a cappella songs have relied heavily on it. The simplest texture produces many of an arranger's most powerful and moving moments.

If you're thinking of this from the perspective of a movie director, big block whole-note chords are like a spotlight shining on your soloist: a clear, open harmonic structure that points directly at the lead singer's melodic motion. It is extremely effective, especially in juxtaposition with a more complex rhythmic underpinning later in the chart.

Build from the Text

This is possibly the next most obvious texture. It is also simple and effective, and it adds one more layer of texture and rhythmic possibility compared to block chords. Obviously, it's a good way to stress an important lyric. It's also useful when the text is bound to a specific rhythmic pattern that you'd like to play with.

Gringo Samba

Words and Music by Dylan Bell

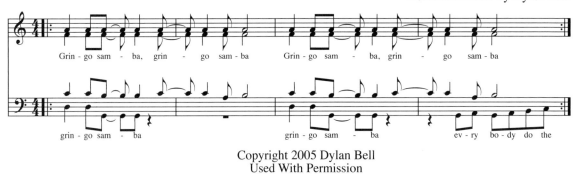

This texture is a common trope in harmonic writing, one well-known example being the Beach Boys' "Barbara Ann." The repetition of "Ba-ba-baaa, Ba-ba-bra Ann" provides a compelling rhythmic-harmonic base upon which the solo can build. It can also serve as a crucial rhythmic hook for the arrangement: soon as you hear "Ba-ba-baaaaa," you know what song it is long before the soloist arrives on the scene.

Repeating a lyric can have a trancelike effect, which has been used to great effect in many vocal arrangements of the folk song "Shenandoah." It doesn't work for all folk songs, however; consider "Danny Boy," which features three difficult syllables to linger on, especially the diphthong in "boy." Below is an example of this technique using Deke's original piece "Dive Into You."

Dive Into You

by Austin Willacy and Garth Kravits
arranged by Deke Sharon

Duet, Trio, Quartet

Think of Crosby, Stills, and Nash, the Dixie Chicks, or the Everly Brothers. There's a great strength in the sound of moving melodic lines, all constantly aligning in harmony. Rarely will you discover a song that wants its entire texture to be so rich, but juxtaposed with solo lines, parallel harmonies offer a welcome alternative. This texture can be especially effective in songs with more than three verses (often ballads or folk songs).

We stated earlier in this chapter that parallel harmonies don't always work in SATB writing. But this is one example where modern a cappella arranging can turn a classical "don't" into an effective "do."

If you're unsure of how to create an effective parallel harmonic line, start by singing along with the original recording. Try singing parallel thirds above the melody, adjusting the few notes that don't fit. You may find that your duet inspires a third line, or that a line above and below are needed to balance the solo—and voilà, a trio is born.

More than possibly any other arranging style, duets and trios practically demand that you sing them repeatedly while arranging, trying slight variations of pitches and chords until each line sits comfortably with the others and the background harmonies. You may want to save this step for last, as such a simple change as background voicings could throw the entire balance off, requiring a rethinking of the passage.

If you're feeling particularly bold, try a quartet, but be very careful of parallel voice leading between the highest and lowest voices, which will happen if you're relying on primarily triadic chords; the ear naturally hears the highest line most clearly, and then the lowest (particularly if either has the solo), leaving the inner voices almost inaudible. If you're arranging a song with more complex harmonies and denser chords, a fourth harmony can be effective.

Adding a duet or trio should work for almost every arrangement, provided you consider where the additional voices will join from an emotional as well as a musical perspective. Some things are well said by a group, but other statements benefit from the purity and clarity of a single voice.

There are times when having a melodic trio works in combination with itself, such as in this arrangement of "With a Little Help from My Friends" that Deke arranged for *The Sing-Off.* The women—soprano 1, soprano 2, and alto—are singing the melody as a three-part choir, and he has the tenors and baritones configured as a secondary trio, filling the space between the women and the bass line and providing a three-part countermelody. Note that he has the bass singing "da," as a more standard "dm" cannot compete with such a huge double-choir sound.

With A Little Help From My Friends

arr. Deke Sharon
Sing-Off Season 2, Episode 4 opening number

In this African-styled original piece, the female trio sings the main melodic theme, while the men sing a rhythmic guitarlike part. In the following bars, the roles reverse: the men respond in trio form, with the ladies taking over the guitar rhythm.

Obama, Twa Wakaribisha
(Obama, We Welcome You)

Words and Music by Dylan Bell

Arpeggiation

What first comes into most arrangers' minds when they think of arpeggiation is the cloying introduction to the 1950s classic "Mr. Sandman." Arpeggiation is actually much more effective when used in slow songs, since it enables you to use a simple repeated pattern without the risk of having the piece grind to a halt during performance. You don't simply have to go up or down the chord; arpeggiated passages are often most effective when the arpeggio is sung "out of order." Arpeggiation is also a good way to declare dissonant and multifactored chords, as well as chords with a unique voicing. Instead of hearing an often imperceptible cluster, your audience is given the opportunity to hear each factor individually, which allows them to "get" the chord more easily. Arpeggiation is a great texture to use to represent a moving piano part or finger-picked guitar parts.

Show Your Face

by Austin Willacy
arranged by Deke Sharon

Don't Fix What's Broken

Words and Music by Dylan Bell

Instrumental Idioms

More and more groups are attacking songs that almost force them to imitate instruments. Trumpets, trombones, and string basses have been replicated in a cappella music for decades, but it's only rather recently that groups have faced electric guitars and drum kits head-on. Moreover, contemporary a cappella, more than any of its predecessors, attempts to create the overall effect of a full band, orchestra, or track, such that the listener is fooled into believing the sound is more than simply voices. The idea is to create a full, compelling sound in which the listener gets lost, and over which the soloists can deliver a compelling solo without the audience's ever feeling as though the sound is too simple, hollow, or choral.

How should instrumental passages be written? That depends on the instruments and desired effect. A string quartet? A rock band? A 1970s funk horn section? There are as many different textures as there are styles of music. Alas, there is not space in this book to cover them all. We can, however, provide you with some ideas on how to proceed.

» Start by listening to music in the style you're planning to replicate, and look at sheet music if available.
» Knowing that the human voice does not cover the range of all instruments, don't hesitate to move the sounds into registers that can be sung. When unsure of the specific octave or placement, make your choice on the basis of where the vocalist is best able to replicate the sound. For example, vocal trumpet sounds usually sound best in a man's falsetto range. Sopranos make a great blistering first trumpet, and tenors and altos make great guitars.
» Be aware that it's not essential that every voice sound exactly like an instrument for the combined effect to work. The more layers, the more the listener's ear will be distracted and not notice any particular part. This is especially helpful when recording with unlimited ability to overdub layers of sound.
» We discussed this a little in step 2 and will describe it later in more detail, but think about the role of the instrument as much as its actual sound.

A background string pad may be represented by simple "oos" and "aahs" just as well as a painfully accurate replication of bows on strings.

The final point is one that will take a little time to explain, but hopefully will help you feel a bit more free when writing vocal parts.

Information is processed in the brain in different ways, with centers for math, spatial reasoning, language, music, and so on. When a person hears a singer, the linguistic and musical centers are activated, so that the brain processes both the lyrics and the musical phrases. However, when an instrument is playing without a singer, only the music centers of the brain are active.

If you heard a person singing a vocal trumpet followed by a real trumpet, you'd probably be taken aback by how different they sound. The human voice is not a brass instrument, and the volume and overtones are significantly different. But for a cappella arranging, this doesn't matter. Your singer does not have to sound exactly like an instrument; he or she simply has to fool the listener's ear and mind into categorizing the sound as instrumental, not vocal.

To this end, it's important to stay away from any sounds that have clear linguistic associations or underpinnings (such as "dum," which sounds like "dumb"; "doo," which sounds like "do"; and so on). Vowel sounds exist in a continuum, and it's possible to choose those that are not clearly a part of your spoken language. Part of the secret is to find a way not only to produce a sound that is closer to a specific instrument than anything else, but to make sure none of the elements of the sound you're creating are clearly linguistic. This is perhaps the greatest folly in the "collegiate a cappella" sound: all too often the singers treat the syllables as words, and the listener perceives them as such. "Jin jenna-jenna joh" may seem like a great choice for a guitar sound. But if pronounced too literally, it sounds like an alcoholic drink followed by a girl's name and a guy's name. Now do you see why it can sound goofy?

How does one figure all this out? Trial and error. Learning from others. And finally, exploring and listening and having fun. Play with sounds using your own voice, see what your singers are able to do, and take some risks in your arrangements. It's usually easy to come up with a safe alternative, so you should lead off with a strange new texture and see if it can be morphed into something usable in rehearsal. If not—no worries; chalk it up to experience and bring something new next time.

》 *Deke says: I'm sure at least one person paging through this book is looking for some cool guitar textures in hopes of being inspired for his vocal rock band. I have some bad news: there's no magic formula. In fact, perhaps the easiest, least impressive-looking arranging I've done is when I'm writing out vocal guitar parts. Why? Because they look like nothing: parallel octaves or fifths, simple rhythms. The magic is in the timbre—the sound that your singers are able to achieve vocally, amplified. If you want a great vocal guitar sound, you'll have to find it through trial and error on a mic, and once you have the sound, keep your guitar arrangement choices very simple.*

Here's an example of a guitar texture paired with a solo and harmony parts, from "Black Horse and the Cherry Tree." The lower four parts are treated as a unit, with the only difference being close voice leading for the upper parts (though not for the bass, who leaps a fifth to remain on the root of the chord). The syllable "zhm" replicates a firmly strummed guitar string with a bit of a scrape at the beginning of the sound. Guitar chords, especially in rock, sometimes work best as parallel open fifths, but this song represents acoustic guitar, using thirds.

Black Horse And The Cherry Tree

Here's one of Dylan's originals, "Don't Fix What's Broken," as recorded by Cadence. This arrangement was conceived as a two-guitar rock-band sound. The "rhythm guitar" part sings open fifths and sixths on the syllable "jn," while the "lead guitar" has a more melodic, arpeggiated part, sung on "gn" or "goh."

Don't Fix What's Broken

Words and Music by Dylan Bell

Instrumental Solos

Instrumental solos, present in a large percentage of pop songs, used to be the bane of many an arranger's existence but are now quite commonplace. The only confusing side effect is that few vocalists have had an opportunity to replicate instruments previously during their training and careers, so it falls to the a cappella arranger and music director to foster this talent within his or her group. This is a wide and largely uncharted territory, but there are some suggestions we can offer to get you started:

> » Nothing is "wrong." It's all a matter of what you want to achieve and what your singers can do. To this end, standard vocal writing rules largely fall away, and cues should be taken from instrumental, not vocal writing.
> » Start by imitating instruments exactly, and only later perhaps build and transform these into other sounds. Otherwise, you can quickly lose focus, and unless your singers are experienced contemporary a cappella singers, the likely result will be timbres and phrasings that are confusing rather than compelling.
> » Don't be afraid to rely in part on amplification. Almost all popular instruments are amplified, altering much of their timbre. Play with microphones and effects, and you'll begin to discover that there's little that the human voice can't do.
> » If you know whom you are writing for, rely on specific voices and specific talents rather than generalizations. This aspect of vocal production is so new and unstandardized that you should know your singer's specific abilities before making choices about your arrangement.
> » If you are arranging for an unknown group or are writing for public consumption, consider offering simple but specific instructions and sonic references (such as "muted 'Miles Davis' trumpet") rather than trying to write syllables, and let them discover how to achieve it on their own.

Rather than exactly replicate the sound of a harpsichord with rock back, for the solo section of the Beatles' "Girl" Deke went with a nonstandard yet easy-to-reproduce "nung" syllable for the soprano and tenor lines, not unlike the way a note on the harpsichord is struck and then resonates quietly. The alto provides a more continuous line, and "noo" allows the line to continue ("nung" would have emphasized the attacks too much and gotten lost in the middle of the other two vocal lines). The bass part is written on "thm," replicating a string bass.

Sometimes an instrumental passage is so well-known as to be nearly impossible to remove without being missed. Moreover, in a song without a bridge, it may function as a necessary departure before a final chorus. Both happen to be the case in the Beatles classic "Drive My Car," which presented a significant problem when arranging for publication, as it would have been foolish for Deke to rely on a singer in every high school to deliver a superb vocal guitar solo.

In addition, the total range of the solo in the Beatles recording is rather significant, which would present problems for any vocal part Deke assigned it to. For that reason, he decided to split the line up between three vocal lines—soprano, alto, and tenor—keeping the bass free to fill the rhythmic and melodic role of Paul McCartney's signature bass line.

The guitar line starts each two-bar phrase with a couple of approach notes, then a high pitch (which Deke knew needed to go to the soprano) that resolves downward with a figure spanning approximately a fourth. He gave the approach to the tenor and the release to the alto so that each would have something to do.

Knowing that the highest voice pulls the most focus, Deke knew he had to keep the soprano line relatively sparse if he wanted people to hear what was happening in the inner voices as the primarily melodic figure. To that end, he chose to have them strike their one note, then hold it for two bars. The altos completing the phrase had plenty to do with simply holding their note at the end of the line. He didn't want the G to clash with the tonic chord that arrives across the bar line, so he had them slide up to the fifth of the chord, an A. The tenor line provided a greater challenge, as they had nothing to do once they sang their brief beginning of the guitar line. The alto above them would be able to hold the focus when they took over so long as Deke didn't write anything too complex for them, so a series of dotted quarter notes would provide some momentum without being overwhelming.

As for the syllables, he started with everyone on the same syllable, but that proved too boring, and any imitative guitar sound he wrote in would sound rather goofy when sung by an entire group of singers. Since the original guitar solo is so well-known, Deke figured it would be OK to write a different set of syllables for each of the parts, leaving the overall melodic guitar figure outlined but not driven home: lyrics for the soprano, a late '60's "na-na" figure for the altos, with the tenors singing the Beatle's classic "yeah yeah yeah" lyric. The end result is somewhat of a period pastiche of melodic lines, each able to stand on its own, with a greater purpose and effect when combined.

This is hardly the only possible nonimitative approach to an instrumental solo passage, but hopefully it does give an idea of how far one can venture from a vocal guitar solo without losing the flavor of the original song.

Girl

Lyric and Music by John Lennon and Paul McCartney
arr. Deke Sharon

Drive My Car

Arrangement by
Deke Sharon

Words and Music by
John Lennon and Paul McCartney

If you want to imitate an instrument well, there are a number of things to consider:

» *The attack of the instrument.* Is it plucked, blown, bowed, or strummed? Hard or soft? The attack is the strongest identifier for an instrument, so this will determine which consonants you use to start (we'll talk about syllable choices in greater detail later).

» *The tone of the instrument.* Is it fat or thin? High or low? Static or constantly moving?

» *Playing characteristics.* This is a little harder to get at first, but once you think about it and listen carefully to the instruments, it begins to make sense. For example, trumpets and saxophones have a broad, full sound, but not a huge change in tone: "bah" would work better than "doing." Strings can have moving dynamics throughout but don't have a loud, percussive attack: try "dee-dee-deeEEE," but not "bonk." Pianos have a clean, percussive attack but no vibrato: "ding" or "den" would work, but not "voooooOOOOOOO."

» *Other aspects* come into play as well when writing for the "instruments." Saxophones and pianos can make wide leaps, but trumpet lines should be more scalar. Strings are great for long, sustained chords and fast running lines, but the gentle attack means that they're not the best choice for rhythmic shots.

» *Deke says: There is no specific place to learn how to imitate instruments. I've taught some classes, alone and with others, that can be found on casa.org and YouTube, and there are others who have done the same. The best way to learn is to sit in a room with someone and learn from him or her (an a cappella event is a good place to find willing tutors), modifying the technique to fit your own vocal instruments. Once you have a core sound, practice along with a recording of an instrumentalist to help solidify your phrasing and technique.*

Individual Lines and Counterpoint

You may have found that many of your arrangements for groups with only four or five vocalists have a similar quality, perhaps because you've always arranged for soloist, a bassist, and a couple other voices singing harmonic lines with unified rhythms and syllables or lyrics.

If you're looking for a different texture, start by writing unique lines for each of the background voices. Cover the same chord factors you normally would, but have each sing different words and rhythms. You'll find that your group will have gone from a fairly homophonic to a polyphonic sound. You may want to assign each voice a specific instrument's part, or you may wish to divide them up so that each has its own rhythmic pattern or repeated lyric. However you choose to do it, the result will be a more intricate sound. With a lot of action happening simultaneously, you'll want to be extra careful with dynamics so that that you can spotlight particular lines that are important, and also so that you don't overwhelm the listener.

The song "Sunshine," written for the Cadence album *Twenty for One*, was conceived on piano. Kevin Fox, who arranged most of the song, had been using a "doot doot doot" piano-chords theme through much of the song, but Kevin and Dylan wanted to end with something different. Dylan eventually came up with the idea of taking snippets of the lead line and singing them in counterpoint with three of the singers while the bass kept the anchor rhythm going. The chords move fairly frequently in this song, and as a jazz-pop piece Kevin and Dylan wanted to keep some of the nice jazzy harmonies—not easy to do in counterpoint! The result provides a nice breath of fresh air with which to end the piece.

Sunshine

If pure counterpoint proves too much for a passage, look for a middle ground between parallel harmonic writing and pure counterpoint. In the House Jacks, with two of the five members on bass and vocal percussion and a third on the lead, everything else has to be covered by the remaining two voices. The top line is the solo, with the other two lines weaving back and forth between parallel harmonies with the melody and parallel harmonies with each other. The result is a cascading vocal figure that sounds as though it has more than three tenors. Note that the lowest tenor sometimes crosses above the middle tenor to continue a melodic line, as seen across the bar from m. 1 into m. 2.

Arranging this chorus was a bit of a logic puzzle. Deke knew he wanted to use primarily parallel thirds and sixths: fourths and fifths sound too "boxy," seconds and sevenths are far too dissonant, and with only three voices any octaves would be a wasted opportunity at which chord factors would have to be dropped. Plus, the harmonic rhythm requires a new chord every two beats, so the tenors need to move quickly between chord factors to cover all three notes in each triad—and do so in a way that's melodic while serving a harmonic function.

Athena

Playful pop

Words and Music by Deke Sharon

Juxtapose Musical Styles

This can easily be done to a nauseating extreme, but in moderation it's clever and fun and can offer a fresh perspective on a piece. Get a pen and paper and list of all of the musical styles you can think of, from Gregorian chant to hip-hop. Many of these can likely be replicated with voices, and you may choose to base an entire song on a completely different style. A good example of this is the King's Singers' album *The Beatles Connection*. They have a slow calypso version of "Ob-la-di, Ob-la-da" and a baroque "Can't Buy Me Love." Both work well musically, beyond being clever. The key is in finding the right match. Another option is to keep a song similar to the original and have one passage shift gears into another style. Again, we advise caution: this practice can easily be overused, drawing too much attention to the arrangement.

Clever is never enough. You might have a cute idea for an arrangement, but cute only gets you about four measures into a performance or recording (perhaps eight if you're extremely clever). Once the laughter dies down and the idea sinks in, it's up to you to make good on your promise and give your audience a reason to care about the next three minutes of music. If you can't do that, come up with a better core idea for your arrangement, and perhaps throw in a brief quote that exhibits your idea but doesn't rely on it at length.

Copy Another Arranger's Style

Since there's no formal way to get an a cappella education, we learn wherever we can. Most a cappella groups start out copying other groups' best songs, and from this experience they learn how to sing and phrase a cappella. The best education you can get as an arranger is to study other arrangements. If you think this is cheap or unfair, then you're denying yourself the only proven way to understand arranging and composing music. That's how we learned to arrange. And besides, if you could somehow get a bachelor of a cappella degree, what do you think you would do in class?

Every great composer and arranger from Bach to Duke Ellington learned by copying, and now it's your turn. Try to arrange a ballad like Gene Puerling, a jazz standard like Mervyn Warren, or a Beatles tune like Richard Greene. (For more information about these arrangers, please see Appendix B.) Chances are your arrangements will sound different than theirs would, and the process will strengthen your arranging tools while giving you new vocal colors and techniques to add to your expanding palette.

Invent New Sounds

In any given arrangement, you're probably going to keep within our tonal system, and you're going to have a melody, chord progression, and a fair amount of repetition. It's literally impossible to invent new chords or rhythms. Just about everything's been done, and a good portion of it is just too dissonant or complex for most people to listen to. The final frontier is timbre. Throughout musical history, just about everything possible has been done with instruments, while people still count on the voice to sing a melody with lyrics. Now that we're using the voice as an instrument, it's time to open up the floodgates and use more than the 1 percent of possible vocal sounds that Western music has limited itself to for the past thousand years.

» *Deke says: When you're looking for a new sound or direction for a passage, remember that there are only four basic attributes of sound: pitch (which, when one or more are combined, creates harmony), duration (which, when divided, creates rhythm), loudness (which, via contrast, results in dynamics) and timbre. I spent 99 percent of my musical education focusing on the first two, with a little of the third woven in . . . but almost never the fourth. Listen to some Meredith Monk and other vocal pioneers.*

Any sound you can get the body to produce is fair game, and given the number of constants in most arrangements, a few strange new sounds are often welcome. Work with your singers and see what they can do. Chances are, if one person can do it, the others can learn. If you're not at liberty to order a bunch of vocalists to make odd noises, it's your job to sit in a room, blinds closed, and mess around until you have a couple of building blocks that can be used in your next arrangement.

And while we're on this subject, let's delve into the world of . . .

Syllables

In the beginning, at least the beginning of Western vocal music, there were only words—real words that made sense. In Western choral music, everyone sang the text, without any sounds that were sung purely for sound's sake. The big exception was the melisma. Sometimes several notes would be sung over one vowel in a word—usually nice, open-sounding vowels like "ah," "oh," and "oo." Sometimes this was used for word-painting. Imagine a word such as "fly" or "soar" sung over a long, ascending melodic line. The sound might be somewhat abstract, but it would still be connected to words.

In the early twentieth century vocalists started looking to instruments for sonic inspiration. Jazz singers such as Louis Armstrong would sing "scat syllables": in essence, he sang his trumpet. Early vocal groups such as the Mills

Brothers were novel and innovative in their imitation of basses and horns. With the arrival of vocal jazz ensemble singing and doo-wop came a wider and more systematized use of these "nonsense syllables." (Incidentally, we've never liked that term: in their own way, the sounds do make sense. They should be called "sound syllables" or something else instead.) Most recently, a cappella singing has evolved into the "vocal band" sound, in which often very literal interpretations of instruments are sung, and the spectrum of syllables has blown wide open.

Having a good vocabulary in background syllables is an important part of the arranging process. An arrangement that uses only "oos" and "ahs" has the potential to become texturally monochromatic, dynamically static, and overall boring. However, the opposite can be just as bad: overuse of wacky syllables can come off sounding contrived, goofy, distracting from the song and melody, and overall unmusical.

Let's start by giving an overview of the basic sounds in the English language. We'll call these "musical phonetics." (For you linguistic experts out there, we know this isn't linguistically correct, and you may gnash your teeth over our pronunciation guides. But we're making music here, not transcribing dialects, so please bear with us).

The following descriptions and tables are taken, with the author's permission, from an article called "A Treatise on Background Syllables," by the a cappella arranger Greg Martin.

Consonants

The following table contains most of the consonants we use in English. Those that are placed in the same row or column share certain qualities.

ng	n	m		hummed consonants
g	d	z	b	voiced basic consonants
k	t	s	p	unvoiced basic consonants
ch	th	sh	f	unvoiced aspirated consonants
j	thh	zh	v	voiced aspirated consonants
y	l	r	w	liquid consonants

Most of them appear just as they would in an English word; the two exceptions are [thh] and [zh]. The difference between [th] and [thh] is that pronouncing [thh] uses the larynx, while pronouncing [th] does not. The [th] sound appears in *thin* and *cloth*, while [thh] appears in *this* and *clothe*. [zh] is the sound represented by the s in *measure*.

Basic consonants are essentially little bursts of air with or without voice, while aspirated consonants are more sustained, like hissing or buzzing sounds. Voiced consonants use the larynx, while unvoiced consonants don't. Hummed and liquid consonants don't require bursts of air or aspiration—only the larynx and a certain position for the tongue and lips. With hummed consonants the air comes out of the nose, while with liquid consonants it comes out of the mouth. Consonants in the same column are produced with very similar mouth positions.

The two major omissions from that table are the consonant [h], an unvoiced aspirated consonant, and the glottal stop, a basic unvoiced consonant, which I'll write with a carat: [^]. A glottal stop is just what it says—a quick squeeze of the glottis (part of the larynx) to stop the air momentarily. For example, there's a glottal stop at the beginning of each syllable in *uh-oh*; and when we don't enunciate [the "t"s in] the word *button*, we use a glottal stop instead: [buh^n].

Vowels

So much for consonants; let's look at vowels. The first two columns in the following table list pure English vowels (in the notation I'm using) and common words that demonstrate their pronunciation. The last two columns do the same with diphthongs.

[ee]	beat		
[ih]	bit		
[eh]	bet	[ay]	bay
[uh]	but		
[aah]	bat	[ow]	bough
[ah]	Bach	[igh]	bye
[aw]	bought		
[oe]	book		
[oh]	boat	[oi]	boy
[oo]	boot		

The order these vowels are listed in is meaningful: if we pronounced them one at a time, starting from the top, our mouths would get narrower and narrower as we went. So [ee] is the widest vowel and [oo] is the narrowest. Also, our mouths would be tallest in the middle of the list and shortest at the ends; [ah] is the tallest vowel and [ee] and [oo] are the shortest. (If you've ever been stung by a wasp and yelled "YEEEOOOW!," you were actually taking a quick tour of those ten vowels in the given order.) The diphthongs, listed in the last two columns, are just pairs of vowels with no intervening consonant or gap. Specifically, [ay = eh + ee, ow = aah + oo, igh = ah + ee, oi = oh + ee], which explains which rows they're listed in. Not surprisingly, the width and height of a diphthong are the same as those of the equivalent pure vowel; so [igh] is the tallest diphthong and [ay] the widest.

A sound syllable basically has three parts: the attack (the initial consonant or consonant blend unless the sound is a basic "ah"-type vowel sound), the vowel (the basic sound), and the sustain or stop ("sustain" could be the vowel, or one of the hummed or vocalized consonants; the stop could be a consonant that finishes the sound such as, well, the "p" in "stop").

This may sound esoteric at first, especially if you haven't studied phonetics, but it's actually rather easy to put into practice. The more free you allow yourself to be while exploring different combinations of consonants and vowels, the sooner you'll arrive on new combinations you like.

Instrumental Imitation

Increasingly, sound syllables in a cappella are used to imitate instruments. The easiest and most natural way to figure out how to imitate an instrument is simply try it yourself and have your singers try as well. You don't have to reinvent the wheel: singers today have already figured out many different instruments (including trumpet, trombone, clarinet, sax, flute, violin, cello, bass, harmonica, and electric guitar).

But making funny noises or being a mimic isn't second nature to everyone. If this is the case, you could try a more systematized way. Using the attack-plus-vowel-plus-sustain model, let's look at some instruments.

Piano.

Attack: percussive, medium to hard: maybe b- d-

Vowel: neutral, varies depending on dynamics: for example, e-, i-, or uh-.

Sustain: short or long, but with a decay: could end with an unsounded consonant like -p, or a sustain like -m, or -n, or -ng.

This gives you:

bep	bip	buhp
dep	dip	duhp
bem	bim	bum
dem	dim	dum
ben	bin	bun
den	din	dun
beng	bing	bung
deng	ding	dung

Now try saying or singing them. Some of them work, some of them don't. In the end, you'll likely only choose one or two. But you've generated no fewer than twenty-four different possible syllables for one single instrument. And we're not even trying that hard. You could use a "k" or "g" for a very percussive piano, for example, and end up with several more.

Let's try the same process with a fairly different instrument.

Strings.

> *Attack:* soft to very slow, and "bow-sounding": v- zh- . . . or maybe no attack consonant
>
> *Vowel:* wide range from dark to very bright: -oo, -ih, -ee
>
> *Sustain:* long, slow release: an open vowel without an ending consonant, or a soft release, like a silent -p

. . . giving us:

oo	ih	ee
voo	vih	vee
zhoo	zhih	zhee
oop	ihp	eep
voop	vihp	veep
zhoop	zhip	zheep

In all these examples we've started the sound out with single consonants, but some of the best and most onomatopoetic sounds will use multiple consonants at the beginning. An obvious case in point: for guitars, try the word "strum." The "str" combination at the beginning beautifully imitates the sound of a guitar pick striking multiple strings, one just after another.

Generating sounds like this can give you limitless possibilities. You'll eventually find some overlap, and this will help you narrow down your choices. Remember the Laws of Good Taste: just because you can doesn't mean you should, and you need to serve the song first. Or go the opposite way: use crazy syllables to exaggerate, caricature, or create comic effect.

» *Dylan says: Don't get hung up on syllables! I've seen so many arrangers pulling their hair out trying to come up with "innovative syllables," usually to end up with contrived and cheesy-sounding results. In general, my own charts use a fairly limited range of syllables, most of them based on pure instrumental sounds that can be rendered easily and naturally with the voice. I liken syllables in arranging to vocabulary in language. Of course, it's great to have a wide vocabulary, but it doesn't make you any smarter or make what you say any more important. In choosing multisyllabic words where a simple word would do, you risk coming off as pompous, confusing, or silly. The same can happen with syllables. Serve the music first and let your own need to be innovative take a back seat.*

Making Your Own Sounds

Who says we have to stick to imitating instruments? One of the greatest things about the human voice is that it can combine so many of the aspects of instruments without some of their limitations. You can have a "piano" with vibrato, or "strings" that sound like they were hit with a hammer . . . or some out-of-this-world sound that even the most advanced synthesizer can't reproduce. For inventing your own sounds, nothing beats pure experimentation. If you need a nudge, use the tables above and the attack-vowel-sustain technique to create new sounds. For unfiltered brainstorming, you could make a "syllable sandwich": randomly choose one attack, one vowel, and one sustain, and see what comes up. This is a great way of shaking up your usual way of coming up with sounds; some of them may be silly, but at least they're something you hadn't thought of before.

You may also decide that it's not all about a literal imitation of the instrument, but rather a representation of what that instrument is contributing to the overall sound. Instead of focusing on the sound of the instrument, you can use a combination of semianalytical description and vague, metaphorical subjective imagery. For example:

» "The piano is the meat and potatoes . . . it's the harmonic grounding."
» "The strumming acoustic guitar is adding a shimmery sound to the whole thing. Almost like shakers, but with notes too."
» "The horns are like a call-and-response to the lead vocal. Very rhythmic."
» "The electric guitar is chugging along, driving the song. It sounds kind of bright orange to me."
» "The strings are moody, like a dark fog."

Hearing the instruments' roles like this is often the first step toward a more compositional and transformational, rather than translational, arrangement style. You might find this process very liberating!

Remember—a cappella music has the ability to shift gears timbrally more effectively and immediately than any instrument or instrumental ensemble. Don't be afraid to change a song from its original inception, however dramatically. That's what arranging is all about.

The Ten Steps in Action: "We Three Kings"

In this song, the BGs will be taking the role of almost everything other than the Bee Gees, as we jump from style to style. For lack of a better moniker, I decided to call one set of three voices the "trio" and the other set the "schmio."

There is too much to say for me to explain every single chord voicing and rhythmic choice, but I will point out a few of note:

» "Dung" was never meant to sound like the word, but rather ring rather cleanly like "dng." Instead of an implied "i" vowel, though, I wanted an implied "uh"—somewhere between handbells and church bells.

» If you look at the figure in the trio starting in m. 6, you'll notice that it's intentionally reminiscent of the descending melody of the *Mission: Impossible* theme. Beneath that part I wanted a more choral harmonic pad, but that wasn't driving enough, so I put a baritone on a pulsing eighth-note figure. When the trio shifts to "oo" in m. 10 (a practical as well as musical consideration: the voices need a break after ringing on a closed vowel in the stratosphere), I shifted the schmio to an arpeggiated combination of bells ("dung") and pizzicato strings ("thm") to continue the orchestral sound.

» After writing a straightforward three-part trio, it was clear the chorus could use a bit more color, so I moved one voice ("trio 3") to sing a series of color notes. I figured this was the safest approach: even though I didn't know their voices and abilities yet, I was sure that a couple of them would have no difficulty holding these diatonic chord tones against the compelling parallel motion of the chorus melody and harmony parts.

» With the exception of the high verse "dung" arpeggio, all of the parts were kept well within standard male vocal range. This was intentional, as I did not yet know their voices. Better safe than sorry.

» I'm a huge advocate of repetition unless there's a strong reason for change. In the case of this arrangement, I felt the second verse could be the same as the first, since the single voice on the solo would provide enough variety. To this day I've never heard a single person comment that the arrangement was great except for the second verse.

» I did feel a need for variety in the second chorus, so I decided to allow the solo trio to reunite after the highest soloist delivered the verse, and gave the trio a rather standard gospel background part that held chords while the soloists had the melody, filling the holes with moving melody. The schmio was given an instrumental figure to create another layer of depth. Everyone joins the lyric in the last measure of the chorus ("perfect light"), because I wanted the contrast of all voices shifting quickly to instrumental textures again.

» Third verse, same as the first (and second, for that matter)—again, nary a complaint. The fact that the bass sings the melody draws enough focus. Pop music nowadays literally copies and pastes entire musical sections with alarming frequency, so it's not something anyone would notice.

» Third chorus, same as the second. We've only heard this iteration once, and it's only eight measures long, so one more time won't get boring, and setting up a similar sound prepares us for . . .

» The reggae section. The schmio is playing skank (reggae rhythm) guitar, with the trio as backing singers. I didn't want the backing parts to be very busy; that way the soloist would be very free to phrase the melody almost out of time and fill holes with ad libs, both sung and spoken.

» The schmio part remains almost the same from verse to chorus, except that I shift from a jangly guitaresque "jng" back to the "dung" sound. I wanted a timbral change here, and returning to the sound from before while staying with the guitar figure subtly sonically marries the earlier and current sections of the song.

» For the coda, a little repetition was called for, and I wanted the voices to break away from their various roles throughout the song, relax, morph back to vocal lines, and cut loose, especially on the last two measures (gospel chords, with a couple of guys ad libbing—with so many doublings, losing a couple of singers wasn't a problem). Live, I wanted a moment where they all drop character, can become themselves again, and share the moment with the audience.

Once I was finished with the last measure, it was time to go back through and add some sprinkles.

The Ten Steps in Action: "Go Tell It on the Mountain"

In my case, I was dealing with far fewer voices. With bass, drums, and lead all taken care of, I was left with three BGs to cover everything else. I wanted their parts to be full of variety, interesting to sing, and interesting to listen to.

I made the decision at this point not to treat the BGs like literal instruments. With only three singers, I'd be hard-pressed to come up with multiple instrument textures at once, and shifting instruments in mid-song might sound a little jarring. It could be done—but I decided instead to keep the BGs sounding primarily vocal, defining their parts by the functions that instruments play in a band.

I already had a rhythm section with my bass and drums. With an R & B/funk chart like this, I imagined that the BGs could fill several roles:

Keyboard/guitar: neutral "doot-doo" syllables, with a little rhythmic life to them

Horns/backing vocals: Parts like these are often interjectory and rhythmic, playing off the lead vocal

Hammond organ/choir: "Oos" and "aahs," usually as a harmonic/textural "pad," meant to sound thick and fat

Lots of ideas for how the BGs could function! Here's how they work.

Intro (mm. 1–4). The BGs' "Go tell it!" line establishes a main theme or character for the arrangement and appears throughout. It acts a little bit like horn shots or a gospel choir.

Chorus 1 (mm. 5–11). The lyric is a strong, joyous statement, and the melody is interesting and spells out the chord changes nicely. Why even bother with chords? I decided to make this a rousing, full-on male unison, almost like a football cheer, complete with the shouted "Go!" For added strength, I harmonized two places: m. 8 ("ev'rywhere") and m. 11 ("Je-sus Christ").

Interlude (mm. 12–15). Same as the intro. Repetition is good here.

Verse 1 (mm. 16–23). Time to put the spotlight on the soloist. I decided to give the BGs a pretty gentle part, almost like a Rhodes piano or rhythm guitar. That said, they still get to interact with the soloist a little. In between the lead lines, the BGs respond, based on whatever the lyric is singing. This is a little free-association game I like to play when writing vocal-style BG parts. In this case, to the lyric "While shepherds kept their watching, over silent flocks by night" the BGs respond with "O Holy Night," then go back to Pianoland. To help with the buildup to the chorus, the BGs switch to open, rising "aah"s, similar to a choir or organ part—with one more added "Tell it, tell it" bit to propel us into the chorus.

Chorus 2 (mm. 24–33). Deke's philosophy of "repetition is good" works especially well in his chart, where he's already throwing variety at the listeners and performers left and right with soloist and style switches. I could have done a straight repeat for the next chorus, but I always like my charts to develop as they get further into the song, and I also like writing things that allow the listener to get something new out of the piece each time. I would typically write more straight repeats for an amateur or unknown group, but these guys are professionals, so I knew I could change things up a little.

The second chorus has the same football-cheer feeling, but on the "ev'rywhere" I added a little extra energy, including a delayed "Go!" on the next bar. Instead of going into another interlude or vamp, we're going into another verse. So I ramped into it with the triplet figure at "Jesus Christ is born!," followed by a couple of added bars (mm. 32–33), to create a little soul "mini-breakdown," sung softly to get us into the softer second verse about the manger. (Though not notated, the drums cut out at mm. 32–33 as well.)

Verse 2 (mm. 34–41). This verse follows the same basic formula as verse 1, with a variation. Instead of a vocal response to the lead lyric, I threw in a musical "Easter egg," a little moment of fun that people may or may not catch (or may hear weeks later). See it? Hint: take a look at Chris's staff at mm. 35–37.

Since the lead line sings "In a lowly manger, the humble Christ was born," I had Chris sing the melody to the carol "Away in a Manger." The rest of the guys harmonize around it to fit the chord changes. I could have had the BGs singing "away in a manger" lyrics; but that would have pulled too much focus from the lead, and also would have made the joke too obvious. Even if you don't know you're hearing a quote from another carol, the descending figure still sounds nice on its own.

Chorus 3 (mm. 42–52). We've now had two choruses and verses; it's time to kick it up a notch. I chose to do so by adding another layer of texture. Instead of another big unison chorus, we'd give the melody to some gang vocals, who would sing it very straight and clean. If they were instruments, they'd be like a sax section, laying it down nice and even while horns dart and dance around, or like a legato cello section in an orchestra. Now the regular BGs play an active role. Pretty much all the rhythmic figures are taken from either the intro or the verse, which helps tie all the sections together nicely. The lead can riff and style around all this. We then step it up again with pedal-tone bass we talked about in the last chapter, and more intro and vamp–like parts for the BGs.

Verse 3 (53–60). And we're back. We dial back on the chorus party and have another verse, which is very similar to verse 1. The melody gets a couple of variations; the BGs respond to the lead lyric, "When I was a seeker, I sought both night and day," with their own line: "seek and ye shall find." But wait—at m. 60, the BGs sing "tell it on the mountain" instead of the usual "tell it, tell it." Why?

Truth be told, I could have just as easily kept "tell it, tell it" the same. But "tell it on the mountain" looks both backward and forward. We heard this figure in the intro, but never since, so I thought I'd tie it back in. It also foreshadows the final section's "get on up and tell it on the mountain."

Chorus 4 (mm. 61–67). We went to a new place in chorus 3, so I thought it was worth a straight repeat here.

Drum solo and final section (mm. 68–76). Nothing new here; the BGs during the drum solo simply use the "go tell it" theme I used throughout the chart. When we go to church at the end, the BGs take full focus. No more "doo-doos": they're full-on horns/gospel singers with some James Brown–esque vocal parts. The gang vocals tie it together with long high notes, like a high string pad. We bring it all home together in the final bar with a rhythmic unison.

CHAPTER 16

Step 9: Final Touches

You've written your melody, bass line, and BGs, and you think the chart is more or less complete. Now it's time to put the finishing touches on it.

During the arranging process, the Dreamer and the Editor ran the show. Now it's the Critic's turn to shine, with the Editor riding shotgun. Whether singing the parts in your head or recording, the process and purpose are the same: look under every rock and eighth note for anything that's less than excellent.

Like the Critic himself, it's easy to portray this as criticism or judgment in the negative sense. But we call this part of the process "refinement," and for good reason. Refining means ridding something of its impurities so that the result is as strong, pure, and perfect as it can be. The process, while seemingly negative on the surface, moves toward the goal of making something better.

Put another way, this process is like "product testing." Car designers may simulate car crashes, but they're not trying to destroy the car: they're trying to make it stronger by finding weaknesses and fixing them before it ever gets to the driver. Approach the refinement process with the same spirit of positivity, and you'll be proud of the results.

It is often smartest to start with general observations and get more nitty-gritty, but the Critic often just grabs what he sees first, in either a linear, beginning-to-end fashion or a cherry-picking, spot-the-worst-things-first fashion. It doesn't really matter how your process goes, but at some point, a combination of a linear approach and a general-to-specific, spiraling-in approach will help make sure your refining process is thorough. There's no point in picking on a piece of bad voice leading if the whole section needs an overhaul.

Here are some general guidelines to approach your chart critically:

Structural: Are you happy with how the form goes together? Do the sections flow well from one place to another?

Energy: Does the arrangement have a nice sense of development? Does it plod along, or lose focus partway through? Are you getting bored as you go through it?

Executional: How well does it sing? Does the voice leading feel comfortable? Imagine teaching this to a group. Are there places where they'll struggle? Challenging sections are well and good, but they should be worth the effort, musically. If there's a musical payoff, great. If not, it may be good to do some adjusting.

Technical: Any wrong notes or rhythms? Any better options for layout and readability? Did you break any of the "commandments" we mentioned earlier in chapter 12 (step 5, "Preparing Your Materials"), and if so, was there a good reason for doing so?

If you see a mistake, your first instinct will be to try to fix it right away. That's the sign of an impatient Editor! Let the Critic finish his job first. Every arranging decision affects the next, so fixing little details higgledy-piggledy may not help. As you comb through an arrangement, you could choose to take notes, like a director watching the run-through of a play. As you go through your notes, you'll be able to prioritize. Fixing one thing might solve another problem. Or you may need to fix several things in tandem to make sure that they stay consistent.

The Rule of Three

The Rule of Three is a very simple but powerful guideline: if you're singing through a part and you stumble over a passage three times, you should probably change it. Why?

You're the master architect behind this arrangement. You know (or should know) why every note is there; you made every decision that led to this passage. So if *you* can't get it after three tries, there's a good chance your group—which is approaching this chart without all the background knowledge and insight that you have—will probably stumble five times, or even ten times, before they get it. It may be a complex part, but something challenging and musically exciting. On the other hand, maybe it's just bad writing: difficult to sing because a note clashes, or because it's unnecessarily complicated.

But first, check the obvious: are the notes and rhythms correct? You may be reading one thing (what you actually wrote) and thinking another (what you *meant* to write), which would cause you to stumble. If that's not the case, consider rewriting the part. If it's a straight transcription of a recorded part, maybe it's just not voice-friendly and deserves to be let go.

If you make the same error a number of times in a row and sing it the same "wrong" way each time, your own musicianship is telling you something. Go with your instincts: it's possible that the "wrong" way is actually the better way.

Read Through the Chart: Know It Vertically

Reading through the chart is more like score study, and more visual than aural. This is a good place to get a bird's-eye view of the chart. Look over all the chord changes or instrumental type parts. Do the chords seem complete? Any errors or missing parts?

One nice thing about notation is that is that it's a good visual representation of how things sound. Very often, what you see is what you will hear. You can see how energy and texture develop as the staves start to look more filled up or sparse. Rhythmic flow is easy to notice.

>> *Dylan says: Melodic counterpoint or interplay between parts is clear to see: I've often written interlocking or contrapuntal parts in part "by eye," noticing the spots on the page where nothing seems to be moving and filling them in.*

Sometimes, without reading the notes at all, you can skim a chart and just look at the density of the writing. Intro—sparse. Lots of white space and whole notes. Chorus—dense, with lots of rhythm. And so on. In more vertical, chorale-type parts, you can see the division of voices, where parts are too close or too far apart.

Not everybody can hear a chart in his or her head simply by looking at it. If this is the case for you, try going though the parts on the piano or playing it back on the computer.

Sing Through the Chart: Know It Horizontally

All the score study in the world will never compare to the actual act of doing. Reading through a chart in your head will give you a decent picture of what the parts sound like, but actually singing through them will let you know what they *feel* like. This is where you can put yourself into the shoes of a singer trying to make sense of what you wrote.

Natural Is Good

We don't mean to suggest that you shouldn't take risks or go out on a limb with some interesting rhythms or syllables—far from it. These are the moments that can make an arrangement stand out and be noticed. But even if the part is "out there," it should be natural—that is, it should have its own internal logic. A vocalist can sing it and "get it," knowing what that part is doing and why it's like that. A singer will be able to do the craziest part if he or she understands it: he or she will internalize the logic and be able to really commit to the part. Particularly in instrumentally based charts, this often separates the truly groovy guitar part from a goofy and forced-sounding "joh, jinna-jinna joh joh."

A part should also feel natural technically. "No pain, no gain" is for body-builders, not singers: if it hurts, strains, or feels bad, you shouldn't ask someone to sing it. If odd leaps are hard to sing, they most likely won't sound all that great either. It's not unreasonable to think that a singer will have a harder time than you when phrasing a line you wrote, but it's unlikely he or she will have an easier time. If you find something to be clumsy, it's clumsy.

Own the Parts

As you sing though the parts, get to know them. A good arranger "owns" the parts in the score, knowing them well enough to practically have them memorized. This shows that each part was very deliberately conceived and written. If you find you don't know your own parts, it might mean:

» You're not writing with the singers in mind.
» You're thinking too "vertically," writing from one chord to the next without paying attention to the line's melodic direction. This is especially common when writing jazz charts.
» If using computer notation, you're writing "from the computer." Read on for why this can be a problem.

The folly of "computer writing." It's a common error—especially among less experienced arrangers—to write something, have the computer play it back, change it, play it back again, and so on. On the surface, it seems to make sense: instant feedback as you write can't be anything but a good thing, right? Wrong.

When you do this, you're not using your inner ear enough. Computer playback is basically good for two things: hearing complex harmonies or melodic interactions that might be outside the realm of your inner ear, and "spell-checking" a section once it's mostly written for actual pitch and rhythm errors. Computer playback can be very misleading. Parts and chords that sound fine may not translate well to voices, since they don't take into account how a singer has to sing them. Computers don't care about odd leaps or terrible voice leading. On the other hand, you can get away with some dissonances in a vocal chart, such as a melodic run that goes through a couple of "wrong" notes on the way up to the right one. These can sound just plain wrong on the computer but come across as delicious moments of tension with voices.

Falling into the trap of write, playback, write, playback means that you lose connection to the part you're writing, basing your writing on moment-to-moment reactions rather than a larger sense of melodic or harmonic direction. Put another way: you're letting the computer tell you what to do, rather than vice versa. Your computer doesn't know how to arrange, so stop asking it to!

There are a couple of ways to solve this:

1. Try to avoid checking every note addition or change with the computer. Write from your head for a while, at least a few bars or even a full section, then check it out to see if you like it.
2. Sing, rather than play, your lines. Trust your inner ear: if you eventually play it back and it sounds bad, it's probably easy to change.

It also bears mentioning that there is a lesser related folly: piano writing. This affects experienced pianists who conceive music essentially through their fingers on a piano. There is rarely a more experienced musician than a fluent pianist, and yet there's a tendency to write lines that make sense on a piano but are sometimes too angular, too mechanical for voices. Of course, playing back each line on the piano will not only prove useless in finding the problem; in fact, it will reinforce the appearance that all is well. So if you're a pianist, make sure to sing through each line in your arrangement before finalizing it.

Once you've looked over the score, it's time for the final step: recording/rehearsing your arrangement.

The Ten Steps in Action: "We Three Kings"

At the top of the song, I was hoping for the sound of a lit match, as we hear at the beginning of the *Mission: Impossible* theme; it can be reproduced with a "fffff" sound performed with a sforzando (I've never heard it done; I just messed around with vocal sounds until I could come up with something that could be represented reasonably well when written down). We don't have to exactly reproduce the sound of Lalo Schifrin's studio orchestra in the opening strains, and in fact a "diddle-iddle" out of time might actually be more effective than a more accurate representation, since it should elicit a smile. Obviously this moment is a very small one and matters little in the overall experience of the song, and yet for those of us who have enjoyed the original television show, it's a little touch that's appreciated.

In addition, I went through and sang each line as a melody in my head (to make sure nothing was too difficult or awkward), nudged a couple of chord voicings, dropped in the occasional pauses and breaths (if I don't choose 'em, they will!), tweaked syllables, and generally made sure things were presentable.

The Ten Steps in Action: "Go Tell It on the Mountain"

I tend to sweat over the BGs as I write them; chances are in my own process I integrate steps 8 and 9 somewhat. So when I got to this point, I was pretty happy with how my parts went.

I sang through them again and made sure everything scanned nicely in my voice. One thing I did was go over the chart for consistency. Did all the parts hang together nicely? I try to reuse rhythmic figures where possible so that any developments in my chart are additive, building on what we already have heard and know. I probably tweaked a few bits here and there, reusing a rhythmic or harmonic figure instead of creating a new one.

I also spent time on the notation side, making sure I had observed (most of) the "commandments" from step 5. Neat, clean charts make me happy, so I made sure the layout was easy to read. After that . . . I recorded it. On to step 10.

CHAPTER 17

Step 10: Record/Rehearse

If you have recording software and a microphone, one of the most effective ways to refine your arrangement is to record it. The experience of actually singing the parts at full volume (as opposed to singing along quietly), not to mention hearing how they land and align, is quite valuable.

If you can sing all parts, male or female, go for it. If you're a non-bass guy, don't worry too much about low bass parts, as singing an occasional note up the octave doesn't change the sound drastically; you'll still know whether or not something works. If parts of the arrangement are just too far out of your range to approximate, find a friend who can cover those parts. In addition, having another singer involved in recording and proofing your arrangement helps uncover little score errors and the like that you might otherwise overlook.

The act of multitracking is best if you have a grid to sing to—both pitch and rhythm—and the easiest way to create one is to export a MIDI file from your notation software and import it into your song file. Make adjustments as necessary for important elements such as tempo changes or repeated sections which may not be represented in the MIDI file (for example, if you used repeat dots or dal segnos in your chart but did not appropriately set the playback).

Next, prepare your tracks. In this case, it's easiest to use the score style we talked about earlier, so that your song file looks just like your chart (top track = solo, bottom track = bass).

Now you're ready to start singing.

Two at a Time

If your arrangement is largely homophonic and chorale-like, try singing "inside-out," starting with tenor and alto (or tenor 1 and alto 2—whichever parts are closest), and ending with soprano 1 and the lowest bass part. One of the advantages of inside-out recording, strangely enough, is that it sounds really weird at first. You won't just assume you know the part; you'll actually have to read it and see if it makes sense. If you can actually get through these parts on their own without too much difficulty, chances are the rest of your chart is quite user-friendly.

If the arrangement is more instrumental, try putting down the bass part first. Then, sing similar parts together. If you run out of similar parts for an "instrument" (for example, if there are three guitar parts), sing two together, then the last one alone. It's not worth trying to sing two different instruments at a time, as they'll just distract from each other.

One at a Time

If there's just one singer (or if you bring in your other singer later), there are a couple of options. For a homophonic or chorale chart, inside-out still works. You can either flip-flop through them (tenor, alto, bass, soprano) or stack down and up: tenor and bass, then alto and soprano. The latter is better if bringing in another singer. For an instrumental-type chart, the principle used for two singers applies: bass, then by instrument, and ending with the lead (or, if the lead helps you find your place in the song, bass, then lead, and finally instruments). There is no right or wrong way, and once you've done it a couple of times, you'll settle on your own preferred method.

As you record, circle or flag all your copy errors, including wrong notes and rhythms, squished-together lyrics and bars, and unfriendly page turns. You can write them in the chart or list them on paper by bar number.

Rehearsal

The final acid test: trying the chart with a real live group. Remembering that all of your work is just a road map or recipe, now it's time for you to see what singers can create using your instructions.

If your arrangement is written for hire or for general interest, this process will be of great help to you in identifying what will work and what won't. If at all possible, resist the temptation to direct the group and teach the part, as you'll immediately inject your own subtle phrasing and nonnotated decisions; you'll learn far more by watching someone make their own choices based on what you have written down. You'll quickly learn where you need to add dynamic markings, articulations and phrasing marks, margin notes, and the like. Your arrangement should stand on its own if you will not be there to teach it, so use this time to figure out anything that's unclear or incomplete.

Once the notes are learned, you can step in and craft the arrangement according to your vision and see if there's anything that still isn't working. Better yet, you can listen with an open mind and open ears to suggestions from the group, explicit and implicit, and incorporate them into your chart.

No, this isn't cheating. Yes, it's still your arrangement.

If you've written for your own group, you'll likely be teaching your own arrangement, and that's fine. It doesn't need to stand up to the rigors of publication, and it's not important that every nuance be on the page, because you're in the room to create magic. Teach what you'd envisioned, then open yourself up to ideas from your singers, tweaking parts here and there to suit their specific voices in ways you wouldn't have thought up alone.

No, this isn't cheating. Yes, it's still your arrangement.

>> *Dylan says: I liken this to the focus-group screenings of a new movie. When a movie is shown to a focus group, the responses are carefully tallied and the movie often rearranged to match the wishes and interests of the group. They may know nothing about movies—but in the end, they are the ones that call the shots.*

>> *Deke says: The movie analogy can be stretched even further. The singers aren't just the audience: they're the actors as well. They will need to feel comfortable with their parts, because they're going to be communicating to the audience with and through them, and singers are not always as flexible and able to assume different characters as actors are. Another analogy: if you consider your arrangement a speech, there will be times when passages need to be rewritten using the speaker's own words.*

Some things can be learned from the process that aren't explicit. For example, pay attention to the length of time it took to learn the notes and which passages or sections needed more time.

Note that a highly skilled group can make almost anything sound good. That's gratifying for you, but it may not be all that helpful in making you a flexible, versatile arranger. If your group is an amateur, collegiate, or community group, you'll likely learn more from the first rehearsal of your arrangement. A pro group might make a mediocre arrangement sound good eventually, whereas an amateur group will probably struggle and may never make problematic sections sound good.

And remember, you are responsible for how they sound.

Even a new amateur group can sound good with the right arrangement, for the simple reason that they *want* to sound good. If they can't sing your chart, rework the chart until they can. Ask them what is difficult for them and what they enjoy singing (although it will likely be very clear).

It's possible that an amateur group may be less likely to criticize, considering themselves ill-qualified to do so. They may assume that it's their fault if the music doesn't come alive. But you wrote it for them, and, like a custom-tailored suit, it needs to fit them comfortably no matter what their shape. Remind them that it's your job, not theirs, to ensure it sounds good. Give them permission to criticize problem areas and make adjustments so that everything works for their voices.

Learn to Let Go

We mentioned earlier, in chapter 1, that the greatest thing you can bring to the refinement process is humility: the ability to accept suggestions or criticism, and to be ready and willing to adapt. A big part of this is knowing when and how to let go.

If you've put a lot of effort into this arrangement, you've also invested it with a tremendous feeling of personal ownership. You wrote those notes, you bonded with them, and you own them. You may feel "precious" about a certain section, a cool arranging trick, or a brilliant adaptation of something in the original. You may have sweated blood over a few bars only to see them on the chopping block.

People need to sing your arrangement. People with opinions, personalities, idiosyncrasies, strengths, and weaknesses. As wonderful as the ideal version of your arrangement sounds in your head, it needs to work in reality with a specific group of singers, and it's unrealistic not to incorporate their input to the extent that they're happy with the chart. You may find that no changes are needed, which is fantastic, but if there's a section that isn't working, pretending that it's entirely the fault of the singers is not going to make it sound any better.

Remember, this is (hopefully) not the only arrangement in the world you will write. One of these things that you had to let go of this time may show up in another arrangement, where it may even work better. In the creative process, *nothing is wasted*. Sometimes you have to go down a wrong path to find the right one. Sometimes a rejected idea transforms into a better one. Like the impurities in refining gold, when you let these go, the end result is all the better for it.

As for wanting every idea to come from you—let that go too. You can have every idea be yours, or you can have the arrangement be better and put your name on it. Choose wisely.

» *Dylan says: OK, I'll admit it. I'm a control freak, and I'm saying these things to myself as much as to all of you. I've lost track of the number of Supposedly Brilliant Ideas that didn't make the cut, or the number of subtle suggestions and changes that may not have been mine but made my chart better. And you know what? In all of the changes requested, suggestions taken and ideas left behind, I've never once regretted the final result.*

At this point, congratulations are in order! Your have a completed arrangement which should be interesting, well written, and user-friendly.

Now it's time to start all over again with another song. And you'll find that the more you arrange, the easier and more natural the process will be.

The Ten Steps in Action: "We Three Kings"

You might know the ending of the story: the label liked the idea and arrangement, the group liked the arrangement, I ended up being asked to do more arranging and subsequently producing the album, we recorded this arrangement, and it turned out very well (you can hear it on *Christmas Cheers* or download it as an individual track). Alas, the label never made the music video I initially envisaged (that honor went to a couple of other songs on the CD, including an original song I cowrote with one of the group members), but the song did make it into their live repertoire and was well received.

I looked at an early draft to see what, if anything, was changed from the first arrangement I delivered. The only change was at the end of the song, where I brought back the early 5/4 *Mission: Impossible* feel with the lyrics "find the manger, find the man-ger!" and a giant last chord, à la the original. Gave it a James Bond feel. Cute, but not as effective as the plagal cadence we ended up using.

It was hugely beneficial for me to be able to teach the song and produce the track, as it gave me the opportunity to make small changes easily and also to clearly present my (rather twisted) vision for the song. Several important musical elements—dynamics, phrasing, relative tempi—can only be made so clear on a piece of paper, and there is significant value in being able to demonstrate an idea to singers and then help craft it once they have it in their voices.

The Ten Steps in Action: "Go Tell It on the Mountain"

These days I record my arrangements before I send them out: not only does it help me tweak a chart and fix any potential notational mistakes, it also gives the group a really clear chance to hear what they'll be doing, including any detailed phrasing or "feel" things that you just can't put on the page.

Chris loved the arrangement. Much like what can happen in the rehearsal process, he gave me a few suggestions for places where he wanted the arrangement punched up. For the most part, these were places where I had done a straight repeat—he wanted a little more variation. The variations in the second chorus (m. 27), and the breakdown before verse 2 (mm. 32–33) were responses to his "more cool stuff!" requests. I wrote and recorded those bits, sent along individual learning tracks for each member, and it was done.

The arrangement went over very well. They chose it to be the opening track of the CD, and along with Chris's own cool-jivin' arrangement of "Rockin' on Top of the World," it was the only track on the album to receive a 5/5 review from all three reviewers at the Recorded A Cappella Review Board. Great fun all around!

In-Depth Arrangement Analyses

Now that we've taken you through the Ten Steps process, we thought we'd open up a couple of our own arrangements, take you under the hood, so to speak, to show you how we put them together and demonstrate not only how they work technically, but what thought processes we went through to make the decisions that ultimately led to the notes you see in front of you.

Each analysis, while providing a general understanding of the piece as a whole, also has its own focus:

1. *Four-part jazz writing: "Christmastime Is Here."* Deke takes this Christmas classic from the *Charlie Brown Christmas* special and explains the harmonic complexity of the song and the steps he took to keep the sophistication of the original, but make it universally accessible and user-friendly.
2. *Instrumental to vocal: "Skating."* Dylan takes this piano-trio instrumental and explains the challenges of translating eighty-eight notes into four voices.
3. *Creativity through limitation: "From Ash You Rise."* Though Dylan wrote the song, much of the challenge came from arranging the piece for women's trio (SSA). Dylan explains how his choice of vocal format led to unexpected creative techniques.

These are in-depth analyses, and we don't pull any punches when it comes to using technical and theoretical jargon to describe the methods and processes. If you're a novice arranger, some of this may be over your head. Fear not. You needn't understand this section of the book to understand the following sections. These are provided for anyone who enjoys detailed musical analysis, and if it doesn't all make sense now, it will in time. There is some further theoretical information, particularly on jazz harmony, in chapter 21 ("Specific A Cappella Styles"). We hope our readers get years of enjoyment and education out of this book, so come back to it later if it doesn't make sense now.

Off we go!

Four-Part Jazz Writing: "Christmastime Is Here"
(Vince Guaraldi; Arrangement and Analysis by Deke Sharon)

Ever since I was a child, the *Charlie Brown Christmas* special has been a highlight of the holiday season, and we'd eagerly await the annual broadcast. To this day, the dulcet tones of an earnest yet slightly out of tune boys' choir warm my heart, and few recordings more immediately and powerfully trigger in me a Proustian flood of memories.

I don't recall the initial impetus to arrange the song for TTBB (it probably was a commission), but I met it eagerly. It's not often that you have an opportunity to arrange a song that has such a strong sense memory and, at the same time, so much harmonic complexity. However, the task at hand was not an easy one, because the song covers a wide range, and a traditional four-part men's choir would not afford me a great deal of flexibility.

My first task was figuring out the key. A traditional men's choir tends to be filled with baritones, many of whom are repurposed to sing other vocal parts. "Real" basses and first tenors are genetically rare, so it's important to remember that the group will likely be mid-heavy and have to rely on falsetto whenever the first tenors get above a G4. Making lemonade from lemons, I decided to use this for effect, as a man's falsetto is closer in feel to a boy treble's sound when sung lightly.

I decided to aim for a key that would put the first tenors in their falsetto range for the lines "Christmas time is here / Happiness and cheer" but then kick into chest voice for "Fun for all that children call / Their favorite time of year." The need to shift from head to chest voice and back again is inevitable, considering that the melodic range spans more than an octave. (Keeping the entire melody in falsetto would likely require them to sing in the range of E4–E5, which is very difficult for most untrained singers and would result in the most memorable line of the song being sung at the screechy, upper outskirts of falsetto.)

There are a couple of keys I could have chosen that would work in this range, but knowing the group was a chorus, which likely meant a wide variance in sight-reading skills among the members, I went for the key of C. Yes, you could argue that a half step higher would have brightened the song, and a C on the top would have still been in reasonable falsetto range, but I'm a pragmatist, and I know that untrained musicians sitting at a keyboard attempting to plunk out a song with seven sharps will likely give up in frustration. This way, every accidental is a black note, and I've given the singers the simplest possible key signature for an otherwise harmonically challenging song.

Looking downward, this key meant that my basses would likely be singing the tonic of the song around the middle of their range (C3) rather than an octave lower. Normally, I'd shoot for a key that keeps the bass singers in the D2–G2 range much of the time so that we have plenty of space between the bass and baritone parts (having a gap of an octave or more between your lowest and next lowest part, when possible, allows easier tuning, as well as a spacing more reflective of the harmonic series), but in this case I was aiming for a lightness and buoyant airiness reminiscent of a boys' choir, so the key didn't present an immediate problem (and a low C2 at the very end of the song was probably still within reach for the lowest basses).

I knew going into the arrangement that the song is AABA form, which means three different iterations of the melody, all in the same key (unless I modulate after the B section, but usually that's completely unnecessary and in the case of this song, would be tacky). To that end, I wanted a very open texture during the first A section, with increasing complexity in the later verses. There are many simple, soft syllables, but none more standard than "ooh," and I wanted the background voices to slip out of focus so that the tenor 1 melody draws all the focus. Also, the signature "loo" during the intro had served its purpose, and using much more of it would likely have become a bit cloying or precious. So "ooh" it was.

As for the rhythm, at m. 5 I wanted the tenor 2, baritone, and bass lines to disappear, so a dotted half note was the obvious choice. Less is more. As for the pitch, a root-position major seventh chord was needed, so the bass note wrote itself (C3, as mentioned before), with the obvious inner voice choices being E and G. Why not a low E below the G? That would have resulted in a muddy sound, difficult tuning, and a wide spread between the lower voices and upper voices. Why not an E4 in the baritone and G4 in the tenor 2 line? That would have been a light, bright sound, but then there would have been a big problem at the top of the following measure, since the tenor 1 line had dropped a fifth, below the tenor 2 and on the baritone note, which would have meant a large leap for the two inner voices if I was to maintain a four-note chord. So the C–G–E–B voicing was the logical choice.

As for the top of m. 6, the bass note needed to drop to a B♭ (following the harmonic contour of the song), with the melody on an E. This is where theoretical knowledge can help one deftly bridge a tritone. As lovely as it would have been to have a fifth note in this chord (the A♭, so the chord would have a strong dominant seventh), there was no way to introduce it without creating a sense of instability in the harmony. The E is a heavy burden for the harmony to carry, so I chose to move all three other voices down to spell out a B♭ triad and then use motion to move the baritone to the seventh. However, there's still a clash between the third of the chord (D) and the eleventh, so first I created a sense of resolution, moving the tenor 2 note down to a C (the ninth of the chord), and then soon thereafter moved the baritone up to the seventh, eventually revealing all of the chord members of this ♯11th chord. However, once I moved the inner voices, the measure felt like it needed more motion, and after a little tinkering around, the natural progression to my ear was to continue the ninth moving down to the tonic, freeing up the bass to move in contrary motion to the other voices (to take some of the edge off the parallel motion at the top of the measure).

To emphasize the motion, I decided to have the moving lines repeat lyrics rather than remain on "ooh," which also draws attention to their moving lines and creates moments of countermelodic interest, as opposed to subtly shifting chord tones. The overall effect of the first four measures of the verse is meant to be perceived as "calm, increasing tension, release/calm, increasing tension." Without the lyrics and motion, the effect would be more static, along the lines of "calm, increased calm, calm, increased calm," which might be perceived as a bit boring.

This chord progression is anything but standard, and the choices I made harmonically and melodically, careful as they were, still were nothing obvious. So, when the third line of the verse restates the same melodic line, I decided to repeat the exact same two measures, as if to reassure a first-time listener that "yes, what you heard was correct." Although it's hard to prove, perhaps you can imagine in your head a series of different choices for mm. 7 and 8 and how those would create an overall sense of instability as opposed to the warm, calm mood I was hoping this passage would evoke.

This takes us to mm. 9–12, which are harmonically just as complex and move twice as quickly.

The descending harmonic line, relying heavily on **tritone substitution**, practically demands that the bass outline the root of the chords, so I went with the flow. I could have unraveled the tritone substitutions and reintroduced a circle-of-fifths progression, but that would have stripped the song of one of its signature harmonic elements, and sent the requisite voice leading into barbershop territory.

Rather than rely on low Ds from the male choir, I decided to continue to keep the voicing close and high, resulting in a seventh between the bass's F♯3 and the tenor 1's E4. The third and fifth write themselves, with no obvious reason to cross voices or otherwise get clever. However, the melodic line drops from the seventh of the chord quickly down to the fifth, and not wanting to reduce the harmonies to a chain of triads, I decided to cross the tenor 2 up above the tenor 1 to grab the seventh.

All is well until the top of m. 10, when the tenor 1 briefly tags back on the seventh of the chord. What to do? Have the tenor 2 line hop down and then back up in the space of an eighth note? I played with this idea, but after singing the line it struck me as needlessly distracting. With a simple, clear vowel like "oh" and a compelling descending melodic line, it was better to leave the tenor note where it was and go without the fifth of the chord for half a beat.

Further distancing the lower three voices from the melody, I decided to have them move on the third beat of the measure, with the melody dropping on the last eighth note. This dichotomy creates tension, as the melodic line resolves the fifth of the chord downward an eighth note later than the other three parts, with alignment only happening on the last three chords of the series, ii–V–I (in this case, it's actually Dm7–G9–CM9). I tried holding the tenor 2 on the C through m. 11, but unlike in the previous two measures, rather than quickly tagging the seventh, the melody spends half the measure there, so after trying several options I settled on having the tenor 1 and tenor 2 lines "do-si-do" and sing complementary melodic lines.

I knew I needed m. 12 to resolve to a tonic chord but then quickly ramp up to the top of the verse again, like the steep incline of a rollercoaster before a big drop. The tenor 1 melody did most of the work through the verse, so it felt right to give them a break in m. 12, passing the focus to the other voices before taking over again in the second verse. With all three other voices moving in this measure, the tenor 2 line (being the highest voice) will pull the most focus, so I wrote a melodic line that resolves satisfyingly to the E they'll have at the top of the second verse and backfilled the other parts with their own ascending lines.

The standard choice for a quick turnaround would normally be a V chord, perhaps a dominant seventh or ninth considering the harmonic complexity of this piece, but those didn't feel right here. After trying a few different chords, the one I liked best was a iv chord, which, in introducing an A♭, feels a bit like a thirteenth chord with a flatted ninth and an implied G in the bass. (If this theory just went over your head, don't worry. It doesn't matter. The important thing is that it sounded good to me.)

Once I finished the first verse, I realized I needed an intro, but as much as I love the original recording, there was no easy way to replicate the initial piano figure, and the closest approximation would feel like a pale imitation. I wanted this arrangement to start with something special, perhaps evoking memories for audience members who, like me, were raised on the television special. Then I remembered: elsewhere in the movie, the *Peanuts* characters all sing "O Tannenbaum," which, luckily, is in the public domain, so it can be used without any copyright concerns.

The *Peanuts* cast sings a pure "loo loo" vowel at some point in the special underneath an important speech, so I grabbed that texture for the introduction—lyrics would have been too distracting. Only a little of the song would be needed—a couple of bars would suffice—and so as not to overwhelm the first iteration of the melody, I decided to start in unison on the "O Tannenbaum" melody, fanning outward after the first couple of notes, heading toward our CM7 chord (C in the bass, B on top). I played with a couple of voicings, but it didn't seem to work to end on a V chord with a high G (not enough drama and sense of motion), and I didn't want to drop to a low G2, which would diminish the impact of the first chord of the melody, so I decided to go with another tritone substitution foreshadowing the verse—a D♭7 chord, which allowed a half-step descent to the first chord of the melody and, with a slight alteration of the top voice, a leap up to an A♭. (It would have been nice to have a B♭ lead up a half step to the B at the top of the next measure, but the D♭7 chord needed all four of its members, being an inherently unstable chord, and the sixth of the chord would have eroded the purity of the tritone-substitution sound).

And yes, the melody does drop down to a B after the F, but it was time at that point to leave the melodic contour behind and ritard in order to make it clear that what you just heard was an introduction and not the focus of the arrangement.

It would have been nice to be able to spell out the entire ii⁷ (Dm7) chord at the top of m. 4, but the melody and bass motion both dictated a D there, so I had to drop the fifth of the chord and have the baritone come down to an F. Keeping the C in the tenor 2 was obvious. I could have taken the tenor 1 line off the melody at that point and had it sing F–G–A (the baritone line, but an octave higher); but after playing with that idea, I decided that dropping from an A to A♭ in the last beat, then leaping up to the B at the top of the verse, was more distracting than the parallel octaves between the tenor 1 and bass voices across the bar line. Yes, parallel octaves can be problematic, especially in the case of pure four-part, close-harmony vocal writing, but ultimately how something sounds is more important than whether it follows the rules, and the parallel octaves bothered me less than the A–A♭–B melodic line on top. Of course, there are other possible solutions.

Speaking a little more about the intro: I decided to have the melody sing a dotted quarter, then an eighth note, at the end of mm. 2 and 3, with the bass on quarter notes (and the inner voices on dotted half notes), as I wanted to draw attention to the expanding melodic elements. Homophony would have been more opaque.

In the end, I was very happy with my choices in this arrangement, and when looking for sweet, melodic songs for the Straight No Chaser *Christmas Cheers* album, I offered this up. It worked well for the group; you can download their recording, or purchase the complete album.

Exercises

» Observe the parallel octaves between mm. 3 and 4 in the introduction. Write some alternate options for m. 4 and see which you prefer.
» Write a different four-bar intro to the song.
» Arrange the same passage for female voices, knowing you can't rely on falsetto. What choices would you make differently, starting with the key?

Christmas Time Is Here

arr. Deke Sharon
for Jordan Wong & the Sounds of Aloha Chorus

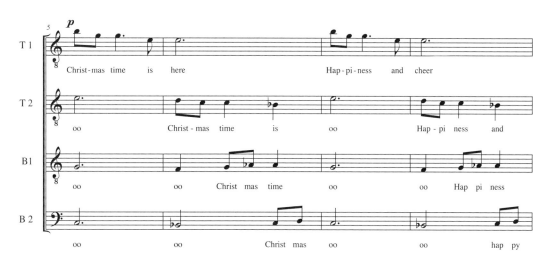

Instrumental to Vocal: "Skating"
(Vince Guaraldi; Arrangement and Analysis by Dylan Bell)

Though Deke grew up in California and I grew up in Canada, we both share the same longtime love of the classic *Charlie Brown Christmas* special and its musical score. For me, it was my first exposure to jazz, and I fell in love with the sound long before I knew what jazz even was. In fact, I credit Vince Guaraldi's piano playing with my first exposure to jazz and my eventual development as a jazz pianist and vocalist.

"Skating" is a beautiful instrumental, a jazz waltz for piano trio that plays while the *Peanuts* characters are all playing on the ice. I remember exactly when and why I chose to arrange this piece. I was on tour with the a cappella jazz/contemporary quartet Cadence in northern Ontario. It starts to snow pretty early that far north, and in mid-October we had our first on-the-road snowfall. Rather than groan at the onset of winter, I was inspired: the arrangement came to me almost instantly, and I grabbed my laptop and started writing in the front seat of the car.

I had some advantages with this particular piece, but I also had my work cut out for me. To my disadvantage: the piece is written for jazz piano trio. This means that the harmonies are lush and complex, covering a very wide range. There are no lyrics to engage the listener, no text to use as a jumping-off place for arrangement ideas, associations, or techniques. The piece would have to stand on its own. And, to top it all off, I decided to write it for Cadence, meaning that I had no more than four voices at my disposal. No *divisi*, no cheating. Just four voices to cover the eighty-eight notes of the piano, not to mention the bass and drums.

To my advantage, I was writing for a professional group, and one whose voices I knew intimately. The guys in Cadence are well versed in jazz on both a theoretical and an instinctual level, so I could stretch the limits of what these four voices could do far more than if I were writing an off-the-rack chart for an unknown group. Deke's challenge was to write within an average group's limits; mine was to stretch those limits as needed to honor the original song.

The original is in the key of C, and wherever possible I like to keep an arrangement in the original key unless I'm doing a radical reinterpretation. I decided early on that this would be a more or less translational arrangement: not a pure lift, but without any serious modification. The original melody starts high, around a B5—way out of range for any mortal tenor, and high even for a soprano. The solution was easy: simply drop the melody down an octave, putting it into a nice place for a falsetto tenor. Since it's a lighthearted jazz waltz, I wanted the melody to be light and feathery, and putting the melody in this register worked nicely.

The opening to the song (mm. 1–4) is meant to be light but rhythmic, with a dancelike quality. A piano is by nature percussive, and my instincts told me that if I wanted a light but warm sound, a pianistic syllable such "dat," "den," or "gong" would translate as intense, rather than easy and warm. It could work, if the approach was light enough, but I decided to try something different. Instead of treating the vocals like a piano, I decided to treat the vocals like trombones. This would take the edge off of the attack ("br" instead of "dat"), and timbrally the closed-mouth resonance would come across with the requisite warmth. Harmonically, the intro follows a simple I–IV–V–IV pattern, with the chord voicings in stacked fourths, giving a nice sixth-and-ninth flavor to the chords. They move in parallel, which makes it simple: no voice-leading concerns, and since the key is voice-friendly, everything sits in a good place. Nice and easy.

The original recording has drums playing a dexterous jazz brushes pattern, driving the rhythm forward. Since I had no drummer for this song, the vocal parts would have to combine well to keep the rhythm going. This is easy in the introduction, where the original right-hand piano voicings (represented by the top three voices) bounce nicely against the left hand and the upright bass (sung by the bass). The bass figure is quite active, and in addition, the backbeat (in a jazz waltz, the backbeat is often still on beat 2, giving an accent pattern of one–TWO–three, one–TWO–three) is implied with a light "ts," similar to a jazz hi-hat, on the second beat.

When the melody starts at m. 5, the top three voices change quite a bit. In the original version, the piano plays slow open-voiced chords in the left hand, the melody in the right hand, and the bass and drums carry the rhythm forward. In this arrangement, the rhythmic drive is primarily taken care of by the bass, who continues the same rhythmic pattern through this section.

At mm. 5–8, the textures separate. We've already got our bass continuing the same pattern, keeping the waltz bouncing along. As in the original song, the melody is in parallel thirds, swirling like snowflakes downward over the range of an octave from B4. Having the melody harmonized like this spells out most of the chordal information quite well, but it also prompts the question: what to do with the leftover voice—the baritone?

One choice may have been to simply write three-part harmony for the melody. I decided not to do this for several reasons. First, I felt it would make the melodic arc feel too heavy: instead of gently drifting snowflakes, we'd have a heavy snowfall. Second, the melodic arc covers quite a range, a full octave before the snowflakes "land" at m. 8. Three voices in parallel harmony would get muddy at the bottom of the arc. Third, I wanted another texture. We have a bouncing one-man rhythm section in the bass and a swirling melody. I wanted something more static and constant, both texturally and harmonically, to glue these textures together. The solution: keep the baritone singing the thirds of each of the chords, one per bar in dotted half notes. Not only does this solve all these problems, but it also makes a nice reference to the original, where the piano's left hand plays simple, open-voiced chords. But rather than a piano sound, I went for a simple, unobtrusive "doo": just enough attack to outline each bar, but not enough to draw attention to itself. I often imagine arranging to be like orchestration, and in keeping with this analogy, the baritone is like a smooth cello section.

In the absence of lyrics, striving for a light, snowflakey sound also meant searching for the right syllable choice. An obvious choice would be a scat-style "doo-ba-doo'dn" kind of syllable, but this still felt too heavy. A Swingle-esque "ba-va-da" would be lighter, but still somehow seemed too self-consciously "vocal-jazz" to my ear. I didn't want this to sound like a show-choir arrangement: I wanted to paint the picture of the *Peanuts* gang playfully swirling around on the ice. I ended up taking inspiration from one of the greatest non-word-singing vocalists ever: Bobby McFerrin.

McFerrin hears syllables as their own language, to the extent that people often confuse his own "vocalese" vocabulary for an unknown African tongue. If one were to carefully analyze what McFerrin does instinctively, they would realize that the syllables in his "language" are the perfect expression of the timbres and rhythmic accents he feels as he sings.

So I just experimented a number of times, singing the melody over and over, finding syllables that tripped lightly and easily off the tongue and still had the right rolling and swirling feel to complement the melody. What I came up with was: "so-va-doh-dn-deh-d'-lo-va-do-dn-deh-d'-lo-va-doh-dn-deh-d'-loh."

It fit beautifully. Feeding people new scat syllables can be like teaching a foreign language, so I knew I had it right when the guys sang it twice and immediately got it. Afterward, I realized that it worked because it was not only light and smooth, but the vowel choices give it the necessary lift to keep the rhythm going. The bright vowels "va" and "deh" land on the *and* of beat 1 and on beat 3, respectively: exactly the same rhythmic-accent structure as in mm. 1–4. This was one of those examples where instinct trumps education. You can't think your way around something like this; you simply have to experiment and trust your instincts.

This gets us through the first four bars of the melody. At mm. 9–12, the melody slows down, but the harmonies become complicated. The chords move in parallel minor thirds—C–E♭–G♭–A—finally landing on C again to take us back to the snowflake melody. These are very hip jazz **changes** and sound great on piano. However, our ears are more accustomed to hearing chord progressions in the usual circle-of-fifths, perfect-or-plagal-cadence type of way. Even the most sophisticated jazz turnarounds are usually based on the circle of fifths. Hearing harmonies ascending in parallel minor thirds is not intuitive and therefore quite difficult to execute. There were a couple of solutions I chose to help the situation.

At this point, hearing solid bass notes becomes crucial. So I dropped the dancing bass line and gave the singer something more straightforward: nothing but roots and fifths, on dotted quarter notes. Now the other singers have something to tune to, but since the bass is still moving a bit, the rhythmic flow hasn't come crashing to a halt.

The good news is that the melody slows down to a dotted half note and becomes less a melody and more a part of the harmony, giving the singers time to lock into the notes and tune the chords. The baritone does exactly what he was doing before, singing the thirds of each chord. This means that, among all the other changes, *something* remains constant. The tenor 2 sings the fifths of the chords (with the exception of the sixth at m. 9, to complete the preceding melodic arc). This means that the baritone and tenor 2 have nice, easy thirds to tune and, alongside the bass, simple triads to hear and execute. That seems more manageable.

I could have left it at that, but I had one voice left over. There were still two elements missing to my ears: some interesting jazz harmonies (now that the rest of the singers were singing simple triads) and some more rhythmic movement (since we had neither the "dancing" bass nor the "swirling" melody). Fortunately, I had a tenor in the group who, once he really understood his part, could sing it with remarkable pitch accuracy. I took advantage of this fact to give him a line that melodically is very difficult to sing, but harmonically makes sense with the parts around it. The part covers the nonessential but more colorful notes: fifths, sevenths, and ninths. It forms an interesting but logical sort of sequence. And, to top it off, I made it easy to get into and out of: the last note of his preceding melody line is the first note of the sequence, and the last note of the sequence is the first note of the following melody line.

As far as rhythm and flow went, even though the original piano version is more rhythmically static here, I wanted to keep the sense of bounce that would have been provided by the drummer. Giving the tenor 1 this quarter-note motif, along with the contrasting "bohn-doon-bohn-doon-bohn" syllables, provided the bounce I wanted. Furthermore, the quarter notes in the tenor 1 against the dotted quarters in the bass give an exciting three-against-two feel, keeping the piece rhythmically interesting.

Mm. 13–16 are the same as mm. 5–8: with so much action in such a short amount of time, there was no point in adding any more layers of complexity.

Mm. 17–20 are similar to mm. 9–12 but give us some new harmonic information: instead of the parallel-thirds chord progression, we have C–E♭–A♭–D♭, leading us back to C. It's still quite harmonically sophisticated but a little more ear-friendly because it follows a more understandable circle-of-fifths progression, ending with a tritone substitution to lead us back to the key of C.

In terms of function, each voice part has a role similar to that in mm. 9–12. The bass goes back to a roots-and-fifths figure on dotted quarter notes. The tenor 2 and baritone have similar, slow dotted-half-note figures, with one notable change: owing to the new chord changes and where they sit in the singers' ranges, the choice of notes is inverted. Now the baritone sings fifths and the tenor 2 sings thirds, so that instead of singing a third apart, they now sing a sixth apart. This gives a rich open voicing with the bass: root–fifth–third. It helps lock the chords as well and provides a slightly different sound than that in the comparable section at mm. 9–12.

Overall I was pleased with what I managed to achieve with this arrangement. I've always enjoyed the challenge of maximizing the use of four voices. Knowing that I was writing for a professional group and with some creative problem solving, I felt I managed to represent the complexity and sophistication of the original in a chart that was still singable.

While all this is fine and dandy from the arranger's perspective, it means nothing unless it speaks to an audience. Despite what I said in the preceding paragraph, my greatest aspiration with the arrangement wasn't to make it hip and complex: it was to represent the joy and playfulness of the original, the sweet sentiment of the *Charlie Brown Christmas* special from which it came, and the wonderful moment of inspiration that first sparked this arrangement on the day of winter's first snowfall. I guess it worked, because I recorded this song myself and sent it around to some friends as an audio Christmas card. They loved it and passed it along to their friends. The arrangement has since taken on a life of its own and has made its way across the world with Cadence, the Swingle Singers, the Hampton Four, and a few other groups. All this from a first snowfall, a childhood memory, and a moment of inspiration.

Exercises

» This chart is a "professional"-level chart. What changes could you make to simplify the chart, and make it more "community-friendly"?
» Imagine this chart being sung by an SATB group. What, if anything, would you have to change to make it singable with sopranos and altos?
» Much of this arrangement is written for a group without a vocal percussionist. If you had one, what would you have him or her do? Knowing that the VP can take care of the rhythm, would you simplify any other parts?
» Come up with your own alternative syllables for the tenor 1 and 2 parts at mm. 5–8.

Skating

Vince Guaraldi
Arr. Dylan Bell

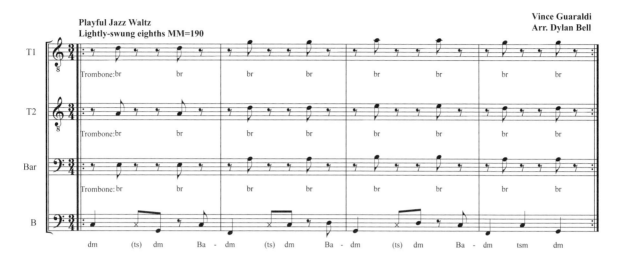

2 Skating

Skating   3

Skating   5

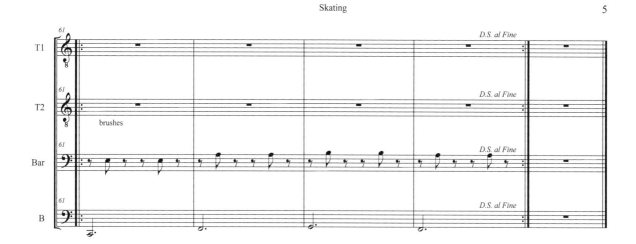

Creativity Through Limitation: "From Ash You Rise"
(Dylan Bell; Arrangement and Analysis by Dylan Bell)

And now for something completely different. Most of this book so far has focused on contemporary a cappella styles written in four parts or more. This analysis will take us in a completely different direction.

"From Ash You Rise" is an original piece of mine. It is written for women's trio (SSA), a less common format with its own unique challenges (see chapter 19 for information on writing for other vocal formats). Furthermore, instead of being a contemporary or jazz piece, this is written in a neo-Renaissance style: I drew inspiration from sixteenth-century motets and madrigals but incorporated modern sonorities. I chose this piece to illustrate three interesting challenges: writing for women's voices, writing for fewer than four parts, and reharmonizing a melody. Though an original composition, most of the challenges with this piece were arranging challenges.

The poetry centers on a mythical bird, the phoenix. According to legend, the phoenix reigns the skies for a thousand years, then builds its own funeral pyre and dances as it burns to death. Afterward the phoenix rises from its own ashes to reign again. When I wrote the poetry, I had a mental image of three angels singing over the ashes of the phoenix, hence the choice of SSA women's trio.

The melody came to me while I was sitting on the steps of the Basilica Santa Maria della Salute in Venice. I guess the atmosphere of the place seeped into me, because the melody came out as a plaintive, hymnlike melody reminiscent of the era when this church was built. The piece is hymnlike in structure, with repeated verses and lacking a chorus or bridge. (There is an extended coda at the end, but we'll get to that later.) Based on a sixteenth-century sense of modal harmony, the melody and basic "chord changes" (such as they are) could be broken down like this (for added effect, imagine it being accompanied by a lute or some such instrument).

From Ash You Rise

Words and Music by Dylan Bell

Though the illustration represents the work as a melody with chord changes, Renaissance music isn't usually perceived in this way. Modal harmony doesn't follow a simple I–IV–V–I harmonic structure: it is more fluid, being built primarily around the melody. Accidentals and non-scale-based sonorities are more common, which in some ways allows more freedom to play with the harmonies. Add to this a modern acceptance of consonance and dissonance, and the color palette opens up considerably.

With a repeated verse and no variety offered through a familiar chorus or bridge, I chose to rely on reharmonization to provide variety and movement. Furthermore, my choice of style and vocal format provided interesting limitations. The use of three voices doesn't permit a lot of easy options for changes in texture, and it wasn't as if, in a quasi-classical piece, I could have the soprano 2 and alto sing guitars, then switch to keyboards and trumpets. Here's how I approached it.

With four verses to get through, I chose to start gradually. The first line (mm. 1–3) is sung solo. The next two lines (mm. 4–11) are sung in two-voice counterpoint. The first more-than-a-simple-major-or-minor harmony moment happens on the word "Now" at m. 11. In my simplified example above, I called this an A♭ chord, but is has a long suspension in the melody, making it more like an A♭$^{\sharp 11}$

chord: something you'd likely find in jazz or **impressionist music**. This can't be represented by two voices, so it was time to add the alto.

Representing complex harmonies with only three voices isn't easy, as one usually wants to define a complex chord with four or more pitches. Furthermore, with female voices, there isn't necessarily a bass voice to ground the chord. As such, this piece makes frequent use of voicings: vertical structures that imply harmonies rather than spelling them out completely. Voicings can be subject to multiple interpretations and often feel more defined when heard in context. For example, the chord at m. 11, on the word "now," is spelled E♭–B♭–D. By itself, it doesn't really spell a chord. Heard in context with the chords in mm. 12–13, the two measures have a flavor of A♭ something, especially once the soprano 1 resolves to the C (the third) and later lands on the A♭ (the root) in m. 13, and the soprano 2 resolves to the A♭. The overall effect is of a long suspension to an A♭ sonority. This is one of the great strengths of SSA writing: with no bass to ground them, chords and sonorities float easily, and with three-part voicings, harmonies can be implied and manipulated with great dexterity.

The second verse sees a few reharmonizations, but since we've heard only one verse so far, there are no earth-shattering changes. There is a color change added in m. 19 between the soprano 2 and alto, with the E♮ (making for a C major chord) in the alto quickly shifting to an E♭ in the soprano 2, darkening the mood. The poetry has such strong images that any arrangement techniques should support it. The phrase "your throat, now stopped, no longer sings" is mournful and benefits from the quick major-minor shift. The second verse makes use of suspensions and voice leading to add movement. In m. 22, the alto has a suspension on the word "beat." In m. 31, the soprano 2 suspends on the word "lie," concluding a moment of extra motion. Overall, the verse contains more movement, such as the parallel voice movement in mm. 24–26 and the polyphonic motion in mm. 31–33.

The third verse represents the death of the phoenix and as such sees the strongest harmonic shifts and developments thus far. In mm. 34–38 the alto assumes a pedal-tone function to allow the harmonies above to shift. A textural shift takes place in moving the melody briefly to the soprano 2. The basic "chord structure" has been altered to make it significantly darker. What was originally G–C–G, D–G–B♭–Am has now morphed into G/D–Dsus–Em, Em–E♭–D (no third). The resulting effect is a suspended, floating, anticipatory sound, followed by darker descending chords.

The next line, "But fire consumes; all songs must end" (mm. 41–45), represents the moment of death, and I tried to reflect this in my arranging choices. The line starts with a powerful three-part unison/octave, then splits into an angular, stacked-fifths voicing (roughly D♭9–C9, with no thirds) for the word "consumes," giving this moment power and drama. Similar angular sounds are used to start the phrase "All songs must end." After the fire dies down, the verse ends softly: the melody is given to the alto, and the voicings are built from there. After some chord clusters and one little moment of canonic writing, the verse ends on a calm, mournful open fourth.

I freely admit that I stole a technique from the great J. S. Bach for this verse. In writing one of his Passions, Bach used a well-known hymn tune, which he reintroduce in increasingly darker keys to represent the depths of despair as the story progressed. I borrowed this darker-sonority idea for this third verse. Although it starts with G/E sonorities, it descends to E♭, D♭, and C, then to A♭, ending not on the G major chord but on that nonchordal open fourth.

The next verse represents hope: "But spirit cannot be consumed / And love, though frail, cannot be crushed." So I did the obvious: I used major chords and brighter sonorities. We start back with a clear sense of G major, and the chord movement on the word "consumed" (m. 54) runs through a more traditional cadential pattern, B7–Em–D–G, giving a clear sense of the key of G major, and of excitement and hope. In contrast with the suspended, static-pedal start to the third verse, this verse bolts out of the gate with movement in each part, and in particular, some scalar movement in the alto, descending to widen the three-note voicings (mm. 52–53) and ascending in parallel motion with the soprano 2 (m. 54) to create a clear sense of rising.

Furthermore, there is a newer, brighter harmony on the word "crushed" (m. 54). This is a good example of harmonizing from the melody line rather than from a typical chord progression. In the first and second verses, the implied chord is A minor. In the third verse, it is voiced as an open D chord (root and fifth, no third) as a result of the descending-darkness harmonies that preceded it. This time, the chord implied is A7sus to A7. Were this chord to be reharmonized according to the usual harmonic conventions, we'd look at other options: the relative major (C major) or possibly F major, maybe even D minor or B♭ major if we were thinking of the harmony in a jazz context. The change to A major, created with a simple color change in the soprano 2, introduces the sound of the C♯, a very bright and noticeable sound in the key center of G minor. Its effect is to lift us out of the current tonality and give a sense of lightness and hope.

The next line (mm. 58–61) isn't much different from the comparable section in the second verse (mm. 24–27) in terms of overall harmony. The main difference is in texture. In the second verse, the parts move in homophony. In the fourth verse, in keeping with the sense of hope and rising energy, the parts are more contrapuntal. The soprano 2 rushes into the counterpoint, almost impatiently, adding a few interesting suspensions: the ninth on the A♭-ish chord on "your song" (m. 58) and a similar suspension on the G minor harmony in m. 59.

I felt this was enough variation for this verse, and it concludes with the same overall harmonies and vocal lines as in the second verse.

The next section, a sort of extended coda, departs from the verse-after-verse structure we've had so far. Mm. 69–80 could be described as pure word painting—that is, using the music to illustrate the words. Most of the piece reflects painting of the sense of the words, largely in sonorities chosen to reflect the text's emotional content, but they stay within the confines of the existing melody. In this section, *everything's* written purely with the text in mind.

The text at mm. 69–74 is "from ash you stir." This is represented with clustery harmonies and call-and-response entries in all three parts. The effect is a soft, rustling stirring. On the next line, "from ash you rise," the announcement starts with the alto, followed by what you might expect: a rising, soaring melody voiced mostly in parallel triads. Being the high point of the text (and the title of the piece itself), this line represents the climax of the piece: it has the fastest movement, the widest dynamic, and the highest range of anything we've seen so far.

The next line, "before us all, the glorious *arc-en-ciel*" (mm. 76–77), gives the melody back to the alto, which takes us through some interesting color changes. On the words "*arc-en-ciel*" (rainbow), we have a crystalline, unexpected sonority: F♯ minor. I tend to hear notes and harmonies as colors, and this particular sound (with F♯s and C♯s, in the context of G minor) sounded to me like bright, primary colors—perfect for representing a rainbow. We stay in this new tonality in m. 78 for the words "reaching, yearning" and eventually settle back into more familiar harmonic territory for "hungry for the sky" in m. 79, reintroducing the familiar sound of F♯s and B♭s.

In m. 81 we're back to our original melody. Since the piece is coming to a conclusion, I decided to make this a strong statement, sung in octaves. This also has the extra effect of clearing the deck, harmonically speaking. Since we had visited new tonal territory just a moment before, I didn't want us to come crashing back into the old key, so to speak. A unison/octave line takes us there, definitively, but still eases us into it.

Mm. 86–90 bring us back to familiar territory, almost like a refrain (I added in one extra bit of word painting here: the soprano 2 has an ascending leading tone to tonic resolution on the word "rise"). To conclude the piece (mm. 91–92), the melody and harmony follow the text—"You rise and fly"—exactly, ascending in gentle triadic harmony and ending on a **Picardy third**-style, high G major chord.

I never thought that arranging a simple hymn tune (especially one I had written myself!) could be so complex. In a sense, I had creatively boxed myself in by my choice of format (SSA, three voices, non-contemporary). But this piece turned out to be an example of how one can find immense creative resources though limitation. I knew from the conception stage that the SSA format was more important than whatever arranging skills I usually used. This forced me to look more carefully at what techniques were left to my disposal: texture changes, reharmonization, and word painting. Moreover, it gave me clearer insight into the unique beauty inherent in SSA writing. I probably learned more from composing and arranging this piece than from most of the arrangements I had written before it. Arranging for SSA isn't easy, but when done well, it is immensely rewarding.

From Ash You Rise

Dylan Bell

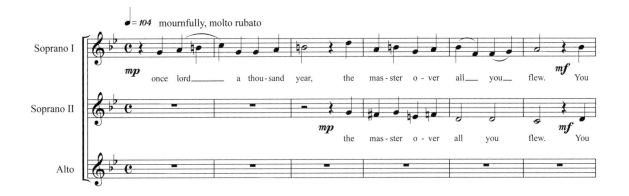

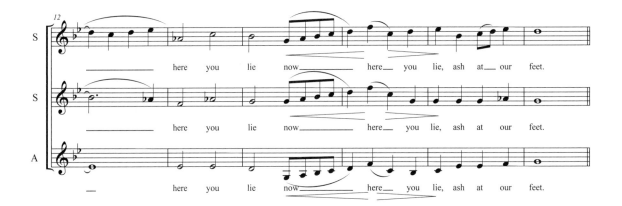

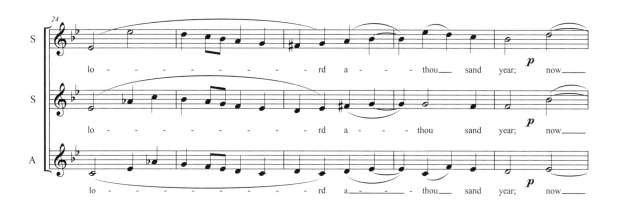

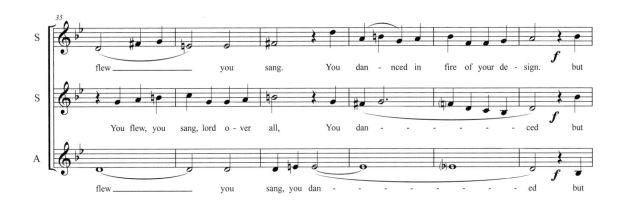

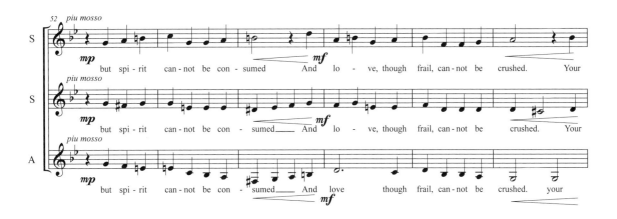

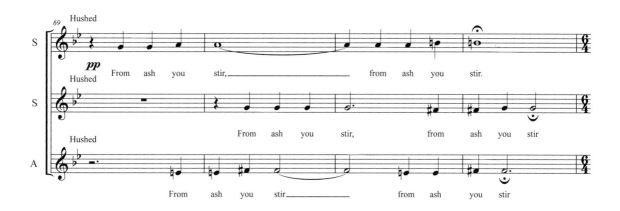

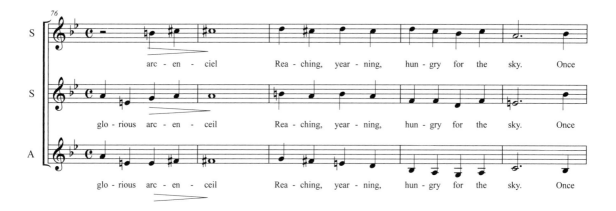

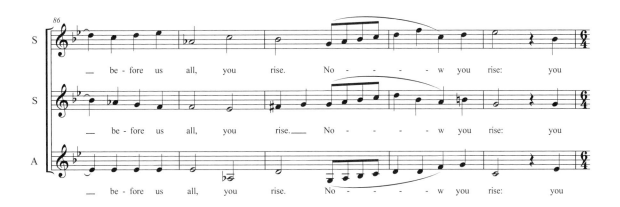

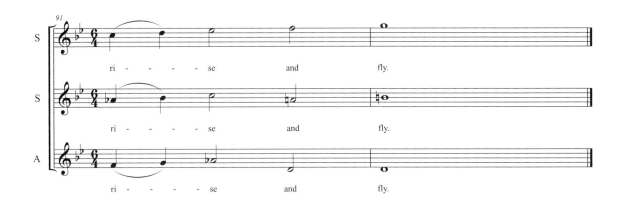

Advanced Topics in Arranging

We started with a general overview and an effective "Ten Steps" method to take you from conception to finished arrangement, taking a general, one-size-fits-all approach and painting in broad strokes. In this next section, we introduce a host of finer brushes.

The following chapters offer specialized tools to help make a good arrangement even better, or to deal with a specific type of arranging or challenge that may arise. If you've been reading this book "reference-manual" style, picking and choosing the chapters you felt were most relevant, this is where you'll find many of your specific queries answered.

Topics for this section were chosen in large part from questions we have received over the years from arrangers of all abilities needing advice on some particular aspect of arranging. We invite you to be part of this ongoing discussion: if you have questions not covered in the section (or in the book as a whole), visit us at http://www.acappellaarranging.com, and we'll keep the answers coming.

CHAPTER 18

Change-Ups and Clever Bits: Adding Spice to Your Arrangement

The basics are in place. All the parts are laid out neatly, properly voice led, nice and consistent. You start reading through it . . .

. . . and you get bored.

And if *you're* bored, the person who put his heart and soul into this arrangement, how do you think the group is going to feel? What about your audience?

What to do? You bury your head in your hands, convinced that this chart isn't going anywhere.

Fear not . . . like a perfectly good (but bland) meal, you may just need something to spice it up a little. Here are a few techniques that will get you there. Like any spices, they're best used sparingly and tastefully.

Start Simple

Your chart may not need a full reflavoring: maybe it just needs a dash of salt. So before tearing the whole thing apart, take a look at a few easy fixes.

Change-Ups

Nothing spells boredom quite like another set of repeat dots, so instead of a straight repeat of a section, try some little variations. These work nicely in a section where repetition is important, like a chorus, but you need just a little something extra to keep it from being a carbon copy. Change-ups can be very simple, such as:

> » *Changing dynamics and phrasing.* Try one verse loud, the other verse soft, or one chorus with broad, smooth phrasing and another with tight, rhythmic phrasing. This is as much a performance change as an arrangement change. You can write it in your own charts and also apply it to others.

» *Changing vowel sounds for a timbral or dynamic shift.* Example: "First time through: sing 'oo.' Second time: sing 'ah.'"

» *Changing repetitive rhythmic parts.* Usually one simple change per section works best.

With these entry-level change-ups, you don't even need to write more material: just add "1st time: Oo, 2nd time: Oh, 3rd time: Ah" to the score, and voilà: instant, simple variation.

You can also use more involved change-ups to develop the piece even further. Take this example, from Dylan's original piece "Don't Fix What's Broken." The piece has three verses. They could have been kept the same, since each verse has new lyrics. But the BGs (in this case acting like guitars) are quite simple and repetitive, even within a single verse. Small change-ups in the second and third verses add just enough of a subtle change to make the piece more interesting.

Here's the first verse:

Don't Fix What's Broken

Words and Music by Dylan Bell

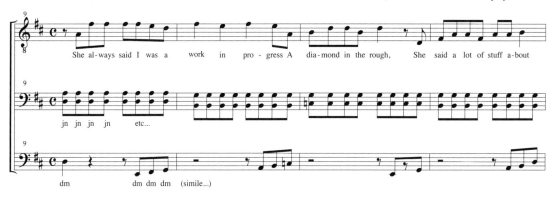

Here's the second verse:

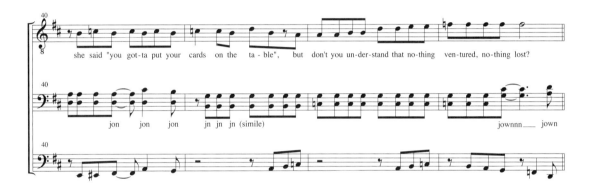

This verse actually has two small change-ups. The first happens in m. 40, with the addition of one little extra rhythmic motif in the bass and lower BGs. The second is a very simple change: the rhythmic shot at m. 43, which was voiced as C–G (an interval of a fifth), is now moved up and inverted to G–C. It's basically the same idea, just a little more intense.

Here's the third verse:

This time there is only one change, at m. 75. In the first verse this figure was voiced low; in the second verse, it's voiced a little higher. The third verse continues by making the rhythmic shot a little more involved and pitching it even higher to sound more like guitar harmonics. Change-ups like this can give a simple part more momentum and energy as the song develops.

It's important to note that change-ups work best when:

» They add to what's there, giving a section more movement, rather than a change for change's sake. "Adding" doesn't necessarily mean "more stuff": it can mean just adding a new element, texture, or dimension.

» They are easy to remember and to articulate. Your singers should be able to describe a change-up easily: "This time around I sing words, and I add an extra note there to make it sound bigger."

Changing rhythms for no apparent reason, for example, will serve little purpose other than to drive your singers loony. "This time I sing 'Jown-jigga-jigga-jown-jown,' but at m. 11, I sing 'Jown-jigga-jigga-JIGGA-jown.' Wait . . . or was it 'Jown-JOWN-jigga-jigga-jown'?" You should be able to explain what a change-up does, and why, in a just a few words.

Reharmonization: Adding New Colors

Reharmonizing is quite common in jazz writing but is often overlooked in most three-chord, triadic pop music. Most arrangements include the tonic, third, and fifth of every chord. How about the seventh? The ninth? The eleventh and thirteenth? Possibly a suspended fourth? There's always the option of altered notes, such as a flat fifth or ninth. There is more information on jazz harmony in chapter 21 if you want to get into it more deeply; otherwise, just experiment. Go to the keyboard and play each chord, systematically adding extra notes. Most will sound bad. Some will sound cool but inappropriate. A choice few will work. If that's too much work, stick to the diatonic pitches (that's the white notes, if you're in the key of C). Try holding one or two pitches from one chord into the next and then resolving them. Or have one part come in on its note a little before the others. If you're in the mood for a challenge, try reharmonizing a couple of passages, remembering to hold constant the pitches in the melody. Use your ears and have fun.

You can also reharmonize by substituting different chords, and sometimes just by changing the bass note. Take a simple C major chord and look at what happens when you change the bass note.

Try experimenting with this on the keyboard. Like the added chord tones, some will work and some won't, but you'll easily develop a sense of what could work for your chart. Remember that whatever new chords you create, they must work with the solo line. Everything else can change, but the solo should remain untouched, with rare exceptions.

Here's an example of basic reharmonization from Dylan's arrangement of "True Colors." The first chorus follows the basic chord changes.

True Colors

Arranged by Dylan Bell

Words and Music by
Billy Steinberg and Tom Kelly

In the first chorus, the harmonies at m. 16 on the words "that's why I love you" are pretty simple: Dm–G7sus–G. At m. 18, on "Let it show," we have E7/G#–Am7: a III–vi, relative minor type of cadence.

The second chorus adds a couple of new harmonic flavors:

True Colors

At m. 37 on the words "that's why I love you," chord changes happen on every word. Our simple Dm–G7sus–G7 cadence has now become a more involved ascending sequence: Dm–Cadd9/E–D6add9/F♯–G7sus–G. At m. 39 on the words "let it show," we still have the same basic chords, but we've added some passing tones to give just a little more color. E7/G♯–Am7 has now become E7♭9/G♯–Am7add9.

Clever Bits and Song Quotes

Clever bits are simply little pieces of ear candy thrown in to add variety, interest, or humor to a section. Clever bits are often built on word association, derived from the main lyric, and are given to the BGs as a response to the lead vocal.

》 *Deke says: When arranging the holiday classic "Holly Jolly Christmas," I wanted to add a little Christmas spice by stuffing in as many snippets of other holiday songs as I could. Scattered amongst the different vocal parts, each is just long enough for the listener to say "What was that?!" before moving on to the next one. In one forty-three-bar chart I managed to include bits of "Jingle Bell Rock," "It's The Most Wonderful Time of the Year," "It's Beginning to Look a Lot Like Christmas," "Let It Snow," "Frosty the Snowman," "Deck the Halls," "All I Want for Christmas Is My Two Front Teeth," and "We Wish You a Merry Christmas."*

Adding clever bits can be helpful on a number of levels. It makes the song interesting for the singers, breaking up endless bars of nonsense syllables. It makes for great live performance, as they easily lend themselves to visual and even theatrical interaction. And in a recorded arrangement, it can add to the repeat listenability of the track: they're often like musical Easter eggs, which the listener may only catch after several plays.

》 *Dylan says: I once had someone call me up and yell into the phone: "Ha! I just caught That Thing you snuck into that song! Six months later!" It was from the song "The Dry Cleaner from Des Moines," and was taken from a line in the lyric where the main character goes to the Vegas casino Circus Circus. The bit in the BGs went like this:*

Clever bits are a little like musical jokes, and like good jokes, they often work best when they are subtle. Have you ever heard someone tell a joke, then ruin it by beating the punch line to death? Don't sweat it if not everyone gets the joke. It's still fulfilling its main purpose, which is to add variety. Sometimes arrangers will sneak in little things for their own enjoyment, regardless if anyone else gets it. So did the masters: J. S. Bach often used B–A–C–H (German pitch nomenclature for the notes B♭–A–C–B♮) as a melodic motif in his fugues. Clever, no?

》 *Deke says: One of my favorite e-mails to receive is when some singer realizes that one of the background syllables in my arrangement of "Hippopotamus for Christmas" was more than just a nice, resonant sound. The syllable? "Dung."*

When it comes to change-ups and clever bits, or any other changes to your arrangement, there are no limits. Countermelodies, new harmonies, playing with lyrics, different syllables, rhythmic changes, different dynamic inflection, weaving other songs into the background, and inserting jokes are only a few of the myriad options you have when considering how to alter your arrangement and keep it fun. You may want to keep a list of things you've noticed and appreciated in other's arrangements so that you have a way to approach this from the right brain. If that doesn't work, just sing your arrangement in the car or shower and see what emerges.

Also remember that clever bits and change-ups are meant to serve the arrangement, not the other way around. Too many of them may cause your listeners (and singers) to roll their eyes and mutter to themselves, "There she goes again." But when used well, they'll help make a decent arrangement sound great and be fun to sing.

CHAPTER 19

Arranging for Other Vocal Formats

So far, we've primarily focused on SATB writing, occasionally adding extra parts and percussion. While all the principles carry over to any combination of voices, it's worth taking some time to dig into the details of writing for other vocal configurations. Each has its own idiosyncrasies.

Men's Ensemble: TTBB and More

Writing for TTBB groups is usually rather easy and straightforward, for the following reasons:

» Each of the upper three vocal parts (tenor 1, tenor 2, and baritone) has a sweet spot in the G3–G4 range. The notes around middle C are where most vocal harmonies in pop music live: they're in a comfortable range for men and women, and they tune well above a bass between an octave and two below.

» There is a well-established body of TTBB writing. From barbershop to collegiate a cappella to doo-wop to vocal rock bands, much of the twentieth-century a cappella tradition has been forged by male groups. You and your singers are used to the sound, and through a hundred years of trial and error, the various common practices tune well and sound great.

» A lot of contemporary instrumental music is still built around the sound of a male singer plus guitars—right where TTBB lives. This means that you can keep the original key, textures, and overall feel unchanged if you wish.

In a TTBB ensemble, the usable range of a male singer is extended both up and down. It looks something like this:

Tenor 1. Full range: G2–F5. Most common range: G3–C5.

Tenor 2. Full range: G2–C5. Most common range: C3–A4.

Baritone. Full range: E2–G4. Most common range: G2–E4.

Bass. Full range: D2–D4. Most common range: D–A3.

Probably the biggest difference in TTBB versus SATB writing is the treatment of the upper voices. As you can see, the average upper range is about a fifth lower than that of an SATB group. Furthermore, the upper voices are much more determined by the timbre of the tenor 1 and tenor 2 singers and where their breaks lie. And this can vary considerably from singer to singer, unlike the case with soprano and alto parts, making it harder to write a standard first tenor part and expect a specific sound.

Fortunately, it doesn't always have to be the first tenor who sings the tenor 1 part. Given the nature of falsetto timbre and vocal breaks, you can have a baritone with a falsetto who, as a result of his thicker vocal chords, is able to sing higher than your tenors. So if you're writing a "generic" chart (that is, not one for a specific group), the best mode of action is simply to write the parts from lowest to highest and let each individual group sort out which voice does it best for each song.

Writing Around the Break

One thing to watch out for in writing for TTBB is writing lines that swim over and around the break. For tenors, the break typically sits somewhere around D4–G4. Most tenors can widen their break a little: that is, if their break is around E4, they can usually sing up to an F4 or G4 in their chest voice and down to a C4 in their falsetto. Tenor 1 lines often work if they stay relatively static, allowing them to stay in one voice for a while without flipping back and forth like an overcaffeinated gymnast.

For a good, basic understanding of homophonic, vocal-oriented (as opposed to instrumental-sounding) TTBB writing, check out barbershop music. It's a long-standing, well-established tradition, and better yet, was written with average, untrained singers in mind. In some ways, it's the TTBB version of eighteenth-century chorale writing. Like chorale writing, it follows more rules than you probably need, but it makes for a great starting place to learn what works.

Melody and BGs

It's common in TTBB writing, especially in homophonic or chorale-style writing, to put the melody somewhere other than in the top voice. Why? If a male lead is in a nice, middle-of-the-road register, you're asking three other guys to squash down underneath him, musically speaking, and that can sound, well, squashy. Plus, you lose any interesting higher melodic and harmonic content. It's like playing only the left-hand notes of the piano: potentially dense and muddy. If this is the case, try the melody second from top, a BG above, a BG below, then the bass. Everybody's in their sweet spots now. This is the standard formula for barbershop writing: in fact, the tenor 2 part is usually just called the "lead." Here is an example of a homophonic TTBB with the lead line in the tenor 2 position.

Sweet Adeline

Arranged by Dylan Bell

Words and Music by
Henry Armstrong and Richard Gerard

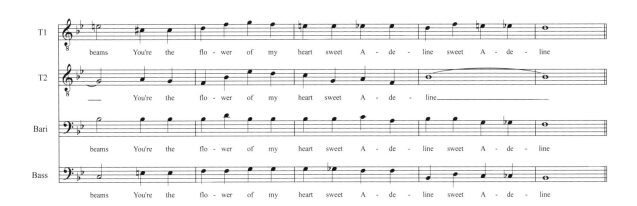

If your lead line is more of a high-tenor rock thing, by all means, put him on top and harmonize down from there. For this kind of writing, you're likely looking at a more instrumental style anyway, and putting the BGs on instrumental parts will further separate the lead texture from the group in a good way.

Don't Fix What's Broken

Words and Music by Dylan Bell

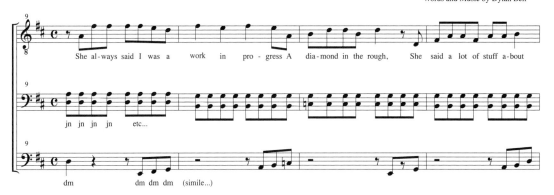

Copyedited by Dylan Bell
Used With Permission

Even in homophonic writing, the tenor 1 can take the lead line if treated more as a male soprano or alto, singing largely in falsetto, or if you have a tenor 1 singer with a lot of height in his sound.

Dona Nobis Pacem

Words and Music by Dylan Bell

In short, you can unlock TTBB writing with an understanding of male falsetto and an eye toward not allowing the BGs to creep down too low.

Women's Voices: SSAA

Writing for women's voices can be tricky. It's easy to do it badly, but if done right, it can be exquisite. Some of the challenges for writing for women's groups are:

» The smaller overall range means chord voicings often need to be tighter.
» The higher bass (or bottom vocal) range can result in murkier harmonic distinctions and increased difficulty in tuning.
» The female head voice is rarely used in pop music, which sometimes results in a difficult choice as an arranger: keep everything in chest voice, resulting in a working range of about two octaves, or use head voice and risk making a pop song sound choral.
» The sweet spot of SSAA voices is approximately D4–D5; it's still useful for harmonic information, but not as rich sounding.
» There's a smaller body of written music for this group, and the sound is less well-known, so your inner ear is probably less familiar with it.

All that said, the drawbacks mentioned above are only drawbacks when trying to write in a typical SATB format. All art is created within boundaries, and there is great inherent beauty in the SSAA format:

» Voices in this range can have a beautiful, angelic shimmer.
» While the male vocal rage works well with harmonic content, the female range works well with melodic content. This is the range where the voice really grabs the attention of the listener.
» The fact that it's overall a less common sound makes it more interesting and notable.
» There are lyrical topics and sounds that are best presented by all-female ensembles.
» Female a cappella is the least explored aspect of a cappella writing, meaning there is more room for pioneering new sounds and textures.

As with TTBB writing, you will use female voices in a slightly expanded vocal range—mostly downward, so that the alto parts cover a "meatier" range, where harmonic information is best heard. The sopranos' extreme range doesn't change, but the average range shifts up about a third to accommodate the voices below it.

Soprano 1. Full range: A3–A5. Most common range: C4–G5.

Soprano 2. Full range: A3–F5. Most common range: A3–E5.

Alto 1. Full range: D3–D5. Most common range: F3–C5.

Alto 2. Full range: D3–D5. Most common range: F3–A4.

You'll notice that the range is compressed: that is, there's much more cross-over between parts, and the full range of the ensemble is a fair bit smaller than that of an SATB group. With this in mind, you may want to write closer, more clustered voicings. And since the voicings will sit higher, they come out with greater clarity. Voices in this register are more likely to compete with each other for your listening attention. While this makes it harder to bury a lead alto part under soaring sopranos, it works really well for textural and contrapuntal ideas, since they will come across with more or less equal force. With this in mind, a chart can almost always be successfully customized to suit the unique sound of an SSAA ensemble.

When I'm 64

Arranged by
Deke Sharon

Words and Music by
John Lennon and Paul McCartney

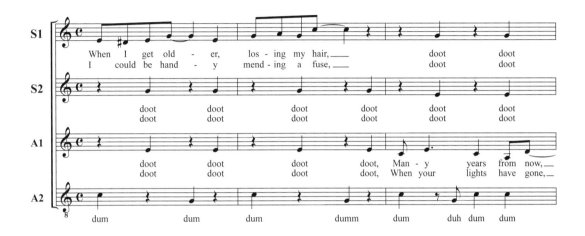

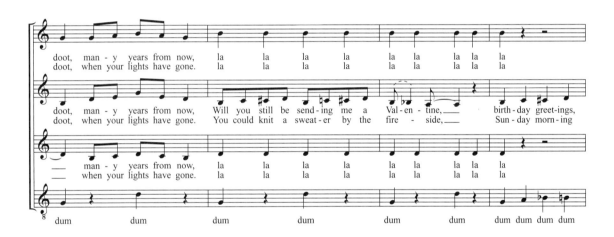

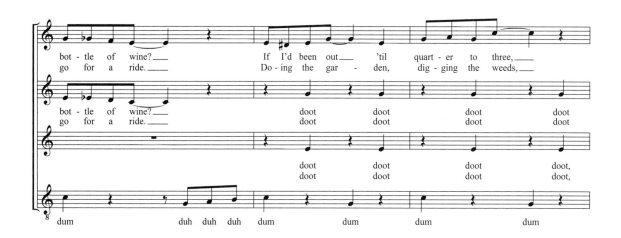

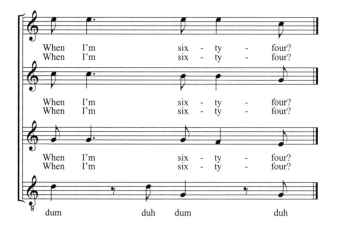

Alto 2 and the "Bass Question"

Our formula so far has been melody + bass + BGs. It works easily with SATB and TTBB since, well, they have basses. And as much as you want it to be, the alto 2 isn't a bass voice any more than a viola is a double bass. There are quite a few solutions to this problem. Some are obvious, but others require some outside-the-box thinking.

First off, what does a bass, whether vocal or instrumental, do? In short, the bass provides a harmonic underpinning and a basic rhythmic drive. Bass lines are often simple, repeated figures. An alto 2 can do this regardless of vocal range. This voice type can be combined with a vocal percussionist to create the same rhythm-section dynamic. And since many vocal percussion techniques are unpitched (see chapter 20), you can still have a slamming kick drum supporting the low end, regardless of gender. If you insist on keeping the alto 2 in bass range or want to do a rock tune without having it sound too light or fluffy, you can always use an octaver.

Our sense of hearing and perception is pretty sophisticated, though, and you can really play with this. Once the ear accepts the alto 2 part as a bass line, it will come across as doing what a bass does, even if it's nowhere near the range of a bass guitar. And let's not forget that, without an octaver, even a (male) bass singer is still singing higher than normal bass guitar range, and we easily accept that as bass.

Same Song, Same Arrangement, Different Configurations: "True Colors" (Arranged by Dylan Bell)

If an arrangement of yours proves popular, you may want to arrange it for different vocal configurations. This makes for an interesting exercise: keeping the spirit of the original arrangement but making it work within the contexts of the new configuration. This can also serve as a measure of your arrangement's durability: if it can withstand the little pushes and pulls of the required tweaking, it's probably pretty good!

Here is an example of an arrangement written for multiple configurations: "True Colors," written by Billy Steinberg and Tom Kelly and originally recorded by Cyndi Lauper, here arranged largely in a homophonic a cappella ballad style. The original arrangement was TTBB, written in C♭. The style in the chorus is a pretty standard four-part chorale style (albeit a little jazzier). This makes it pretty tried and true and easy to translate to other parts.

True Colors

Arranged by Dylan Bell

Words and Music by
Billy Steinberg and Tom Kelly

Here we go in SATB. Thanks to the four-part chorale style, it didn't require much revoicing or tinkering. The first task was finding a good key, one that was high enough for the soprano voice to ring nicely, but not so high as to give the tenors an aneurysm. The best choice was to move up a major third to E♭. This put the melody in a medium tessitura for the sopranos (E♭4–E♭5). Their top note is a F. The tenors have a relatively high tessitura in this section (fortunately it's balanced in other sections of the song) and a high note of G4.

True Colors

Arranged by Dylan Bell

Words and Music by
Billy Steinberg and Tom Kelly

Adapting for SSAA proves more challenging. The arrangement can't go much higher without the sopranos getting squeaky, yet the bass line is out of range for the altos. The only solution, even though it's a hassle, is to revoice it.

As is often the case, this results in taking the chart in a new direction. The goal is to create an arrangement that sounds like a "true" (no pun intended) SSAA chart, rather than a lazy, botched-up wrangling of an arrangement that's perfect for SATB or TTBB but simply doesn't work when the vocal range is quickly condensed without much thought (and sadly, there a lot of those out there).

First, we had to find a key that works for the melody. E was the ideal choice, for a couple of reasons. To begin with, it was practical: it fitted nicely with the melody in the first sopranos and allowed a solid low tonic from the second altos. And besides, in this style and with these voices, the key of E has a bright, crystalline quality, yet still feels tender and true to the lyrics.

Once the key was chosen, the next thing to do was to modulate the existing chart and see what was out of range. Please note that clefs have been changed to reflect proper SSAA usage.

True Colors

Arranged by Dylan Bell

Words and Music by
Billy Steinberg and Tom Kelly

For example, that low B at mm. 34–35 in the alto 2 line has to go. Same with the voicing at m. 39, "let it show." Even if it's technically possible, it makes for too many parts singing at the extreme low end of their ranges, which will sound weak and not have a bright, shimmering effect. So instead of voicing for the nice B pedal that the bass sings on the word "shine" at the bottom and building up, we'll go from the top and build down. It goes to the soprano 2, and the "shine" B pedal becomes a sort of descant from which the other parts hang. Instead of being an anchor, as it was for TTBB, it now makes the chord float. Different, and still nice.

True Colors

Arranged by Dylan Bell

Words and Music by
Billy Steinberg and Tom Kelly

Next, the chords at "let it show." Having the alto 2s down at C3–C♯3 is too low, and that pretty little moving bit in the original tenor 2 part would get lost. So the old baritone line is flipped up to the soprano 2, the alto 2 sings the fifth of the chord instead of the root, and now that line has some room to be heard.

Writing for More Parts

If you're accustomed to four voices or parts, writing for more can feel like a luxury: more parts equals more freedom, richer harmonies, and more clever bits and ear candy. Below are some general suggestions.

Five and Six Parts

Use the extra voices to make three- and four-part BGs. This is almost essential when writing jazz charts, which typically call for richer voicings and more advanced harmonies. If you're arranging pop music or dealing with triadic harmonies, you have an extra voice to double a pitch up the octave or at the unison.

Add a bass or baritone part. The bass line is the "second melody" of the song, so you can help enrich it by adding a second bass-function part. This voice could double the bass at the unison or an octave above, add fifths in places to make the bass line richer, or any combination thereof (see chapter 14). If a bass line is particularly angular or hard to execute, it can be split between the bass and baritone parts. This is great for things like disco bass lines, which sometimes have regular and fast-moving octave leaps that would leave a bass singer doubled over in pain and likely out of tune.

"Floater" parts. You could simply write a normal SATB chart and have one or two "floater" parts that fill any number of functions as needed. They may add an extra *divisi*-type note here or there to the BGs, cover extra bits such as guitar lines, lead doubles, or harmonies, or all of the above. This works best when writing for your own group: you can custom-make a part to suit your chosen singer and, if you wish, make it as crazy as he or she can handle.

More than Six Parts

More BGs! Especially when you're writing a jazz chart, you can add still more BGs. The late, great Gene Puerling regularly wrote jazz charts with up to eight parts. One possible configuration is to have a double set of BGs: one triadic unit on one texture and a second unit on another—for example, a triadic whole-note "ooh" pad with another arpeggiated trio overlaid.

Arrange by "instrument." With this technique you can, for example, designate multiple voices as "guitars," "keyboards," or various "horn sections." In these cases, you're not thinking vertically, writing SATB from highest part to lowest. You're thinking texturally, with multiple voices (often in multiple ranges) covering different things. You can also combine this with ranges if you want, which further helps to separate the textures.

Here We Come a-Caroling

Traditional, Arr. Deke Sharon

In this particular case, the soprano lines are covering the horns, while the alto, tenor, and baritone parts are covering the electric piano.

You can also allocate people to occasionally jump out of their regular part to sing specific bits of ear candy, "fly-honey" background vocals, and so on.

While writing with no part limitations, keep in mind the golden rule of musical taste:

» *Just because you can, doesn't mean you should.*

Research has shown that, in music, most people can concentrate on only two to three things at a time. So if you insist on using twelve separate voice parts to do different things at once, they won't just go unnoticed and unappreciated: they'll likely come across as a dense, cluttered mess.

It's even worse when writing for voices. Real guitars and trumpets come across as two very distinct things. Vocal approximations of these instruments will be much harder to distinguish: after all, they're still really the same instrument, meaning that you can have fewer separate textures before muddiness sets in.

There's also the practical consideration of strength in numbers. The more parts you write, the more you thin out your ensemble, and the idiosyncrasies and weaknesses of individual voices may become apparent.

Writing for Fewer Parts

Four-part writing is the standard because it allows for one lead melody and three other parts to cover triadic harmony. Take one (or more) away, and what are you left with?

First of all, when writing for fewer parts, song selection becomes more important.

» *Dylan says: I've always felt that a well-written song is one that could be performed with just guitar and voice and still sound complete. Songs that require lavish orchestration, textures, or production to sound good may or may not be strong songs, but regardless, if the song requires lots of textures to sound good, it won't be the best choice when writing for fewer voices. Focus on songs with a strong melody and/or bass line and fairly straightforward harmony.*

Three Parts

It's not easy, but it can be done. One way to approach a three-part arrangement is to consider the various combinations of voices:

3 + 0: Three voices, singing in homophonic, triadic harmony. Think of Crosby, Stills, and Nash or the Dixie Chicks: a melody with two parallel harmony parts. This kind of three-part vocal writing is very pleasing to the ear, but it cannot sustain a song throughout, for whenever the melody pauses, the music stops. Also, parallel vocal harmony results in the absence of a clear harmonic underpinning—a bass line—or any other rhythmic element to ground the song.

2 + 1: Two voices singing lead/harmony, plus bass. In this texture, there's a solo line and an independent bass line, with the third voice harmonizing the solo line. Duet writing can be very effective (think Simon and Garfunkel), and the bass line can outline the roots of the chords and provide a rhythmic element. The key here is to stagger the bass line's breaths so that they don't occur at the same time as the other two voices. When writing this way, you'll find frequent doubling of the tonic—anytime, in fact, that the melody or harmony line lands on the root of the chord. Write a bass line that doesn't sit entirely on the tonic of the chord throughout the measure, instead outlining chords by moving to the fifth and/or third, perhaps with color notes between, and you'll find periodic doublings less of a problem.

1 + 2: One lead voice, two harmony voices. This is a nice, semicontrapuntal texture. It combines the free-flowing feel of the first option above, but separating the melody from the harmony parts adds one extra layer of texture; it also solves the problem of the music's stopping when the melodic phrase stops, keeping the piece flowing.

1 + 1 + 1: One lead, one BG, one bass. Writing two independent lines that interweave with your melody is not as easy as it sounds. In this case, the BG has to be fairly agile, as he or she may be spelling out chords in two-note chunks (for example, where the bass sings the roots and BG sings the third and the fifth). That dictates much of its shape, and what remains is an assortment of leftover pitches and rhythmic holes. You can treat the remaining voice as if it were one of a section of BGs, knowing that it both has to cover important chord members and make melodic sense.

1 + 1 + 1: Three melodic parts, in counterpoint. This will likely give your arrangement a "classical" feel reminiscent of a Renaissance madrigal. It's a beautiful texture but can drastically change the feel of your average groove-centric pop song.

You probably won't want to use just one of these for a whole song: rather, your arrangement will likely use a combination of these. Think of it as a palette with several different colors to choose from.

One advantage of writing for three voices is that, since the human ear can focus on up to three things at once, the voices don't need to be stuck in one role. The parts are more fluid, allowing the singers or parts to swim around from one function to the next, with your listeners still able to keep up with what's happening.

Hey Jude

Arrangement by
Deke Sharon

Words and Music by
John Lennon and Paul McCartney

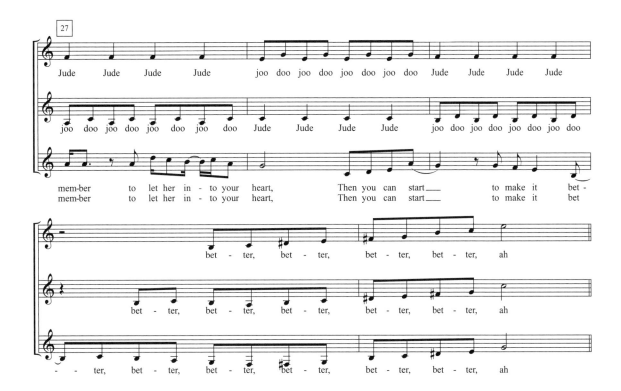

Two Parts

You won't often find yourself writing for two parts. A cappella duos are pretty uncommon (though they're out there), and if you're in a choral situation, you have enough singers to write for more anyway. But if you're in a duo or want to add a new texture to your show by featuring a duo piece or two, it's nice to have some duo-arranging skills in your pocket. Your color palette will most likely be:

» Lead voice, and accompaniment
» Two voices in harmony
» Two voices in counterpoint (this is possibly the most interesting)

And as in three-part writing, you may want to mix up the colors in any given song.

Earlier in the book, we talked about different arranging methods: arranging by ear, through recording, and through notation. In two-part writing, if you're writing for a specific duo, you'll probably find that you want to arrange with those specific voices in mind, utilizing their strengths (and avoiding weaknesses) in great detail. If this is the case, you're probably best off arranging by ear. As you break down a song to its basic elements of melody, lyrics, and harmony, you can decide by section, or even by lyric, which arranging colors you want to use where. Two-part writing may seem limiting, but it's also beautiful, intimate, and, if done well, very engaging for the listener.

Here We Come a-Caroling

One Part

Solo a cappella is an idiomatic art form: it is entirely about the individual singer and his or her abilities, and there is no standard for writing for solo a cappella voice. Solo a cappella artists usually arrange for themselves by working out the song in their own voice and choosing what works.

There is no better reference for solo a cappella arranging than Bobby McFerrin's album *The Voice*, in which he uses his voice to weave multiple lines, jumping from lead to bass to background, much in the manner of a Bach solo cello suite movement. Beware that very few vocalists have the dexterity to replicate this kind of vocal virtuosity; make sure you're arranging within your singer's ability.

CHAPTER 20

Vocal Percussion

Vocal percussion is a rich, diverse subject and practice deserving of its own book. Several instructional materials exist in a variety of forms, primarily video; but very little has been written explaining how it should be notated and integrated into an a cappella arrangement. We'll do our best to rectify this lack.

» *Deke says: In all the arrangements I've written over the past twenty years, I've notated vocal percussion in no more than a couple of dozen (and even then, usually only a measure's worth). Vocal percussion, like beatboxing, is an aural tradition, best learned and practiced by ear. If notating VP is a hassle, or you're busy enough with the sung notes, you can do without it and work it out in rehearsal.*

» *Dylan says: I am a vocal percussionist and I also play drums, and I sometimes like to use vocal percussion creatively in an arrangement just as I would any other voice part. If my arrangement is based on a well-known recording and I just want to have the vocal drummer represent that, I often won't notate the drum part. But if I'm writing with a particular drum part or pattern in mind, I'll write some of it out.*

We're going to focus on how to write and represent vocal percussion parts in your arrangement. Most vocal percussionists, however, do not rely on notation. Instead, they create parts by ear, usually by mimicking the percussive elements of an original recording, then modify as needed or desired.

Many people classify different vocal styles such as vocal percussion, vocal drumming, beatboxing, and so on. For our purposes, we'll use the general terms "vocal percussion" and "vocal percussionist," shortened to VP. (Apologies to any vice presidents or vice principals reading this, unless you are also vocal drummers.)

VP, among all practices within a cappella music, has been the most recent to develop. Choral writing has had a thousand years of development since the first notated music appeared around 1000 A.D., and a cappella has followed alongside in the popular idiom from madrigals through folk music, spirituals, barbershop, and doo-wop into contemporary a cappella.

VP developed out of necessity as it became increasingly difficult to represent popular music, given all its rhythmic elements, without it. It's a new practice, a highly individual art form, and each of its best practitioners brings a unique set of skills to the table. As a result, there isn't an established, academic-sounding common vocabulary of techniques. We won't try to create one here, but we'll give you some basic information on this art form and make some sense of how to use it.

For arranging purposes, the use of VP could be broadly classified like this as shown below.

The Single Drummer

Many modern groups, particularly if they focus on pop music and/or have a vocal-band format, have a single dedicated VP. This one percussionist usually fills the role of a drummer in a band, weaving together a complex pattern of kick, snare, hi-hat, cymbal, and other sounds (with a few auditory tricks) to create, amazingly, the sound of an entire drum kit. The tradition of beatboxing has similarities but also differences: a beatboxer, especially in its current competitive form, exists primarily as foreground, alone or with a rapper, while a vocal percussionist usually coexists with a group, integrating his or her sound into a tapestry of many voices. Beatboxers primarily create sounds reminiscent of programmed drums and turntables, with hip-hop at their musical center, whereas vocal percussionists replicate live drum kits, more within the rock tradition.

» *Deke says: When forming the House Jacks back in 1991, I met a soon-to-be graduate of the Brown Jabberwocks who not only sang extremely well but could sound exactly like a rock drum kit. This was a truly unique self-developed skill derived from the now legendary Andrew Chaikin (aka Kid Beyond). He joined up, and we developed our "rock band without instruments" sound and style around his incredible talent.*

The Drum Section

Vocal drums can be divided among individual sections or singers. This approach can be used for pop music but is most effectively used for interlocking percussion parts, such as African or Latin music: one person can do congas, another shakers, another cowbells or agogo bells, and so on. It is also useful for multilayered drum loop– or rhythm machine–based sounds, or for studio-recording arrangements where parts can be overdubbed.

Note that percussion does not only have to be vocal. Keith Terry is famous for his pioneering work with body percussion, and Cuba's Vocal Sampling amplifies their hands as well as mouths, creating the sound of claves by one hand forming a tube and the other hand slapping the top of it.

》 *Deke says: Back in the late '80s, while I was directing the Tufts Beelzebubs, it wasn't like I was consciously trying to form a new class of a cappella singer. Frankly, I just wanted to figure out how we could sing all the cool college rock songs, and that meant casting aside doo-wop idioms and using our voices like, among other things, drums. My first arrangement with VP was Peter Gabriel's "In Your Eyes," and it featured four people on VP: kick and snare, hi-hat, shaker, and talking drum.*

Many standard VP sounds aren't strictly vocal. For example, there is a frequently used kick drum sound that isn't a low pitch but is actually created by sending a short burst of air at the microphone head ("puh"), creating a sound like a drum head being hit that's lower than the human vocal chords can create.

Interwoven Percussive Elements

It is possible that your arrangement neither wants nor needs a dedicated drum-kit sound. Or, if you're working with a smaller group, there may not be an extra voice handy for dedicated drums. VP elements can be given to different sections at different times: the altos could take a shaker part, for a verse, if you can afford losing a pitched voice. Or, VP can be woven into a vocal part, like this:

jown-ga ch-k-ch-k jown-ga ch-k-ch-k   jown-ga ch-k-ch-k jown-ga ch-k-ch-k

It is common to imply a backbeat in a bass part, like this:

dm (dzh) dm dm (dzh) dm   (dzh) dm dm dzhm   (simile w backbeat)

Notice in this example that if the bass has to sing a note on the backbeat, you can still imply the percussion with a change in syllable: "dm" becomes "chm," "tm," or "dzhm." Sweden's a cappella masters, the Real Group, are experts at this: with five voices singing sophisticated jazz chords with implied vocal percussion, plus the bass singing backbeats, you hardly miss having a drummer. Also, you'll see that the drums aren't notated after the first couple of bars: in fact, you could even just write "bass sings snare on backbeat" and avoid notating it altogether.

VP for Your Group

If you are writing for your group and you have a dedicated VP, you can be as vague as you like with drum notation and instructions or even not notate anything at all. Presumably you know what your drummer is capable of, and more often than not you may just want to tell him or her to go with it, and learn something similar to the recording. If you want to provide general instruction, follow the steps listed below.

VP for Other Groups

No VP sounds exactly like another. With voices, though individual timbres may vary, you know what a soprano or alto can do, and you can write within those parameters. You can write specific notes, words, and rhythms and know that they'll be replicated as you ask. The VP vocabulary is so varied that it can be hard to know what you can ask them to do. You may not even know what's possible. So we need to set a common "minimum standard" of sounds you can expect to be able to use.

Basic VP Vocabulary

Here's a basic building block of sounds you can write for a VP part.

> » *Kick drum:* "dm" or "bm"
> » *Snare drum:* "pf"
> » *Cross-stick (the "click" instead of the drum sound):* "kh"
> » *Toms:* "dng"
> » *Hi-hats:* "t," "tsss"
> » *Cymbals (crash and ride, plus cymbal rolls):* "kssssh," "pshhhh"
> » *Shakers:* "shk"
> » *Congas/bongos:* "bng"
> » *Talking drum:* "doong"

No matter how the VP approaches these, you should be able to get the sounds you want within these parameters.

Notating Vocal Percussion

If you are writing for a percussion section, it's pretty straightforward: assign a note (or two or three, depending on the layers or "notes" of the percussion instrument) using percussion-style X noteheads:

Basic Groove

The basic function of the drummer in a band is to keep time, and the same can be said for VP. In most pop music, the 4/4-with-a-backbeat holds it all together, usually a combination of the kick and snare.

In some songs, the drums have a signature groove: if this is the case, be sure to notate it specifically if you want the drummer to follow it.

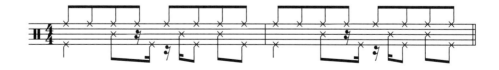

» *Dylan says: Two parts on one staff? What gives? Although it's being sung by one mouth (instead of four limbs), I like to notate VP the way real drumming is done,*

which sometimes involves showing more than one layer of drumming. In these cases, the layers are kick and snare on the bottom and hi-hat on the top.

It's possible that the VP won't be able to articulate all eight hi-hats, and it may not sound good even if they can. VP notation is representational rather than literal, telling the VP basically what a drummer would play. You leave it to the VP to figure out how to put that in his or her face. The key is for the VP to understand the part in layers, rather than indicating exactly what syllables to use in what order.

Syllables

» *Dylan says: I rarely write syllables in drum parts: in keeping with the interpretive sprit of drum notation, I'd rather have the VP find those sounds on his or her own. Instead, I give verbal descriptions of what drum sounds I want.*

Even if you don't want to notate syllables, doing so may help guide a less experienced VP. This is most important for the snare drum, which is also the sound where you'll find most sonic variety, both in real drums and in their VP representation. If the sound you want is specific, but hard to imagine unless you know the exact reference, use a combination of words and syllables . . .

> » *'80s electric snare: "dzh"*
> » *'70s tight, dry snare: "bf"*
> » *Big rock snare*
> » *Sloppy rock hi-hat*

. . . and let the VP use his or her imagination to bring it to life.

Notating Changes

Drum parts don't usually change from bar to bar: they find a groove and stay in it. They may change the feel in a new section, but often they keep the basic feel throughout. Instead of writing out the whole part, use this:

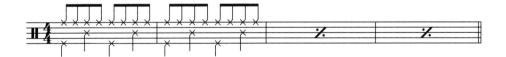

It's easier to write, and easier for the VP to understand.
For specific drum fills, try this:

(You don't need to notate the crash on the next bar; that's usually implied.)
For a nonspecific drum fill, this will do:

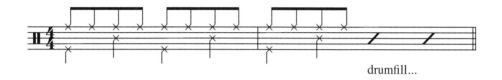

drumfill...

For any places where you want to VP to hit particular shots (common in jazz
and funk charts) within the usual groove, you can write this:

What Do I Keep from the Original?

That tells us how to write it. But if we're representing a particular recording,
what do we choose?

On the recording, it's often not a single drummer taking care of all the percussive elements: there may be tambourines, shakers, or any number of other
percussion bits involved. Do you have to cover all of them?

It's not all that different from the choices you probably made when representing instrumental parts. There may be seven guitar overdubs, but they're playing
90 percent of the same notes. Chances are you let a few parts go, amalgamated
them into one part, or figured out the role of that part and put it somewhere else.
In short, you covered the important textures and functions of the instrumental
parts. You can do the same with drums and percussion.

Drums and percussion in most pop music can be broken down into three
main functions:

» *Basic rhythm.* Kick and snare, downbeat and backbeat. This is the heartbeat
of the song, and if you're doing any VP at all, you'll definitely want to represent this.

» *Surface rhythm.* The lighter, faster stuff such as hi-hats, shakers, and tambourines. This is nice to have but more important in some songs than others. Sometimes this rhythmic drive comes directly from the drummer, but often the surface rhythm is covered somewhere else, like a rhythmic guitar/keyboard part. If so, you may not need any extra layers beyond hi-hat—if even that.

» *Decorative rhythm.* Congas, cowbells, and other percussion instruments. These usually have interesting repeated patterns and add spice to the song. The nice thing about these types of rhythms is that they don't have be done with VP.

This should give you a pretty good start on using VP in your arrangement. For more in-depth understanding of VP, we've also included some resources in the appendices.

CHAPTER 21

Specific A Cappella Styles: A "How-To" History of A Cappella

Throughout this book, we have been giving tips and techniques that were used in a contemporary-music context but can be applied to any genre of a cappella arranging. Now, imagine that someone calls you and says, "I need this heavy-metal song arranged in a barbershop style." While this chapter won't make you an expert in all styles of music, we will take a look several common styles of a cappella music, examine the unique qualities that define them, and give some pointers on how best to convey that style of music in your arrangement.

To make this comparison of styles easier to see and hear, we'll use the well-known hymn "Amazing Grace" for each style of arranging.

A note to all you Serious Music Scholars out there: the descriptions of each music genre are, of course, drastic oversimplifications. Consider them an "introduction to . . ." rather than a detailed and fully accurate stylistic analysis. However, they also explain, in condensed form, the history of Western a cappella music.

And remember, nothing beats repeated and varied listening to understand a style of music. If you *really* want to understand barbershop music, read the section on barbershop, then listen to a hundred barbershop recordings and sing a handful of barbershop charts. It will all start to make sense.

Let's start at the beginning, with . . .

Classical Music

"Classical" music (or, more correctly, Western European art music) is at the root of much Western music as a whole. If you've ever taken a course on theory, harmony, or basic arranging, many of the terms and conventions here will be familiar: this is where they all come from.

In the beginning, there was only melody, in the form of plainchant. Plainchant is as old as the human voice, but in music studies it is usually associated with Roman Catholic church music. The first manuscripts of plainchant date to around the ninth century, so it's probably a lot older than that. Rhythms were simple and free-flowing, since the church authorities viewed rhythm, dancing, and other visceral music expression as suspect. Sound syllables were not used: no doo-wops or hey-nonny-nonny-nos. The closest you might get to sound syllables were melismas, where one syllable of a word would be stretched over several notes. Since it made sense to stretch a word over an open vowel, this is likely the origin of "ah," "oh," and "oo" as sound painting. Our example piece, in plainchant, would likely look like this:

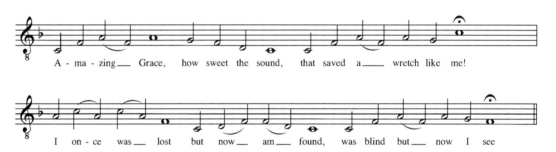

(Well, except that it would be in Latin, and not in typical Western notation!)

The first thing you'll notice is that there is no time signature, and the rhythms are greatly simplified. Plainchant is smooth and more or less nonrhythmic: gone are the pulse and the "swing" of the original. The rhythm comes from the natural rhythms of speech and natural places to pause or breathe. To get a rough sense of how to feel this, simply read the words of your melody, following the melodic phrase, but without any pulse. You'll feel some natural movement and stops-and-starts, and that's as far as you'll go rhythmically.

Eventually a second part was added, usually in parallel fifths, fourths, or octaves, below the melody. Some theories suggest that this was simply a matter of vocal range—if the low singers in the monastery couldn't hit the notes, they simply sang the whole melody at a lower pitch. This led to organum, and it looked something like this:

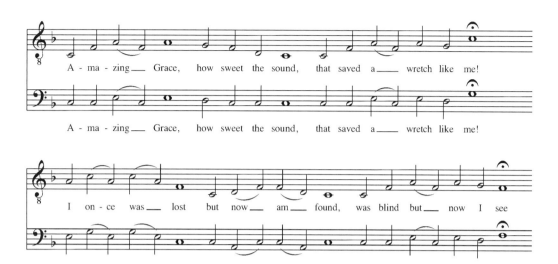

Organum is the sound that people often associate with medieval religious music. The singing monks in *Monty Python and the Holy Grail*? They're singing organum.

You'll notice that the second part is mostly in parallel fourths and that it starts and ends on a unison. You won't see many thirds in organum; back then, a third was considered a pretty far-out, "imperfect" sound, unlike "perfect" fourths, fifths, and octaves.

Music from this time is associated with terms such as

» Plainchant
» Organum
» Gregorian chant
» Medieval music (more correctly, early medieval music)

or, colloquially, by more vague terms such as "church-mode" music or "monk-style" music. If someone says, "Write me something that sounds like a bunch of monks singing," this is probably what he or she is asking for.

And Then Came Polyphony

People have been improvising, riffing, and styling since music began, so it's no surprise that these practices made their way into church music as well. **Polyphony** most likely started with one person singing the melody, slowly and simply, and another singer improvising up, down, and around it. Eventually, by about the twelfth century, this was codified into a more consistent and written-down form. The slow but steady melody became the cantus firmus (literally, "fixed song"). A more developed form of organum, this eventually became the basis for counterpoint.

You'll notice that the stylized line may flit and fly about but always comes to rest at an important stopping point in the melody, such as the end of a line of text or a breathing point. With the idea of harmony not yet developed, the counter-line would stop on a "consonant" interval such as a unison, octave, or fifth (thirds were still considered dissonant). Also, the melody has been "squared-out" with a 4/4 time signature and simplified rhythms, in keeping with the static nature of cantus firmus.

By about the sixteenth century, during what's usually called the Renaissance period in music, the number of voice parts had increased, and the cantus firmus had disappeared. Now instead of a single melody with one or more decorative parts, there could be multiple lines, each its own separate melodic part, and each equally important. Melodic ideas could be passed back and forth between parts, giving each part a little moment of focus, weaving them together like a tapestry.

arr. D. Bell

In this particular example, the melody is divided among the four vocal parts: alto, soprano, tenor, then bass. This doesn't have to occur in **polyphonic** music, but since one part doesn't dominate over the others as the designated melodic part (as became the norm later on, from eighteenth-century chorales right up to today's pop soloist), it can easily happen. You'll notice some surprisingly advanced-sounding harmonic developments, such as the use of a "modal-sounding" E♭ accidental in some bars (though the concept of harmony and chord changes didn't really exist yet) and several syncopations and rhythmic pushes-and-pulls between parts. You'll also see plenty of interaction between parts such as the "sharing" of running eighth-note lines, creating a constant flow.

Polyphony is a compositional style rather than a musical genre, so it shows up in various forms. In instrumental music, you start seeing fugues. In vocal music, you would find polyphonic writing in motets and madrigals. Though they are considered two different types of music, musically they are essentially the same. The difference is in the choice of language. Motets, like other sacred music, were sung in Latin, usually religious in nature. Madrigals were sung in the "vernacular" (the local language) and were often nonreligious, or secular. Secular madrigals were the sixteenth-century equivalent of vocal pop music. And surprisingly, a lot of the subject material was similar: songs about dancing and having a good time, and falling in love (or lust).

This type of writing is associated with terms such as:

» Motet
» Madrigal
» Early music
» Renaissance music
» Medieval music (late medieval music)
» Polyphony
» Fugue-style writing (a fugue is usually instrumental, but the word is sometimes used colloquially as a catch-all phrase for polyphonic writing)

So if someone asks for an arrangement style and uses one of these terms, this is probably what he or she is asking for.

Since we now have three or more parts singing at the same time, some attention was being paid to what those three or more notes sounded like together. But while people talked about consonant and dissonant intervals, this was still modal (melodic, scale-based, "horizontal") writing, rather than harmonic (major/minor/dominant chord–based, "vertical") writing. This would come later with . . .

Chorale-Style Writing

Simply put, chorale-style writing is the essence of harmony. When people take theory classes in "harmony," they usually study eighteenth-century church chorales. It not only formed the basis of harmony for the next two centuries of classical music, but informs all harmony today.

Johann Sebastian Bach is widely considered the father of the chorale. While he didn't invent chorale writing, a large set of his chorales was published after his death that represent a perfect distillation of this style of writing and essentially became a harmony teaching tool.

The main shift here is the use of homophonic instead of polyphonic or contrapuntal writing, meaning that, instead of several vocal parts of equal importance, there was a main melody (in chorale writing, usually the soprano), with the other parts usually singing the same words at the same time as a secondary accompaniment. Little bits of contrapuntal motion show up here and there to make for better voice leading and to create an overall sense of flow. Chorale writing is generally in four parts, representing both an easy way to divide vocal ranges (female high, female low, male high, and male low) and a sensible way to represent three-note harmony, allowing for doubling and emphasizing of certain chord tones wherever necessary. Our example, in chorale style, looks like this:

arr. D. Bell

The first thing you'll see is that, compared to previous examples, the parts are much more simple and static. Now that the voice parts are divided between melody (soprano) and accompaniment (everyone else), the accompaniment parts serve to support the melody and don't overshadow it. You'll also notice that there is far less interplay between parts: they largely follow the melody in rhythm and lyric, except for a few places where parts move under a static melody line, or for voice-leading purposes.

This model was carried on well into the nineteenth century and is pretty much the default setting for an overall classical-music sound. Most modern choral music is an evolution of this style, adapted to include a more advanced harmonic vocabulary.

Barbershop Style

Barbershop writing is pretty much a direct descendant of standard chorale writing. Developed in the United States in the late nineteenth century and codified and "revived" beginning in the 1940s, it in some ways combines traditional chorale harmony with contemporary popular culture in an informal setting. It's designed to be singable by anyone.

We can start by looking at the similarities between chorale writing and barbershop writing:

» Four-voice writing as the standard approach
» Homophonic in character
» Simple, singable melodies (in chorale music, this was to allow the congregation to sing the hymns; barbershop was originally based on the catchy, singable tunes of the day)
» Use of typical Western harmonic development (major, minor, and dominant chords, with chord progressions based on the circle of fifths and eventually leading "home" to the tonic)

There are also characteristics that separate it from chorale writing:

» Songs and lyrics based on popular, secular songs
» Originally all-male groups, with all-female groups arriving in the 1940s (mixed ensembles are rare)
» A writing style based on quartet singing (though large choruses are common)
» Melody or "lead" part in the second-highest voice, rather than the highest (owing in part to its same-sex, close-harmony style)

Barbershop writing, having been codified, preserved, and propagated mainly by a specific organization (the Society for the Preservation and Encouragement of Barbershop Quartet Singing in America, or SPEBQSA, now thankfully known as the Barbershop Harmony Society), is one of the only musical styles that deliberately and self-consciously applies rules to its art form. Doing so allows us to have clear instructions on how to create and perform the music, allowing even untrained singers to follow the instructions and "sing it right."

To arrange a piece in barbershop style, start by following some straightforward rules:

» Song choice is important. Choose a song with a simple melody and a straightforward chord structure. In addition to standard barbershop repertoire, three-chord pop and rock songs work, as do Tin Pan Alley songs and jazz standards. Songs with parallel harmonic structures, unusual harmonic development (or trancelike, no-harmonic-development songs) are much more difficult. Barbershop relies on the sense of having a "home key," moving away from it, and coming back home. If your song doesn't do this, you'll have to find a way to make it happen!

» The backbone of barbershop harmony is the dominant seventh chord (for example, C7, that is, C–E–G–B♭, in any inversion). This chord type is so important that for a song to be considered "barbershop" (for the purpose of barbershop competitions, for example), a song must have a minimum of 30 percent dominant seventh chords. The dominant seventh chord is also a key component in the "chord-ringing" aesthetic of barbershop singing. When certain chords are sung with the right blend, balance, and resonance, you can actually hear a "fifth voice" as a result of the combination of overtones and frequencies in the chord. The dominant seventh is not just harmonically important: it is also one of the easiest chords to make ring.

» Keep your parts largely homophonic. Barbershop, unlike vocal-band singing, is not about separating vocal textures: it is about combining them into a whole that is larger than the sum of its parts.

» Barbershop harmony has a very specific harmonic vocabulary. In addition to dominant seventh chords, you can use major chords (which should be turned into dominant sevenths wherever possible), minor chords, and major and minor chords with added sixths. Other chords (minor seventh chords and augmented and diminished chords) can be used, but only if the melody requires it. Avoid chords that are missing the root, third, or seventh (they sound ambiguous), major seventh chords (and minor-major seventh chords), and augmented or otherwise harmonically complex chords (unless dictated by the melody).

» Though a barbershop song can have a solid pulse, it is not groove-centered music. Avoid vocal percussion, overly syncopated parts, or anything that requires strict timekeeping in order to work properly. Barbershop harmony works well when it can be sung *rubato*, stretching and milking the harmonies and allowing plenty of time for the chords to ring at the ends of phrases.

And then there is the tag.

The tag is the last part of the song, similar to a coda in classical music. It's the grand finale of the song and usually contains the most harmonic interest and complexity. It often includes a "hanger," where one singer holds a single note and harmonies are woven around it. Tags are most often big and loud, with ringing, "paint-peeling" chords to wrap the song up. Barbershop tags are so highly stylized that they are often taught (and informally performed) as stand-alone pieces independent of the songs they come from. All barbershop songs (according to the Barbershop Harmony Society) must end with a tag, and there are infinite resources devoted solely to barbershop tags. Go to a barbershopper's party, and inevitably groups will gather in various corners, and burst into song—for a single, dramatic, four-bar tag.

It makes for a lot of rules to consider (and remember what we said about rules earlier in the book?), but the well-defined parameters can make it a lot of fun to write a barbershop-style chart. And the upside: follow the rules, and you'll pretty much have a guaranteed-singable barbershop piece. Here's what happens when our example is arranged in barbershop style:

arr. D. Bell

The first thing you'll see is that the key has been changed from F to A-flat: a simple, practical consideration now that we have an all-male ensemble with the melody on the second-highest part. The parts look similar to those we saw in the chorale-writing example—largely homophonic, with not much going on in the way of voice leading or extra rhythms. Where you start to see differences is in the harmonies. We have our requisite number of dominant seventh chords, a couple of diminished chords, and of course the tag, starting in m. 15. With the melody fairly low and on the tonic, the parts moving around tend to aim high—you'll see that the bass finishes on a high E♭. While this gives a sense of tension and drama, it also represents a range extreme: if this were too high for the bass, the simplest fix could be to have the bass sing the hanger and the lead take the bass part. Such simple part-swappings, done in order to best suit the voices in the particular group, are common in barbershop quartets.

Doo-Wop

Doo-wop is the term for vocally centered (but not always a cappella) rhythm-and-blues music. It originated in the 1940s with African American groups in urban centers. Its heyday was in the late 1940s to the early 1960s, and the name "doo-wop" (though applied quite late in the evolution of the style) refers to the non-word-based sound syllables used in the backup vocals, often as a form of instrumental imitation. Though connected to the pre-revival barbershop tradition, it represents a departure from barbershop in its use of scat syllables, instrumental imitation, and separation of the vocal parts into different textures (lead vocal, BGs, and bass singer).

Doo-wop, like barbershop music, is often associated with the music of its day—in this case, popular music that represented the era of post–big band, pre-psychedelic R & B and early rock and roll. It developed in parallel with instrumental music, both following and leading musical development.

When people talk about "street-corner a cappella," they usually mean a cappella doo-wop, which, in the late 1950s and 1960s, was a pretty accurate description: groups coming out in the evening, singing on a street corner or around a lamppost. The songs were either original music or a cappella versions of radio hits. Since the sound of doo-wop (and music of this era in general) is ingrained in the North American cultural memory, it isn't all that hard to imagine and recreate. Here are a couple of factors to consider.

Doo-wop is typically written for four to five singers: a lead singer, a bass, and two or more backup singers. Like barbershop music, doo-wop groups were primarily male, though female groups did exist: '50s and '60s "girl groups" were based on the doo-wop sound, though they were not usually a cappella.

Doo-wop songs are often tied to the harmonic structure of I–vi–IV–V, later known as "'50s changes" or "ice-cream changes." Background vocals typically cover simple major or minor triadic harmonies, following the chord changes with a repetitive sound-syllable motif. Background rhythmic parts will often contrast from section to section: for example, long, open "ah" syllables are sung in a chorus or bridge, with a "shoo-wop, shoo-wadda-wadda"-type motif in the verse.

In direct contrast to barbershop style, doo-wop is primarily groove based. Many doo-wop songs are swung or in a triple or compound meter such as 6/8 or 12/8. Background parts are meant to drive the song's rhythm, juxtaposed against a solid and simple bass line and often a smooth, crooning lead vocal.

Doo-wop is probably the most direct ancestor of contemporary a cappella arranging. The sound was based on that of instrumental groups, and while the sound syllables didn't always directly imitate the sound of instruments, they imitated their function. A "shoo-wop, shoo-wadda-wadda" vocal part might represent a horn section; "da-doo ron, ron, ron" might be a piano or guitar, and "dip-dip-dip-dip bohm" a bass. When arranging doo-wop style, keep the vocabulary simple and more "vocal": you won't find much "zhing-joh-joh" literal imitation happening.

Here's our piece in a doo-wop arrangement.

In this case, we've kept the same male-friendly key of A♭, and also changed the key signature to 4/4 to give the piece a bouncy, swinging, late-'50s feel. The lead singer's rhythms have been modified to give a little swing and syncopation. The bass line is fairly straightforward, starting with a signature "bom bom di-dip, ba-dm" and otherwise outlining the chord changes as expected. Near the end, the bass includes a I–vi–ii–V turnaround typical of doo-wop and jazz. The BGs take a repeated rhythmic figure through the chord changes on basic triadic harmonies, moving to static block chords partway through. All in all, you can imagine this being played by a '50s-style rock-and-roll band and sounding very similar.

Vocal Jazz

Vocal jazz writing can be basically broken down into two types: chorale style, and close-harmony or big-band style.

First, a primer on jazz harmony. Jazz harmony is the evolutionary result of what Bach was doing three hundred years ago. The difference, in two words, is simply: *more notes*. Basic jazz harmony isn't really a new or different way of conceiving harmony: it is simply an extension of classical harmony. Classical harmony is primary tertian, meaning that the chords are imagined by stacking thirds on top of each other. This is usually triadic: major and minor chords with roots, thirds, and fifths. Dominant sevenths are added for harmonic motion, to help resolve one chord to the next. Other notes, such as major sevenths and ninths, or other chords, such as diminished or augmented chords, may show up, but usually just to add color or to serve as a source of harmonic tension, which is eventually resolved to a more stable major or minor chord.

a "static" major chord   a dominant-7 chord...
                                which "expects" resolution

Jazz harmony simply extends the limits of what a "normal" chord might be to include sevenths, ninths, even elevenths and thirteenths (aka fourths and sixths). Well, that's about all the notes in the scale, isn't it? We can turn the "normal" major chord into a major seventh just by piling another note on top of the old major chord. Now it seems that just about every note in the scale is fair game in a static, going-nowhere chord.

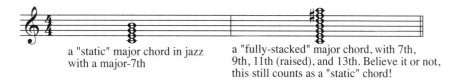

a "static" major chord in jazz   a "fully-stacked" major chord, with 7th,
with a major-7th   9th, 11th (raised), and 13th. Believe it or not,
                                        this still counts as a "static" chord!

In the case of dominant seventh chords, the situation becomes even more varied. In classical harmony, a dominant seventh is usually a "moving" chord, creating tension and resolving to the "resting" major chord; this is the good old V–I cadence. Keeping with the more-colors-in-the-palette sound in jazz harmony, a moving dominant seventh chord can have its upper partials (the ninth, eleventh, and thirteenth) raised or lowered in just about any way you see fit, giving several variations or colors to choose from.

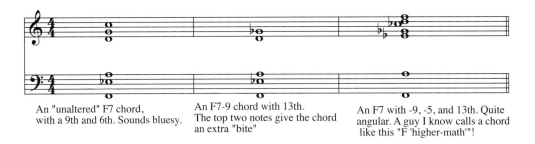

An "unaltered" F7 chord, with a 9th and 6th. Sounds bluesy.

An F7-9 chord with 13th. The top two notes give the chord an extra "bite"

An F7 with -9, -5, and 13th. Quite angular. A guy I know calls a chord like this "F 'higher-math'"!

Not only does jazz harmony offer more colors, it offers a finer brush. Jazz harmony uses the same circle-of-fifths approach to harmonic motion as classical music, but goes further around the circle. A typical classical cadence needs to get back to the tonic, or I. The usual route is V–I, the perfect cadence, or IV–I, the plagal ("amen") cadence. The standard jazz cadence backs up a little further: ii–V–I.

D-7   G7   C (major 7th)

Or, it can start from even further away: iii–VI–ii–V–I.

E- (with 9th)   A7 (with 13th)   D- (with 9th)   G7 (with 9th and augmented 5th)   C6/9

A iii-VI-ii-V-I jazz progression. Note that extra partials such as 13th, -9s, etc are common.

Or even: ♯iv–VII–iii–VI–ii–V–I. Round and round we go.

Jazz harmony also makes use of reharmonization: using substitute chords, often a minor third down. If the song moves to the IV, try its "relative," ii. V can be substituted by iii, and the tonic by vi. If this sounds vaguely familiar, it probably is: it's the same principle behind the relative minor key signatures that you learned back in theory class or piano lessons.

Chords can often be substituted for their relative equivalent:
by simply changing the bass note, an F chord becmes a D-7 chord,
and will work similarly in the chord progression.

Don't forget the substitution unique to jazz writing: the tritone substitution. Simply put, it works like this. The main notes in a dominant seventh chord are the third and the (lowered) seventh. In a G7 chord, you'll have G (the root), B (the third), and F (the seventh). Now, try a different bass note, a tritone (augmented fourth or diminished fifth) away: D♭. Now you have D♭ (the new root), B (the seventh—technically a C♭, if you're feeling fussy), and F (the third). It's now a D♭7 chord, created just by swapping out the bass note.

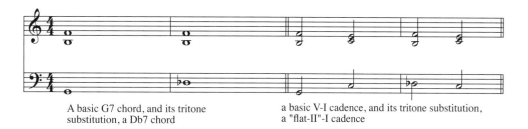

A basic G7 chord, and its tritone
substitution, a Db7 chord

a basic V-I cadence, and its tritone substitution,
a "flat-II"-I cadence

Despite all these explanations of jazz harmony, jazz chorale isn't all that much different from writing classical or barbershop harmony. Whereas barbershop has a unique style defined in part by a very focused harmonic vocabulary, jazz chorales diverge by expanding the harmonic boundaries. But the same principles of homophonic writing and good voice leading apply to all.

All these extra notes can be quite a challenge to cram into a four-voice chorale. There are a couple of solutions:

1. *Write for more parts.* Like doo-wop, vocal jazz doesn't have a standard four-voice format as classical or barbershop writing does. Five, six, even eight voices are often used to allow for the lushness of jazz harmony.

2. *Drop the root.* Most of the time you won't have to: "basic" jazz chords have four notes, and you have four voices to deal with. But when you want to stuff in a few extra colors, you *can* drop the root—something that's almost unheard of in barbershop or classical writing. As our collective understanding of harmonic conventions has developed, our ears will fill in the implied root of a chord, or at least understand where the chord is going even without it. It's similar to modern films, in which a flashback scene can be recognized and understood even without the wispy, going-back-in-time visual effects

seen in old movies. We know what a flashback is without its being spelled out; the same can be said for more complicated jazz chords and progressions.

So, to write a piece in vocal jazz-chorale style, try the following:

» Write in a primarily homophonic style.
» Keep the tempo slow, possibly with generous use of rubato, to allow time for the harmonies to be heard and understood.
» Use harmonically rich chords such as major and minor sevenths. Experiment with adding upper notes such as ninths/seconds, elevenths/fourths, and thirteenths/sixths. You can even try altering (raising or lowering) the upper notes, especially with the V7 chords.
» Use many of the conventions of standard choral writing: good voice leading, small moments of motion between parts, and the like.
» Add more harmonic motion with extended cadences, especially the "standards" in jazz: ii–V–I and iii–vi–ii–V–I. Not only will this offer more harmonic interest, it will also offer more opportunities for interaction and voice leading in the inner parts.
» Try substituting chords, especially if you have another section with the same chord changes.

If we try these techniques, "Amazing Grace" could go like this:

At first glance, this arrangement seems somewhat similar to the chorale and barbershop versions, though it's in six parts. There's no major groove or rhythmic action. It's in the harmonic examination where things get interesting. Basic chords have been included to help you follow along.

First of all there are simply more chords. Where once we had a single chord per bar, we see numerous chord turnarounds. In m. 2 we see a Cm7–F7–B♭: a ii–V–I "mini-cadence" to the B♭ chord. Over mm. 5–8, we see a reharmonization of the I chord (F) to its relative, vi (Dm), and in m. 8, we see what looks like a tritone substitution: where we expect a C chord, we have a G♭ chord, which quickly slides into a Gm chord, leading to a full reharmonization of the next section. On the words "I once," instead of a V–I cadence leading to the tonic F chord, we have a III–vi cadence leading us to the relative minor.

At m. 9, this section is reharmonized under a pedal tone in the bass, allowing for some sad-sounding "lost" chords (to reflect the lyrics), followed by some more hopeful-sounding "found" chords. At mm. 13–15, we see what looks like a III–vi–II–V cadence, pausing on the V chord (with a few of those altered upper notes just to make it interesting). But instead of ending on a tonic chord, there's an added coda of chords descending from the ♯iv chord (Bm7b5 mm. 16 to the end). This is a fairly conventional jazz-harmonic ending.

In addition to all this extra chord action, we see more voice-leading moments (usually to add extra passing colors) and a clear break from classical-harmony rules. In many cases these passing bits are voiced in parallel fourths or in other ways usually *verboten* in chorale writing; so why are they acceptable here? Back in the discussion on harmony in chapter 15 we mentioned that parallel writing draws attention to itself. While this is undesirable in smooth, unobtrusive classical-chorale parts, it's being used here for exactly that reason, to give the moving parts a little moment to shine and be noticed.

Jazz harmony (especially chorale style) is considerably more complex than most of the other examples so far, and if the numbers and chord-speak are starting to sound like the math classes you nearly failed, don't sweat it. Much of the essential harmonic knowledge is probably in your ears anyway, regardless of the theory and numbers behind it, so you can probably hear major sevenths and other harmonies in your head already and can discover much of your harmonizing by noodling around on the piano. Many jazz arrangers were not fully versed in the theory behind why things work: they just wrote what sounded good to them. And while this example is fairly stuffed with jazzisms, a jazz chart doesn't need every chord to be retooled to sound good. In fact, simpler is often better, and more complex can be exhausting!

Big-Band Style

This is a catch-all term we'll use to describe non-chorale vocal jazz writing. Like doo-wop and contemporary a cappella writing, it can take on many different forms and often involves using different vocal textures. Whereas chorale style tends to dominate in down-tempo pieces, this style is more often found in medium- to up-tempo songs.

All the same concepts of jazz harmony mentioned above will apply here—and we'll include one more: close-harmony writing. Close-harmony writing is not much different from the homophonic barbershop style. The voices move together as a single group, often in similar motion (all going up or down together, as opposed to chorale writing, which often uses contrary motion to keep the sound grounded). Close harmony in vocal jazz is a little different: since there are often four notes in a close-harmony voicing, the interval between inner parts is often as small as a whole or half step, giving close harmony a tight, almost buzzing sound. This sound is used often in a big band, particularly in the saxophone section. Here is an example of "Amazing Grace" done in close harmony.

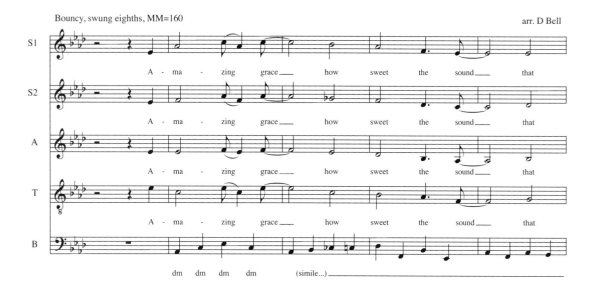

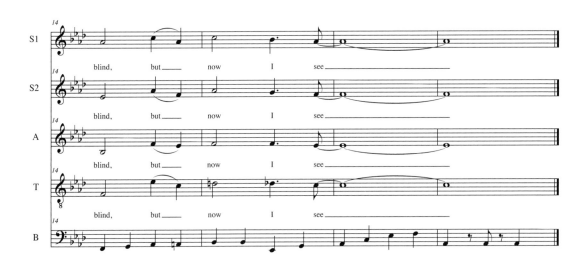

This one is in five voices: four for the close harmony, one for the jazz-style walking bass. We're back in A♭, to make the chords and melody "pop and ring" a little more, and back to 4/4 for a jazz-swing feel. The writing is nearly always parallel, with a couple of places (such as the chord on the word "blind" in m. 14) where the voicing opens up a little to give a nice all-fourths voicing. There are a couple of ii–V–I chord progressions (easy to follow in the walking bass line), and some interesting jazz colors (such as the chord on the word "I" in m. 9) but overall there is much less harmonic complexity than in the jazz-chorale style. There are two reasons for this. For one, the tempo is much faster, allowing less time for the singers to sing (and the listener to hear) any complex movement in the parts. Also, this type of sound is based on the swing and dance-band sounds of the 1940s, which generally wasn't as harmonically dense as other forms of jazz.

This arrangement had an ensemble lead. For a piece with a soloist, you could try a format we'll call "doo-wop plus": bass, lead vocal, and four BGs. As in the previous example, the bass takes on an instrumental-bass role. The lead vocal stays the same (this time as a baritone or tenor solo). The BGs will function similarly to a big-band horn section, adding "shots" in response to the lead vocal line.

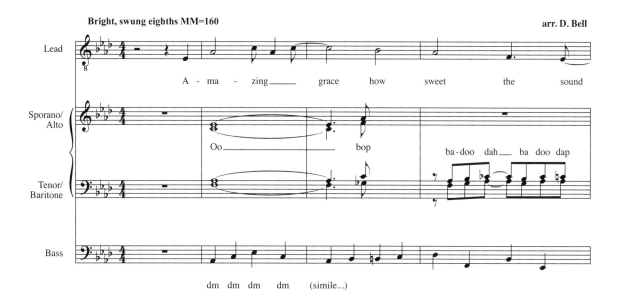

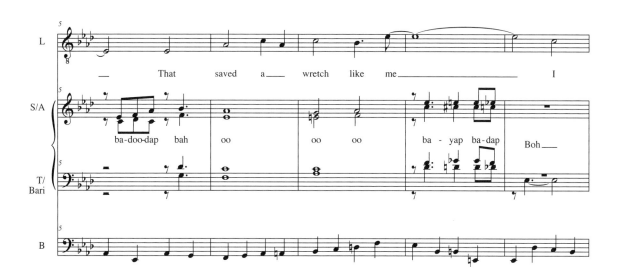

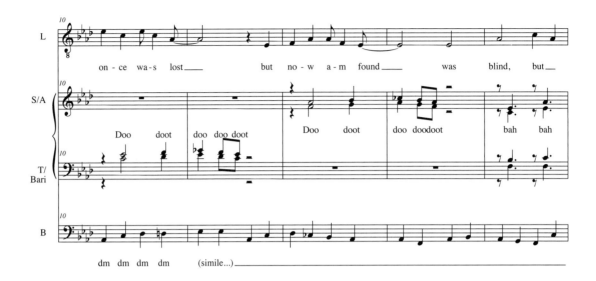

Unlike in doo-wop, the BGs don't provide a constant, repetitive motif. The parts are energetic and varied against the lead vocal. Also, there is less need for the BGs to constantly spell out the chord changes. Most of the harmonic information is provided by the lead line and the bass line, so the BGs can add interesting melodic motifs and comments to the lead.

Gospel

Gospel is another church-based style, this time based in the African American Christian tradition. A traditional gospel choir includes instrumental accompaniment (usually a piano, often a full rhythm section or band). An accompanied gospel choir is usually in three parts—sopranos, altos, and men—though it can also follow the usual SATB format. The tessitura is generally high, with all parts singing in full chest voice. The harmony is triadic, the sound is homophonic, and the parts generally move in similar motion. All voices generally sing words, without much use of sound syllables. The lyrics, by definition, are spiritual in nature.

The sound of gospel is the heart of many other styles, including R & B, doo-wop, and some vocal jazz. Many singers in these genres had their start in gospel music and brought that sound into these other styles.

A feature of many gospel songs is the "breakdown." Whereas most of the song has everybody singing together, the breakdown is a kind of polyphonic ostinato. Each part will have a short musical phrase, two to four bars long, which it repeats. The parts are layered in one by one, building the song back up in dynamic and energy.

As in vocal jazz writing, a cappella gospel does not have a set format, and the music itself is not as tightly defined as is a genre such as barbershop. Some guidelines for writing in gospel style include:

» Music of a spiritual nature, as this is the basic definition of gospel
» Groove centered
» Three-part harmony, though other parts may be added to approximate the role of the band
» Mostly homophonic (except for the breakdown and any instrumentally based parts)
» Text based, with little use of sound syllables
» Intense energy: gospel music is sung to inspire and excite the listener
» Wide dynamics, often sung in full voice
» Even in ensemble singing, use of individual vocal ornaments and improvisations to add energy to the overall sound (not notated, but if writing for a group less familiar with gospel, suggested riffs could be added)

While the above characteristics describe most gospel, it is the message and intent that ultimately defines the style. Related styles such as doo-wop and R & B, if they have the gospel message, may still be considered gospel even without the church-choir sound. Take 6, our early example of a vocal jazz group, could be described as a gospel-jazz group owing to the spiritual nature of their music, their individual vocal stylings within their ensemble singing, and the occasional moments of full-out use of range and power.

Here's our example written in a gospel flavor.

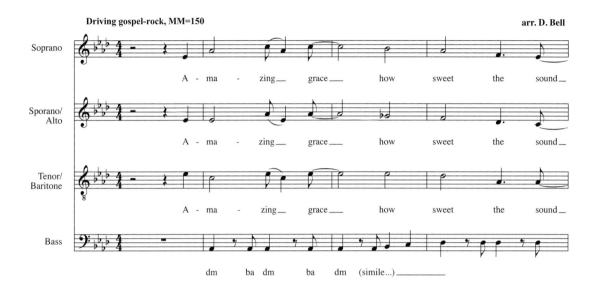

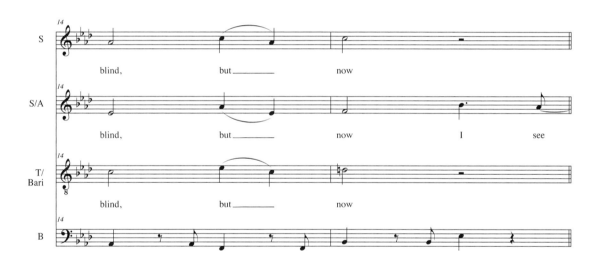

Now we have an instrumental-style bass line, with three-part harmony above it. The harmonies are primarily major/minor and triadic. The rhythms are syncopated a little to suit the straight-eighths, driving-rock feel. A few bluesy notes sneak into the melody at m. 10: this descending triadic figure is a common convention in gospel writing. Similar blues sounds show up in the alto part in m. 13.

Then we have the breakdown, something we haven't yet seen in our other writing thus far. The writing style is contrapuntal, almost like the polyphonic work we saw much earlier in the chapter, only it's R & B flavored and groove based, harmonically vamping on the I and IV chords. The parts enter one at a time: the alto (the simplest part, almost like a cantus firmus), the tenor countermelody, the bass (singing a very R & B–style bass line), and the soaring soprano.

Since a cappella is, above all, a choice of "instrumentation," we have chosen to focus on styles that are, by nature, vocally centered. And we haven't even touched on indigenous a cappella vocal styles around the world. Ultimately any style of music, from country to technopop to Chinese opera, can be arranged a cappella with a little imagination. All it takes is an understanding of the genre and some creativity to translate it into an all-vocal ensemble. We hope this small sampling will get you started.

CHAPTER 22

Writing for Your Own Group

Up to now we've been focusing on general arranging principles that apply to all groups. We've talked about standard ranges, textures, and what you can expect from most singers. A one-size-fits-all approach to an arrangement ensures that the chart will be at least somewhat universally singable and by a specific combination of voices. Something for everybody.

But what about your own group?

Chances are, unless you are a professional arranger-for-hire, much of your writing will be done for your own group, with you as one of the singers and/ or director. If you sing with a larger community choir or school group, many of the general principles of arranging remain important, because a change in the ensemble's membership a few months from now could render a carefully custom-tailored arrangement effectively unsingable. However, if yours is a small group, you should be making every decision with your specific singers in mind.

As an a cappella arranger and/or music director, your instrument is the sound of the combined voices in your group, much as a classical composer or conductor "plays" a symphonic orchestra. The human voice is more varied and versatile than any orchestral instrument, and the abilities and idiosyncrasies of each a cappella vocalist can differ more radically than within, say, any violin section or brass quintet.

Every a cappella musician will instantly acknowledge the obvious unique nature of her and other's voices, and yet some arrangers find themselves arranging for traditional combinations of voices (SATB or TTBB) and traditional vocal ranges even if they know each singer personally. Other arrangers break traditional choral-arranging guidelines to accommodate many of their vocalists' strengths, but still conceive of vocal arranging more or less as it has persisted for centuries in choral music. Occasionally groups will stumble upon an interesting vocal effect or imitative instrumental sound, only to blandly layer it on top of their otherwise rather standard arrangement. The result of these practices is that many a cappella arrangements have a similar sound, drawing upon a small fraction of the capability of the human voice.

In the early days of contemporary a cappella, a group's sound was its most defining characteristic. Arrangements were fairly simple (at least by today's standards), and the voices brought them to life. When Rockapella sang a Persuasions arrangement, they sounded like Rockapella. Also, in those days, there were far fewer groups, making them easier to distinguish.

Nowadays, the a cappella world has exploded with thousands of groups, professional and amateur. Moreover, the use of modern digital recording (including pitch correction) gives many groups a sound that's indistinguishable from that of others.

How can you rise above the crowd and find your own unique, definitive sound? By using great, carefully crafted custom arrangements that take advantage of the full range and depth of your voices and personalities.

Your group, no matter what size, age or ability level, is truly unique. Your job, as an arranger, is to highlight whatever qualities make them so. No one can tell you how to arrange for your group—you will be the best judge of that—but we can give you a number of ideas and techniques that will help you unlock the tremendous potential of your group sound.

>> *Deke says: It has been a long-standing tradition in the House Jacks that we will provide our arrangements of any of our original songs free of charge. Some of our arrangements translate well to other groups, but some are simply unsingable by most groups in their current form because they rely heavily on our idiosyncrasies and unusual vocal techniques. We still gladly e-mail any arrangement in hopes that the group receiving it will be able to make sense of what's written and come up with their own version.*

Know Each Person's Voice

This is the obvious first step in realizing the potential of your group. By broadly categorizing your singers' voices, you fall into the largest trap that classical choral tradition has set for small ensembles. Choral music relies on homogeneity of sound, within each section, within the group, and from choir to choir. But you're looking for your own sound, one that's exciting and original, so it's dangerously limiting to think of any of your vocalists as simply a soprano, lead, or bass. Falsetto, for example, isn't a valid traditional choral practice in most cases, whereas for us, it's often essential.

Take some time with each of your vocalists and explore. First consider range and the effect that the various regions of your singer's voice have on different vowel sounds. Is your alto darker when she goes lower in her register? Does your first tenor cheat toward an "ee" vowel within a fifth of his break? Don't judge, just listen and take notes, and use words that you'll understand, even if they're not explicitly musical terms. One of my former singers gets "punchy" around a high F; another becomes "throaty." If you're prudent in your choice of words, it will allow you to discuss these qualities with each group member and help you explain to them the sound that you want. (Of course, you'll have to be prepared for a few raised eyebrows at first.)

Eventually, you want to be able to hear each individual voice in your head as you're arranging. Listen closely during rehearsal to the way a particular line is sung; later, look at the arrangement and follow the line, trying to hear it in your head as it was performed. It will be tough at first, but within a short time you should be able to take a line from an arrangement you're currently working on and hear how it will be sung by the singer for whom it's intended. This will aid you in many ways—and the most important one is that you'll begin to arrange for the specific voices in your group instead of textbook voice parts.

Change Voicings

With your newly gathered knowledge, try an arrangement that rearranges your singers, crossing voices and otherwise scrambling expectations. Don't do this in-discriminately—envision the outcome before you start by listening in your head to the sound of each vocalist singing each line, then choosing who you want where. Don't simply put the highest voice on top.

You might have guessed that putting your baritone above the first tenor on a falsetto line will result in a less controlled, raspier sound, but then again you might find your baritones have a fuller falsetto that they can push higher (the lower a man's voice, the higher his falsetto). Unexpected tone colors may result.

Survey the notes you collected regarding each vocalist, looking for places where you used the same or similar words to describe different people's voices in different ranges. Call on this information when, for instance, you want to set up a high, breathy texture and each of your voices has only a limited area where the sound you're seeking is really controlled. For example, in women's voices this often means paying close attention to where chest voice becomes head voice; you may realize that your first alto belongs above your second soprano by reason of the specific pitches in the bridge of one arrangement. By playing to each of your vocalists' strengths, you can easily create blends and textures that were very difficult to execute before. And—when you're not striving for a precise blend—by moving and crossing voice parts for effect, you're allowing each vocalist an opportunity to exercise and express a far wider repertoire of sounds.

》 *Deke says: When arranging "Wake Up" by Arcade Fire as an opening number for the third season of The Sing-Off, I wanted to maintain the high, powerful chanting nature of the original, so I found myself often crossing the tenors above the altos and even sopranos. First tenors belting out a high A have a bright, tense impassioned quality that women can't reach on that note. Later in the arrangement, I push the sopranos up toward the top of their break as well on a countermelody so we have the sound of men and women at the top of their chest voices. If I'd stuck with traditional choral voicing, the effect would be pretty, but never as powerful.*

» *Dylan says: When I was in Cadence, I was the top tenor; but as we started arranging more carefully for the group, we found ourselves flipping the top two voices quite often. I have one of those voices with a medium-high break and a smooth transition from chest to falsetto. Our second tenor had a lower and much more pronounced break and a very noticeable difference in tone from chest to falsetto. But he had a beautiful light falsetto and a killer bright soprano range. So in songs where we needed a full-sounding top voice or a melody line that jumped all over the break, I sang the tenor 1 line. For songs where the first tenor had to "float" over a stronger second tenor, or where we wanted a brash top-trumpet line, I sang second tenor and the other guy sang first, which always sat well above his break.*

An interesting case in point: the male chorus Chanticleer. A chamber-sized group of twelve singers, they don't consider themselves a TTBB ensemble, but rather an "orchestra of voices." The conductor knows his twelve "instruments" intimately, and even when performing traditional TTBB arrangements, he hand-picks his instruments, song by song or even section by section according to the way each voice can best give the sound he envisages.

If properly executed, you'll have audiences on their feet, amazed by the variety of sounds that came out of only a few vocalists. But before you do, you'd better find out what those amazingly varied sounds are.

A Library of Sounds

Take the time to collect and eventually utilize all of the unique sounds that each of your vocalists can make. Do this at a different time from the first cataloguing of sounds, because you don't want the excitement and variety of this exercise to overshadow that very delicate and precise task. Before you get together for this session, however, give each singer at least a week to make notes and try things out. Start by suggesting he or she imitate instruments and sound effects, then delve slowly into unique, nonderivative sounds.

Critics of a cappella music as a genre point most often to the similarity and homogeneity of sound within the genre. But this is certainly not a limitation of the instrument—it's a limitation of imagination. You should let imagination take you wherever your mouth and throat can go. Consider Bobby McFerrin: he spent years playing around before he fully developed his signature sound, and he has not stopped pioneering an increasingly exhaustive repertoire of sounds. Be playful, weird, whatever it takes. Remember the only rule of brainstorming: no criticism. There'll be plenty of time for critique later when you're arranging.

There may be all sorts of vocal textures you haven't even considered. If you want to explore these further, check out the unusual, playful book *Mouth Sounds* by Fred Newman. More information can be found in Appendix C.

Putting It All Together

Once you've gathered all of this information, you're ready to start. You no longer think of your vocalists traditionally; now it's time to start considering your options as an arranger beyond the traditional restrictions. Take, for example, vocal spacing. Challenge what you know of the traditional spacing of voice parts. (While exploring, however, never forget why the tradition exists. In the example of spacing, be careful not to make tuning a virtual impossibility.) Also try at first exploring only one or two aspects while leaving the rest more or less unaltered. It helps if there's a reason, either within the song or in the concept of the arrangement, that motivates the change. To continue with our example: bass solos often mess with traditional vocal spacings, and your next arrangement with a bass solo might be the perfect time to explore new answers to those specific problems.

The Essence of Your Group

All the above suggestions focus on the sonic personalities of the singers. There's also the personality of the group to consider. Although your group likely performs many styles of music, it still has an overarching personality, or essence, that shines though. Take some time to think of what that mean. We're talking about general adjectives, such as:

 » Playful/humorous
 » Precise
 » Serious
 » Innovative
 » Preservational (such as a tribute group, or a group devoted to a particular style such as barbershop)
 » Improvisational

If your group were a person, how would you describe him or her? Obviously there won't be just one aspect, but many. When you arrange, keep these adjectives in mind; they'll help you write a chart that suits the nature of the group as well as it suits the voices.

Remember, there is no one right way of doing things—only what appeals to you, your group, and your audience.

CHAPTER 23

Writing Medleys

At its worst, a medley can be awkward, cheesy, exhausting to sing, and a drag to listen to. They're so frequently done poorly that it has become almost a cliché to hate medleys. And yet, when done properly, a medley can be the highlight of a vocal group's performance.

Crafting a great medley is difficult. First, you're not just arranging one song: you're arranging at least two, perhaps several. Even if you are only using pieces of a song, you still have to expend the same amount of effort to listen to and internalize different versions of the song so that you're fully prepared to arrange.

Next, you've got to marry these pieces in a way that makes sense to the listener and is not effectively impossible for your group to manage (difficult, immediate key and tempo changes are far easier on instruments and in the studio than they are with live voices).

Finding the right song sections and soldering them together will take some tinkering and will draw heavily on your arranging skills, both creative and practical. Assuming you're now comfortable with basic arranging and our ten-step procedure, you're now ready for the four additional steps needed to tackle a medley: conception, distillation, assembly, and transitions.

Conception

First, the medley is likely based around some sort of concept, or at least it should be. If you're stringing together two or more songs, there should be a reason you're presenting them as a unit. Maybe you're showcasing the work of a single artist, or perhaps a suite of songs from the same style or era (for instance, a late 1970s disco medley or an up-tempo, foot-tapping ragtime medley). Medleys can also be a practical catch-all during a group's song selection process. Can't decide on the best song to cover by Artist X? If the artist has enough good songs, perhaps it's best to present a brief survey.

Medleys can also be a wise choice when you want to cover songs that are well-known and catchy, but not really strong or interesting enough to demand their own three-to-four-minute vocal presentation.

You might want to think of a medley as performing the same function as a montage in a film: it's a way of distilling key information in a creative, condensed way. A montage may show the passage of time in a movie: in one minute, ten years can pass, and we understand the essentials of what happened in those ten years. In the same way, a medley can highlight the entire career of an artist in a few minutes or present an overarching view of a particular era or style of music. If you approach your medley concept like this, it will help keep it cohesive. It will also help with the next step.

Choosing the Songs

We've already gone into some detail in previous chapters about what to consider when choosing songs. For medleys, the trick is not only choosing the right songs, but making them fit together well.

Let's say that we're doing a medley of a single artist. Keeping in mind the concepts mentioned above, brainstorm all the pieces by that artist that you can think of and scribble them down. Once you're done, it's time to narrow down the list. Keep some of these factors in mind as you start focusing your choices:

- » *Best of.* If you had to choose a handful of pieces, which would they be?
- » *Cross-section versus snapshot.* Do you want to present a cross-section of the artist's whole career or focus on one particular era or timeframe?
- » *Recognizability.* Medleys are essentially distillations, so they work best with songs that are easily and quickly recognizable. If a song needs to be heard in its entirety to be recognized, it may not be the best choice. Go for songs with clear hooks or choruses.
- » *Key, tempo, and style.* If there are two to three songs in your overall list that are quite similar, you may want to choose only one. Or you could do just the opposite: slam them together back-to-back in the medley, or present them in one section as a mash-up (more on mash-ups later).
- » *Mini–set list.* A good medley can be like a mini-concert. With this in mind, imagine that you are putting on a concert with full songs. What combination of songs would make a great set list, with a good overall musical, energy, and vibe balance?
- » *Number of songs.* How many songs you will want to include depends on a lot of things. A medley can be hard work for both the singers and the listener, so you don't want to wear them out. A good medley shouldn't be much longer, in terms of duration, than two full songs: four to six minutes, possibly even shorter. This could be two or three songs where we hear a good amount of each song, or five (or more) songs with some excerpts being only a few (very memorable) bars long.

When working on medleys, it's important to remember that less is more. If you're trying to give someone a taste of a song, a verse and chorus are usually enough. Sometimes just the chorus is enough.

» *Dylan says: And here's the exception to the rule! In my 1980s group Retrocity, when we came up with our first song list, we had a lot of leftover songs; these made it into the "K-Tel Top 24 Monster Medley." Yep, that's right—twenty-four songs representing a cross-section of nearly every genre of Top 40 '80s music. Some pieces had full verses or choruses, some had only a drum or guitar solo. It was ten minutes long, a demon to sing . . . and the highlight of every show.*

» *Deke says: Whereas Dylan has experience with long, many-song medleys, I almost never tackle a medley with more than three songs. If the focus is humor, it works well to quickly feed a rapid-fire progression of song snippets, but if you're presenting the songs as a series of stories and moods, I find more than three to be exhausting. Each season on The Sing-Off, we've had a week featuring three-song medleys from the same artist, and this formula proved to work well.*

Even after you've chosen your songs, keep your brainstorming list handy. Getting all the elements right in a medley is a pretty fluid process. If, during the assembly process, you find that one song just doesn't fit, you may want to try one of the alternate pieces on your old list.

Distillation

The distillation process is fairly straightforward. With each song, imagine a few ways of distilling the essence of the song in a minute or less. Examples might be:

» Just chorus
» Verse and chorus
» Instrumental hook
» Memorable solo, lyric, or moment in the middle
» Opening riff

Remember, it's best if the piece you choose is easy to recognize. Choruses are obvious. Verses may be less recognizable, but if you follow it up with a chorus, people will get it. Instrumental hooks and opening riffs are great if you just want to give a little eight-bar slice of the song. Instrumental solos have to be really obvious to be recognizable outside of their context.

Give yourself a few options for each song, since the assembly process will factor into which pieces get used.

Assembly

Assembly is basically the heart of the process, and you'll probably find it best to tackle it before actually notating the arrangement. If you can't hear the pieces going together well in your head (even if you don't think you have a strong inner ear), it's a good chance that they won't flow together well on paper or onstage.

If it helps to hear the songs out loud and you have access to music software, you can make "radio edits" as mentioned earlier in chapters 8–17 detailing the ten steps. In this case, you're not just splicing one song, but mixing and matching all the songs in the medley to see what sounds good together. This will give you only an approximate sense of how they'll fit, so don't worry if they don't sound perfect together; with one ensemble singing them (and a master arranger making the transitions smooth!), they'll likely go together much better than the spliced recordings.

As you're assembling the songs, keep a few things in mind:

» *Keys.* Unless the songs are traditional, jazz, or other songs recorded by multiple artists, you'll probably find that there is a particular recording or version that people know. You may wish to arrange in the original key where possible, as the tonality is part of the familiarity factor for the listener. So, as you put songs beside each other, make sure the keys work together well. If the songs are in the same key, that helps. If they are a fourth or a fifth apart, they'll be easy to connect through turnaround chord progressions: cadential-type chord progressions based on the circle of fifths, connecting two key centers together. Songs that are in unrelated keys will be harder to put together: you'll have to do some careful transitioning to connect them smoothly.

» *Tempi.* Similar principles apply here. Songs with very similar tempi are easy to put together; if you're going for a continuous-sounding medley, you can even "cheat" by matching tempi. If one song is at 120 beats per minute (bpm) and another is at 126, you can usually meet in the middle without its feeling any different. Conversely, highly contrasting tempi also work well, providing a nice change in the middle of the medley. These will take a little more work to put together. Songs that are close but noticeably different may be more difficult to manage, but it can be done, especially if there's a clear purpose to the order of the songs (such as a survey through an artist's biggest hits in chronological or some other order), or perhaps if the tempi increase, one after the other.

» *Style.* Consider whether you want the medley to have a constant "hooked-on-classics" steadiness or lots of contrast. Too much of the same thing may blur the songs together, while too much contrast might make the singers seasick from tempo, key, or style changes, may break the flow of the medley, and will be harder to write and to execute. We've noticed that it often works well if the first couple of pieces are similar in style so that the medley has some momentum; then, once you're well inside the medley, you can provide contrast.

For the time being, don't worry too much about how you'll actually connect the pieces together: we'll worry about that later. Right now, you're just going for overall flow. Be prepared to move the puzzle pieces around a fair bit, and don't be afraid to change or drop songs if they simply don't flow together. And remember: in a medley, flow is the name of the game.

You've got your pieces chosen, distilled, and in order. Time to put them together. Since we've already discussed general arranging ideas, we won't go into them here. Instead, here are some tips and considerations:

» *Flow versus variety.* There is a benefit to a medley where each song has a distinct feeling: the audience is given a clear sonic picture (and often musical memory) immediately. At the same time, it's pleasing when the songs in a medley flow smoothly from one to another. Which approach will work best for your songs?

» *The songs themselves.* If the songs have enough contrast themselves and you've ordered them well, much of this will take care of itself.

» *Change soloists.* If the songs still seem too similar, simply change the soloist for the next song. It provides a sonic change-up and easily alerts the audience that we're on to something new.

» *Change arranging techniques.* If the key, tempo, and/or style are close enough, you can change the arranging style without sounding abrupt. One piece may be static, homophonic, and choral in style, and the next one full of percussive or instrumental vocal parts.

Transitions

Although an almost limitless number of challenges present themselves when moving from one song to another, we've found that there are a few key categories into which most transitions fall. To demonstrate these techniques, we'll be using one of Dylan's medleys. The "Tin Pan Medley" is a survey-style medley using four songs from the Tin Pan Alley era of songwriting, in this case from the first two decades of the twentieth century.

Back-to-Back Songs, No Transition

If your tempi are similar and your key changes easy, you can simply go from one song to the next. In the example below, we connect the songs "The Entertainer" and "Sweet Adeline." The tempo and key are the same between the songs, so nothing's needed to help the singers or listeners transition. Only one change was made. "The Entertainer" ends on beat 3, and the pickup to "Sweet Adeline" starts on beat 2. Left as is, this would leave two beats of "dead air," so the last bar of "The Entertainer" is turned into a 2/4 bar, and the pieces flow nicely without any extra help.

Tin Pan Medley

Immediate Tempo Change

In the same medley, there is a change in tempo from the first piece ("Alexander's Ragtime Band") to the next piece ("The Entertainer"), and again, the keys are related—F and B♭, respectively. Immediate tempo changes in medleys can be tricky: the performers need to be able to hear the new tempo while still singing in the old tempo. Not everyone can hear it, and it's nearly impossible to agree on the new tempo change!

The solution: put one person in charge of changing tempo. This can be the director, or the soloist if he or she has a pickup. In this case, it's the person who has the "trumpet" melodic pickup.

Tin Pan Medley

Another good choice is to have the vocal percussionist establish the new tempo. Firstly, he or she is focusing on tempo already, and if the performer is singing VP in your group, his or her sense of tempo is probably strong. Second, drummers work best off their own sense of tempo; trying to get a drummer "on-line" with someone else's tempo can be challenging, and if the drummer doesn't get it, the audience can usually tell. Since there is no VP in this section of the medley, the melodic pickup works just fine.

Tempo and Key Change

When the transition between the pieces is going to require a major shift—key and tempo—your best bet may be to try to maintain the flavor of one piece while transitioning into the next. This requires a little arranger's license and can sound quite cheesy if it's not done well. (But if your medley is intentionally campy or silly, embrace the cheese!)

In this case, we're going from an up-tempo feel ("Oh, You Beautiful Doll") to a relaxed ballad ("You Made Me Love You"), meaning a large tempo change. The key change goes from F to E♭: similar in flavor, but not immediately related. The solution in this case was to reach the final tonic chord of the first song, which was made the beginning of a II–V–I turnaround to get to the new key. This takes care of the harmonic side. The new tempo is established clearly, obviously, and immediately by the bass, who starts a walking bass line into the next piece. The three upper voices are singing long notes on top, making the notes sound more like a couple of long pauses rather than the start of a new tempo. Having the bass singer set the new tempo also has a practical side, as it allows one singer to drive the bus rather than having all of them try to feel the new tempo at once.

» *Dylan says: Remember how we mentioned earlier that you should allow your arrangement to evolve even after it's written? This is one of those instances. When I wrote this medley, the bass sang long notes like everyone else, to give a "fake fermata" feel: it sounded like paused notes, even though they were counted (in our heads) in the new tempo. The only problem was that the bass and lead had to start the new song together, and they couldn't feel it the same way. So we had the bass set the new tempo alone, and thus the tempo was well established by the time the new song started.*

Tin Pan Medley

Arranged by Dylan Bell

Full Stop

You can also simply stop one song, pause, and start the next. This works best when:

» *The two songs are very different.* The full stop makes for a good reset, and you're not stuck trying to create any contrived "connecting tissue" between two very different songs.

» *The second song is a ballad.* Free-time ballads aren't easy to transition into, especially if the previous song is a solid, chugging groove: the energy change is just too abrupt and awkward. So wrap up the other piece, make a little pause, and start fresh. Note: in performance, the audience may interpret a pause as the end of the medley and start applauding. Your best bet is to make sure that you keep your visual energy active. Stay focused; don't relax or drop your gaze. This lets the audience know that something else is coming. You can then start the new song or tempo as mentioned earlier, with the conductor's gesture, a melodic pickup, or, if your choir is well rehearsed, a simple breath cue.

In this case, the two songs are quite different: the first song, "You Made Me Love You," is a ballad, and the second song, "By the Light of the Silvery Moon" is up-tempo. The keys are related—E♭ and B♭, respectively—so the transition is fairly simple. The last bar of "You Made Me Love You" includes a transitional setup chord, moving from the tonic E♭ to the dominant of the next song, F7. This works particularly well since the melody note here is an E♭, meaning it can stay the same while the chords shift around it. There is a pause on the F7 chord, a break, then we go straight into the new song and tempo.

Tin Pan Medley

Ending Your Medley

When it comes to ending your medley, you have a number of choices.

Simple Ending

Much of the time, you can simply end your medley with the last song. It's simple, it doesn't require any arranging tricks, and works nicely. Ideally, this is something you've considered when choosing your songs and their order. It would obviously be a mistake to have "The End" by the Beatles in the middle of a Beatles medley, but if it's the last song, nothing more is needed.

Grand Finale

You might, however, want to expand or amplify your ending beyond that of the original song. If you think of your medley as a mini-set, imagine that the ending is the grand Finale and write an ending that suggests this. You could play with a chord progression that's somewhat epic (like $\flat$VI–$\flat$VII–I), use the signature blues ending to many a rockabilly song (bass line: 1–$\flat$7–6–$\flat$6–5–6–7–1), or a big gospel IV–I plagal cadence with ad libs over the top. Some endings are heard in many songs and performances because they work well, and you may find one that fits your medley's style.

Conclusion or Wrap-Up Ending

You can also include elements from previous songs in the medley, which gives a real sense of conclusion.

The following example combines a grand finale and a conclusion or wrap-up ending. The "Tin Pan Medley" ends with the up-tempo song "By the Light of the Silvery Moon." This song choice helps bookend the medley, since it started with "Alexander's Ragtime Band," which is roughly the same tempo. First, the final piece is concluded with a half-time ending, typical of many forms of music, where the last few bars are doubled in length to suggest a grand finale ending. On top of that, melodic material from the opening piece, "Alexander's Ragtime Band," is woven into the mix. But rather than a simple recap of the first song, it is presented as a Dixieland party, where other instruments extemporize around the melody and come together at the end for a snappy finish.

Tin Pan Medley

"By The Light of The Silvery Moon"
Words by Edward Madden, Music by Gus Edwards

Arranged by Dylan Bell

Mash-Ups

Born from the creative overlapping of multiple dance tracks, mash-ups are a modern form of medley in which two or more songs are overlaid, existing simultaneously for some or all of the length of the song. It's almost like a twenty-first century form of counterpoint, where entire song elements are interwoven. There are a few elements that need to be in place to make this work:

The bits of songs you use should be simple and easy to recognize when divorced from their context. You might take a bass line, a groove, and a single guitar lick from one song. To work in a mash-up, they need to stand on their own, clearly recognizable and sonically cohesive. For example, the beginning of "Another One Bites The Dust" by Queen is a clear, simple musical statement over which you could sing another song and still never lose sight of the Queen element.

The pieces should all be in the same or closely related keys and tempi, and if they're not, you'll have to be able to make the keys fit yourself. Mash-ups are generally created through the manipulation of digital musical samples. It's clear that when grabbing and digitally altering a song snippet, one can cheat keys and tempi a bit, but don't stray too far from the original key or tempo, as it will make that snippet hard to recognize. In some cases, singing a theme at half tempo works well, since it adds a new, almost cantus firmus–like texture to the mash-up; or drop the groove to a half-time feel and it will sound like a cool remix.

The themes should be very short, and they should repeat. Try for one- to four-bar hooks, and treat this section as an open repeat. If you repeat, the audience will have more chance to get the parts.

Harmonically, the less motion, the better. There are some songs with the same chord progression (you could mash up several doo-wop songs rather easily), but most vary to the extent that they clash sonically. A simple, repeated harmonic progression, or even the same chord over and over, works well. Some modern hip-hop songs have very little in the way of chord progression and would work well for this purpose.

Consider layering in the parts, starting with the song you've just been singing. If you repeat, it allows the audience to catch each part as it gets added in.

» *Dylan says: I chose to end my "Michael Jackson Dance Medley" with a mashup. In this case, I knew I wanted a mash-up ending right from the conception stage and chose my pieces with this in mind: "Don't Stop Till You Get Enough," "Workin' Day and Night," and "P.Y.T (Pretty Young Thing)." I chose these pieces because the keys and tempi were similar. I also added one extra performance element: I made it an audience singalong. After the final piece ("P.Y.T.") in the body of the medley, the arrangement breaks down to just drums. We divide the audience into three groups: one group sings the "P.Y.T." hook, another sings the "Workin' Day and Night" hook, and the third sings the "Don't Stop Till You Get Enough" hook. We add these in one at a time. Not only does the audience get to understand the mash-up—they get to participate!*

If you're looking for some good examples, check out "Best of the Bootie" online (http://bootiemashup.com/blog/). It's a long-standing club series where DJs submit their mash-ups; each year's winners are compiled and made available for free online. If you're not sure what a mash-up is, or if you're looking for inspiration, there are hundreds of examples, weaving together songs old and new in a variety of astoundingly creative ways.

» *Deke says: A key plot element of the movie Pitch Perfect revolves around a female a cappella group that's stuck in the past; only through a new member who introduces the concept of a mash-up are they able to excel. When arranging their final performance, I needed not only to weave together the songs musically, but also to make sure they had emotional resonance. Because it was a comedy, I took the arrangement from the sublime to the ridiculous, mashing up something like eight songs. Don't try this at home.*

Writing a medley may be hard work, but it is a great exercise for an arranger: in a sense, it's a crash course in many of the principles of arranging. When you write a medley, pay very close attention to step 10: workshopping the piece with your group. The transitions are always the hardest, and your group will help you determine which ones work and which don't. Don't be afraid to go back to the drawing board, or even start from scratch. When you're finally done, you'll have arranging muscles like Arnold Schwarzenegger, and a sparkling gem of a piece for your concert.

CHAPTER 24

Breaking the Block: Overcoming Creative Barriers

Some people may think this topic doesn't exactly belong in this book, but since creative barriers can and will happen when you're arranging, having some tools at your disposal to deal with them when they arise may prove valuable. Creative barriers usually fall into a few general categories, each with its own solution.

Earlier in the book, we mentioned the Dreamer, the Editor, and the Critic, and they'll be making appearances here. If you've been darting around this book rather than reading sequentially, take a moment and skim chapter 4.

Block No. 1: The Blank Page

This is the first and most obvious one, and unless you're some kind of divinely inspired Mozartean genius, it's probably happened to you. You've got the will, the time, and the enthusiasm. You're psyched, ready to unleash a torrent of music. You sit down, take a deep breath, and . . .

Nothing.

No problem. You get up, pace around a little. Make a sandwich. Answer a few e-mails. You come back, still somewhat enthused.

Still nothing.

This is ridiculous. You stare at that page, willing it to give up its secrets to you. Utter a few choice words. As your will drains away, you give up, and spend the rest of the afternoon watching TV.

Sound familiar?

It happens to all of us. Creativity is powered by its own momentum, and often the hardest part is simply overcoming inertia. How do you start from nothing? This is the Dreamer's job—and he hasn't shown up for work. You need to figure out how to invite him to join you.

Create an Inviting Physical Environment

Give yourself open-ended time, if you can. The Dreamer doesn't work by the clock, and being overly time conscious will work against you. Hide or get rid of your clocks and watches. If you do have somewhere to be, set an alarm fifteen minutes ahead to give yourself a little wind-down time . . . then cover the alarm clock and forget about it.

Get rid of distractions. Shut down your computer. Don't just close it or put it to sleep: *shut it down*. Unplug it. Take the battery out if you need to. You need to make it just annoying enough to check e-mail or surf the web that you won't be tempted. Turn off your phone: you have voicemail, right? Is there anything so important that it can't wait for an hour or two? If your workspace is full of little reminders of things you need to do, put them away, hide them, or work in another room.

Now that the distractions are gone, make the room inviting. If you've got a nice sunny window, get close to it: if it's nighttime, adjust the lighting so it's warm and inviting. If you're into candles, incense, or any of that kind of stuff, go for it. Anything that makes you feel good will foster your creativity as well. Preparing your space also prepares your mind: while you're setting out candles and hiding your timepieces, you're also clearing your head of distractions. You may even be starting to create stuff without realizing it.

Sometimes new surroundings are better. Go out for a walk. Walking is a great way to get ideas happening: your body's busy, but there's nothing really to think about, so you can let your mind wander. And there's something about moving that feels a lot better than just staring at a page, waiting for something to happen. Don't forget to take a notebook or portable recorder!

Create an Inviting Mental Environment

This is an idea adapted from a fantastic book on creativity, Julia Cameron's *The Artist's Way*. Cameron calls it "Morning Pages," and here's what she suggests. First thing when you wake up, write three pages, uninterrupted, of whatever's in your head. Don't think it through; it could be pure stream-of-consciousness rambling, or some thoughts about your coffee. It doesn't matter. Don't go back and read it, don't edit as you go. Just write. Three pages. The purpose is to clear your head of any analytical processes and just start a flow. Put another way, it's about letting the Dreamer in to play.

》 *Dylan says: I don't do morning pages regularly, I don't always do them first thing, and I don't always write three pages. But when I'm starting a creative process, and I can feel that there isn't anything already there, I start writing my own "Starting Pages." Eventually, the flow happens, the Dreamer shows up, and I know I'm finally in a creative space.*

You may have your own similar processes, such as meditation, breathing, working out, or something else. Regardless of the method, they all share the same goals: focusing on one single thing, clearing the mind of the annoying here-and-now clutter, and allowing a clear mental pathway for creative flow. It's always in you; it's just a matter of giving it a clear way of getting up and out where you can consciously reach it.

Creativity is a mental muscle, and as such, it benefits from regular training. Try some of these tips on a regular basis (even if you don't have a specific goal or chart in mind) and you'll find it gets easier and easier to slip into a creative headspace. Build that muscle up, and you may even get close to the Holy Grail: creativity on demand.

Get the Dull Stuff Done

In some cases, you may already know the basics: what song to do, how many parts, and the overall form. It's just getting the actual notes-to-paper process happening. If this is the case, start with what you already know. Prepare your score: map out bar lines, key and time signatures, even more detailed things such as repeats, rehearsal marks, dal segnos and codas, and so on, if you already know them. Don't worry if you end up changing it later. This process helps in a few ways. First, it's work that needs to get done anyway, so you're at least keeping busy while waiting for the Dreamer to arrive. Second, by mapping out the chart in advance, you won't have to slow down your flow in the middle of a rush of creative work to do something mundane like figure out what the road map of the chart will be. Third, this organizing process will subconsciously get you in the headspace for writing and provide that starting momentum you need. It's the musical equivalent of getting your room in order.

» *Deke says: During the busiest times of the year when I've had to arrange as many as five songs in a day, I sometimes find inspiration impossible to muster. So I download a MIDI file, listen to the original, open a Finale file, start typing in lyrics—all the things I know have to be done that require no creativity, yet still take time. If I'm not inspired by the time I need to be creative, I move on to the next song. It's like I'm moving all the boxes into a new house and unpacking but not decorating.*

Don't Force Expectations

The Dreamer works when he wants to, not always when you want him to. Part of the downward spiral of a blank-page block is the rising feeling of frustration from a lack of tangible results, aggravated by a ticking clock. When it gets bad, you may even start watching the clock and getting upset. At these times it's important to remember:

Creativity happens in the background. Your computer may look like it's doing nothing, but there's all sorts of maintenance, file checking, and other computer things happening in the background that you don't know about. Creativity works the same way: all sorts of things are being worked out in your subconscious. That's why there are times when things "just happen" and a song or arrangement seems to practically write itself in a matter of minutes: most of that stuff probably got worked out hours, days, or even weeks before and you just didn't realize it.

Creativity is a process, not a product. If you're a results- or goal-oriented person, this is a tough one to swallow, and it can take years to fully get it. Of course, we *are* looking toward an end product—the arrangement—but it won't happen without process. Trust the process: even if you're not writing anything down right now, something's probably happening, even if you don't know what it is.

You may even walk away from this session with nothing tangible. Trust yourself: something probably got done, and the next time you sit down (or even when you least expect it), something will show up.

» *Deke says: Tried and true formula: think about everything you need to do, get everything organized, go to sleep, wake up, take a shower. The next morning you'll find you have far more insight, because your brain has been working overnight. Problems are worked out while you dream, ideas are considered, thoughts coalesce.*

Block No. 2: Everything Stinks!

This can happen at just about any stage in the game. Maybe you're brainstorming ideas, and they all seem terrible. Nothing seems to stick. Or you're a ways in and find yourself hating everything you've done. Worse yet, you finish a chart, sit back to look at it, and feel like setting the whole thing on fire.

This usually means the Critic is a little too hard at work. He's jumping around, slashing and burning everything you worked so hard at. And you feel lousy. There are a couple of different responses, depending on what stage of the process you're at.

Early in the Process

If you're getting blocked when you are brainstorming, it usually means you're judging your work when you're not supposed to. Remember: *don't let the Critic into the room until the Dreamer has done his work.* Ideas are not meant to be judged; they're meant to float around freely until someone sees a use for them. Some may even float away for good, and that's fine too. Do your best to see the Critic as a helpful, *but separate*, piece of the puzzle, and tell him politely that you're not banishing him. He'll get his chance—later.

If you find you're automatically going into fix-it mode, developing and tweaking a half-baked idea, your Editor barged in. The problem is, if the idea is *too* raw, it will fizzle while the Editor's doing her thing. Tell the Editor the same thing you told the Critic.

》 *Dylan says: I'm a compulsive Editor. I want to tweak and fiddle with every idea that comes out, no matter how half-formed it is. There are a couple of problems with this. One, the idea never has a chance to fully form. Two, by seizing on one idea and working with it, you've stopped allowing the flow of raw ideas. You may be working on a semi-useful idea, but there was an absolutely inspired idea coming along—which you just choked. A good rule of thumb for compulsive Editors: when you see an idea you want to pounce on, wait five or ten minutes. If the idea was worth it, you will probably remember it. If not, it wasn't ready for editing yet.*

Later in the Process

If you're well into the chart and if feels like everything's awful, it can simply be a matter of warped perception. The longer you work on something, the more each detail (good and bad) gets magnified, until you can't see the forest for the semiquavers. In this case, the answer's pretty simple: take a break.

For one thing, you may be exhausted and not thinking straight. But even if you're not, there's a good chance your brain is going though the same circle of thoughts and associations for a given phrase or bar, like a hamster on a wheel. So jump off. Do something completely different for at least an hour: have some food, go for a walk, watch TV: preferably something unmusical, brainless, and unrelated to what you're currently doing.

》 *Dylan says: When I need a break, what's my favorite activity? Housecleaning. Seriously. I hate cleaning almost any other time, but when I need a break from creative work, it's a great brainless, distracting activity that allows my thoughts to calm down and sort themselves out. And now my room's clean. Win-win!*

When you come back, look at the chart from a different place. If you were obsessing about the middle section, work on the end. Then come back. Hopefully by now you've forgotten some of the hamster-wheel thoughts that got you into trouble in the first place.

If there were ten things you hated, they're maybe down to two or three, and you can honestly say that they're worth changing. But now you're recharged and able to do it. If you're still bothered by everything, you may need a longer break, so if you can, come back to it in a day or two.

Block No. 3: Painting Yourself into a Corner

Everything's going along wonderfully. Ideas are flowing, and you've gotten a lovely trail of notes and phrases behind you. As you work your latest idea in, you realize that the altos can't move up, or your tenors were doing something that doesn't work here.

You're trapped. Worse yet, you can't get out.

This is as much a logistical issue as it is a creative impasse. But it's going to take some creative problem solving to dig yourself out. There are a few solutions that usually work here.

Unravel

You've found out by now that arranging consists of hundreds of little decisions made from bar to bar and from part to part. Usually they're pretty straightforward, and usually either/or in nature: "should I resolve the tenors up or down?"—that kind of thing. What's tough is that every single decision affects every other one down the line, and one decision is often enough to cause problems later. It's not "wrong," which is why you didn't catch it. It's just that this decision doesn't play well with another one several bars later. It's like knitting: there's an odd stitch somewhere, and you need to find it.

If this is the case, start with the line that's giving you the most trouble. Back up four bars or so and see what happens if you alter the line a little. (This will likely mean changing all the other lines around it. Go ahead.) Still trapped? Try going back another four bars. Hopefully, you will have found that funny little knot and figured out a way around it. If not, try the next strategy.

Work the Other Side

Sometimes it can help to start from a point later on in the piece and work backward. If you're stuck on a chorus, try working on the bridge that follows it; then work backward to the section that was troubling you. Often you'll find a better way to approach that chorus. You may even have some new ideas, informed by what you came up with in the bridge.

» *Dylan says: I rarely arrange in a linear, front-to-back fashion. Like songwriters, I'm often inspired by a hook, or a chorus. So, I start there and find myself "writing around" the sections that came first.*

Try Another Idea

Sometimes, two ideas are great separately, but no matter how hard you work, they just won't play together. If this is the case, and you've tried all you can, something has to go. Before you tear apart that section where you got trapped, ask yourself how important that idea or section is to you. It may be that you keep this idea, but change the idea or section that leads up to it, or the one that follows it. Zoom back, look at the whole chart from a bird's-eye view, and start to prioritize. It's important not to get too attached to all your ideas here. As the author William Faulkner once warned: "In writing, you must kill your darlings."

Usually at this point the Editor's been running the show, happily putting things together and doing what she does best. If you get trapped like this and can't see a way out, call on the Dreamer. Sometimes this will help you break out of the what's-already-there box. Sometimes these traps end up being the source of unexpected creativity, and you discover a new way of getting from point A to point B.

» *Dylan says: I was trying to write a four-song medley, and try as I might, I just couldn't get all four songs to play together well. I switched up the order, I tried changing keys on one of them, I tried using different sections, using different ways of connecting them. It turned out that there was one song that just wasn't working. So I held my breath and decided to let go and cut it. Suddenly everything flowed together. By the time we got to performing the medley, I didn't miss the fourth song, and pretty much forgot I had even considered it.*

There may be other blocks and issues that will slow you down, but remember: they're nearly all fixable. There are few music "problems" out there without a solution, and after you hit a few barriers and break through them, it will be that much easier the next time it happens.

CHAPTER 25

Final Thoughts

This book was truly a labor of love. Through the last twenty-four chapters and countless examples, we've tried to present a comprehensive approach to arranging contemporary a cappella. But that doesn't mean that there isn't more to say. A cappella arranging—the art form, and the book itself—is an ever evolving process. We intend to continue sharing our thoughts online and hope you will as well. Please visit us at http://www.acappellaarranging.com.

If we've missed something, please tell us. If you have your own stories, ideas, and techniques, please share them with us. The craft is best served by an open exchange of ideas, and we encourage you to be part of that. Hopefully, new ideas and techniques will be included in future editions of this book, and we hope this book will help you in your own development for years to come.

We'd like to conclude with a few parting thoughts.

Give Yourself Permission to Stink

Fear of failure is a big problem in our society. We're often so afraid of screwing up that eventually we are afraid of making even the tiniest mistake, and this leaves us paralyzed and disempowered. Not everything you do has to be the Greatest Thing Ever Written. Besides, if you're not willing to screw up, or do something badly, you'll never take chances. If you never take chances, you'll never learn. So go ahead: be mediocre, sub-par, even awful sometimes. Most of the time no one's going to see your mistakes anyway. And if they do see a few, and you can be graceful and humble about them, you get a great reputation for honesty and humility.

It's Not About You

From creative blocks to stage fright, our biggest enemy is usually ourselves. Why is it so easy to fumble around for fun on an instrument you don't play "for real," or play a game of touch-football that would make a pro-level player cringe with embarrassment? It's simple: *you don't care*. We mean that in a good sense: you don't have your ego, identity, and self-image wrapped up in what you're doing, which means you can do it free of cares. It's natural, when you're passionate about something, to put your whole self into it. And you don't want to lose the passion: you just want to lose the baggage that comes with attaching your self-worth to the thing that you're passionate about. Put the music first, take your ego out of the equation, and you can simply focus on the job at hand: serving the music.

It Can Take Ten Lousy Ideas to Make a Single Good One

You really think those great arrangements just happen? For every mental image of Mozart transcribing the music in his head, error free, there's an alternate (and more realistic) image of Beethoven, furiously scribbling and scratching, fixing and revising. Remember, for any finished product that you see, you're seeing the final distillation, the very best of what the creator came up with. If you want proof, check out the deleted scenes of any movie on DVD, or the alternate takes on a rerelease of some classic album. While it's interesting to get a glimpse into their process, most of the time you'll watch those scenes (or hear those takes) and say, "Yep, I see why they cut that. It wasn't particularly good."

Practice Makes Perfect

For arrangers who want to be professional, working at the top of their field, a reality check: anyone can be great from time to time, but according to recent theories advanced by Anders Ericsson and Malcolm Gladwell, it takes somewhere in the range of ten years or ten thousand hours to become an expert. It takes time to develop a fluency in any craft, resulting in a consistently high percentage of excellence in your output. No, there is no shortcut. If you want to be one of the best, you have to put in the time. Many of you reading this do not need to worry about that bar; just arrange when you need a song for your group, and have arranging be a labor of love. But for the few eager future experts out there, find a way to make arranging (as well as coaching, directing, singing, editing, and/or producing a cappella) a major focus of your time, starting now.

Just Notes

There are times when everything you're writing seems extremely important, and you're challenged by a decision, knowing that it's the climax of the song, biggest moment, pivotal emotional statement, whatever. When you're paralyzed in this way, try to remember that it's all just notes. Yes, it's important within the context of your arrangement, performance, and group—but not in the big picture. If you need a little perspective, pick up a newspaper.

» *Deke says: My wife, Katy Sharon, deserves credit for the expression "just notes," as it's paraphrased from her experiences working in the Gap corporate offices. Anytime she or her colleagues would get too frustrated by a problem or conflict, they would remind each other that it's not brain surgery or antiterrorism, it's "just pants."*

Simple Beauty

As much as a cappella (or any art) is not a life-or-death endeavor, it can also be one of the most rewarding things you do. There is something simple and beautiful about voices singing together, and you help make that happen. Sometimes you might take yourself and your work too seriously, but if you ever despair that it doesn't matter, remember how much joy your music brings people and allows them to share with others.

Harmony through harmony: that's why we arrange and sing a cappella. A little music makes the world a little better, and when people sing together, it brings them together. That's in part why we wrote this book: we need you to help others sing and spread harmony—in your city, your state, your country, around the world. In person and online.

Now you've got the tools. Get out there, write, and sing!

Appendix A:
"We Three Kings" and
"Go Tell It to the Moutain"

We Three Kings

Traditional, arranged by Deke Sharon
for Straight No Chaser album "Christmas Cheers"

Go Tell It On The Mountain

Traditional
arr for Home Free by Dylan Bell

2   Go Tell It On The Mountain

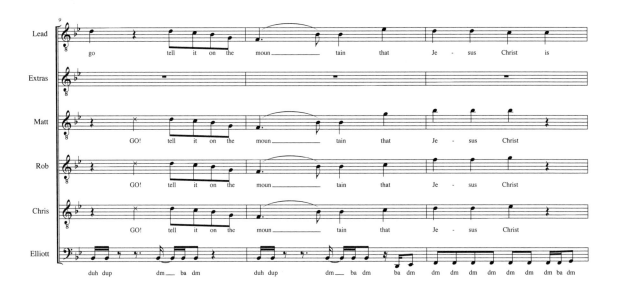

Go Tell It On The Mountain 3

4   Go Tell It On The Mountain

Go Tell It On The Mountain   5

6   Go Tell It On The Mountain

Go Tell It On The Mountain 7

8

Go Tell It On The Mountain

Go Tell It On The Mountain   9

Appendix B:
Notable Arrangers: An Incomplete List

There are hundreds of fantastic arrangers out there—far too many to mention. For each name we've included, there are a dozen we've left out, to the point where we even debated adding this list for fear of excluding someone terrific. We eventually decided that some information is better than none, so without further ado, here is our Incomplete List of Notable Arrangers.

There have been many fantastic a cappella and vocal arrangers in the past century, spanning a wide range of styles and techniques. The list below is a broad survey and in no way definitive.

Rene Baños: It's rare for someone to singlehandedly conjure a new branch of a cappella, but he did when forming Vocal Sampling. You cannot believe that only six voices can create this much sound and this deep a groove. If it weren't for the Cuban embargo, they'd be a household name in the United States. They certainly are in the rest of the world.

Ysaye M. Barnwell: Sweet Honey in the Rock forged a powerful, earthy, and deeply spiritual sound and style that stands as one of the pillars of the female a cappella tradition. If you think women's writing is light—both in theme and sonority—take a lesson from Dr. Barnwell.

Roger Emerson: If for some reason you didn't sing one of Kirby Shaw's arrangements in high school (see below), it's because you were too busy singing Roger's. Clear, elegant writing for young singers, with some lovely, more complex published arrangements as well.

Richard Greene: Grammy-nominated arranger who, along with his Bobs cofounder Gunnar Madsen, invented a fresh new a cappella sound in the early 1980s that paved the way for the contemporary a cappella explosion. His work is humorous, unexpected, and always fresh.

Jester Hairston: Amen! He was the understated master of the spiritual for choir, a torch that was later picked up by Moses Hogan and others. There is much to be learned from this tradition and Jester's light yet powerful touch.

Mac Huff: Say what you want about show choirs—the fact is that they are one of the most effective and inviting ways to get students interested in singing. Some of the arrangements are quite impressive, none more so than those done by Mac. For all that *Glee* has taken from his lead, the producers should be sending him a monthly check.

Derric Johnson: Best known for Epcot's Voices of Liberty, Derric's rich, sonorous, often homophonic arrangements of folk and holiday songs are transcendent. If you're a fan of dense, closely stacked chords, look no further.

Keith Lancaster: Beyond prolific; if you have heard any contemporary Christian a cappella, there's a very good chance that Keith is behind it. Bright and inviting, Keith's style is a hybrid of religious themes and secular stylings.

Jerry Lawson: The Persuasions carried the torch virtually alone through the 1970s, bridging the street-corner and modern a cappella sounds. Not much of his work exists in written form, but as his arrangements were created and taught by ear, listening is the best way to understand them.

Phil Mattson: Synonymous with vocal jazz, the PM Singers were a breeding ground for future arrangers (such as Michelle Weir) and educators. When it comes to clever, compelling vocal jazz writing, there is none better.

Gene Puerling: Often imitated, never duplicated. From the HiLos to the Singers Unlimited and beyond, Gene's dense, idiosyncratic chord voicings are instantly recognizable and have influenced vocal jazz writing perhaps more than any other arranger's.

John Rutter: With his warm sonorities and pop sensibility, Rutter is as much conductor and classical composer as he is arranger, with a body of work that is as inviting to modern ears as twelve-tone writing was challenging.

Kirby Shaw: If you grew up singing in a choir, you almost certainly have sung one of Shaw's arrangements. But don't be fooled by your memories into thinking his body of work is rudimentary, as he's a master of vocal jazz and complex part writing.

Ward Swingle: From the first strains of *Glee*, the instantly recognizable sound of "da va da va da" is classic Ward, whose trademark marriage of classical melodies interpreted through vocal jazz became universally known in the 1960s, with a tradition that continues through today.

Mervyn Warren: Founder of Take 6; his legacy continues with Mark Kibble and Cedric Dent. All three are masters of their signature "gospel melodies, jazz harmonies, [and] R & B stylings" sound.

There are too many other talented people to name, including Mark Brymer, Greg Jasperse, Ed Lojeski, Philip Lawson, Yumiko Matsuoka, Darmon Meader, Bernice Johnson Reagan, Paris Rutherford, Roger Treece, Michelle Weir . . . the list goes on.

In addition to these well-known published arrangers, there are several fantastic young arrangers in the contemporary a cappella community who are not (yet) world-famous names but have created some fantastic charts. Look for Tom Anderson, Ed Boyer, Ben Bram, Christopher Diaz, Robert Dietz, Andrea Figallo, Oliver Gies, Nick Girard, Kerry Marsh, Anne Raugh, Gabe Rutman, Jon Ryan, Kurt Schneider . . . too many to name.

Appendix C: Recommended Texts

There are countless resources nowadays to help you learn and understand music theory. We have not read them all, so we feel most comfortable mentioning only the ones we know well. They worked for us, so we know they'll work for you.

Callahan, Anna. *Anna's Amazing A Cappella Arranging Advice: The Collegiate A Cappella Arranging Manual.* Southwest Harbor, ME: Hal Leonard, 1995.

> *Written when contemporary a cappella was young, with a collegiate a cappella perspective, there is plenty of good information in here.*

Cameron, Julia. *The Artist's Way: A Spiritual Path to Higher Creativity.* New York: Penguin Group, 1992.

> *A fantastic book on the creative process, and on harnessing one's own creativity. The book has a somewhat spiritual bent in places that may not appealing to everyone, but the "12 week program," reminiscent of many self-help programs, is both practical and inspiring.*

Fux, Johann Joseph. *The Study of Counterpoint.* Translated and edited by Alfred Mann. New York: Norton, 1971.

> *A translation of Gradus ad Parnassum (Ascent to Mount Parnassus), this masterwork of Renaissance vocal writing was used by Bach and Mozart. Remarkably conversational in tone, it's the definitive treatise on what we now call counterpoint. Even if you have no intention of writing a sixteenth-century madrigal, you'll learn much of what you need to know about the interweaving of voices here.*

Levine, Mark. *The Jazz Piano Book.* Petaluma, CA: Sher Music, 1989.

> *Next to lifting Take 6 charts, it's one of the best places to learn about jazz harmony and voicings. You don't need to be a pianist to get years of learning out of this text, since it's more about theory and harmony than about learning to play like Oscar Peterson.*

Newman, Fred. *Mouth Sounds.* N.p.: Workman, 1980.

Russo, William, with Jeffrey Ainis, and David Stevenson. *Composing Music: A New Approach*. Chicago: University of Chicago Press, 1988.

An arranger needs to be a composer, since much of what you create never existed in the original song. Superlative approach, starting with very basic principles, yet never boring or condescending.

Schoenberg, Arnold. *Theory of Harmony*. Berkeley and Los Angeles: University of California Press, 1983.

There are far easier texts with which to learn eighteenth- and nineteenth-century four-part writing (do not start here!), but none more filled with wisdom and insight. Although he is best-known for the development of twelve-tone theory, Schoenberg was an absolute master of tonality and taught at UCLA for many years. His wisdom is now yours.

Appendix D:
Online Resources

There is an ever growing and changing list of online resources, and we'll do our best to update the list on our own site at www.acappellaarranging.com. The list below is a start.

www.casa.org: the Contemporary A Cappella Society of America is the mother ship of the a cappella community. Don't let the "America" fool you: though based in the United States, this is now a worldwide resource, with "ambassadors" in dozens of countries around the world spreading joy of a cappella music.

www.a-cappella.com: CDs, songbooks and more.

www.singers.com: Another source of CDs and songbooks.

www.barbershop.org: Barbershop harmony for men.

www.sweetadelineintl.org: Barbershop harmony for women.

www.chorusamerica.org: Organization for professional and recreational choirs.

launch.groups.yahoo.com/group/ba-acappella: A cappella e-mail Listserv for the San Francisco Bay Area. Similar groups exist for several other regions around the United States.

www.dylanbell.ca: Dylan's site.

www.totalvocal.com: Deke's site.

www.capublishing.com: Some of Deke's published arrangements.

http://www.mouthdrumming.com: the website of Wes Carroll, former House Jack VP and vocal drumming pioneer.

www.mouthoffshow.com: Hosted by Dave Brown and Christopher Diaz, this weekly podcast stays on top of what's new in the a cappella scene.

www.vocal-blog.net: This a cappella site gives us a European perspective on the a cappella world, written by Florian Stadler and the Swingle Singers' own Clare Wheeler.

www.vocalasia.com: The pan-Asian a cappella organization's site.

www.inside-acappella.com: Contemporary a cappella YouTube channel.

Glossary of Terms

BGs Shorthand for background parts. We coined the term to mean any part that's not the lead, bass, or percussion.

break The place where the voice switches from **chest voice** to **falsetto**. Generally more pronounced in men's voices and in less trained singers. Put another way, it's that place where the voice seems to "flip" from a strong sound to a higher, usually softer sound. Trained singers spend years ironing out this part of the voice so that singing "over the break" sounds unnoticeable.

changes Shorthand for "chord changes" or the harmonic structure of the song.

chart Informal term for a piece of music, a score, or an arrangement. This seems to be more common in North America, particularly in the contemporary genres. Ask someone from the United Kingdom or a classical musician, if you can see their "chart," and they'll think you're asking about their medical history.

chest voice Put simply, the voice that sounds closest to your talking voice. Some people define it further as the "strong" singing timbre.

diatonic Commonly used to refer to scales or melodies based upon combinations of half and whole steps, such as the major and minor scale. A "diatonic melody" is one based on such a scale, as opposed to a "chromatic melody," based on half steps or "accidentals" that fall outside the scale.

*****falsetto** Italian meaning "little false"; the upper register of a voice created with only the edge of the vocal cords. Very distinctive in a male voice (think of Frankie Valli, or the guys in Monty Python when they speak like women), hard to identify in most women. Note that the lower a man's voice, the higher he can usually sing in falsetto (with practice).

*****head voice** The register above **chest voice** that's lighter in tone. Note that a woman's head voice is rarely used in popular music, and when it's relied on heavily in an a cappella arrangement, it can make a song sound choral as opposed to pop or rock.

homophony/homophonic From the Greek for "same sound"; refers to vocal parts moving together, usually singing the same words and rhythms. Examples are

---

*The terms "falsetto" and "head voice" have very fuzzy definitions and are a subject of endless debate among singers. For the purpose of clarity and simplicity, in this book we've chosen to use the term "falsetto" for men's above-the-break voice, and "head voice" for the same in women.

most chorale writing, hymns, barbershop writing, and block-voice vocal jazz writing.

horizontal Another, more general way of saying "melodic." Horizontal music reading involves one line: a string of notes, or melody.

impressionist music Refers to a style of classical music of the late nineteenth century, exemplified by such composers as Claude Debussy and Maurice Ravel.

lead sheet A piece of printed music consisting only of melody, lyrics, and chord changes; the bare bones of a song.

lifting Colloquial term for transcribing.

octaver A.k.a. *octave pedal*, an electronic effect used to add a lower octave (or two) to a voice. This can be used to make a bass singer's range similar to that of a bass guitar, or an alto's voice sound like a bass singer.

polyphony/polyphonic From the Greek for "many sounds"; refers to vocal parts moving independently of each other. Examples are fugues, motets, and to a certain extent, "mash-ups," where different sections interweave different song lines.

Picardy third Also called a *tierce de Picardie*; refers to the use of a major third in a chord at the end of a cadence or musical section in a piece that is primarily minor. The result is a "happy" sound in a song with primarily minor, often "sad" sonority. Originally found in medieval and Renaissance music, it is also used in barbershop music. No one is sure exactly who or what "Picardy" refers to . . . but we know that it predates *Star Trek*'s Jean-Luc.

tessitura From the Italian for "texture"; refers to the average range of a piece or a vocal part. For example, a vocal part may cover two octaves: if most of that time is spent in the upper octave, the part has a *high* tessitura. If it's all over the place, it's a *wide* tessitura.

tritone substitution A jazz harmonic progression wherein a dominant seventh chord is swapped for a dominant seventh chord a tritone away. That means that a Dm7–G7–C progression would become Dm7–D♭7–C. The reason this works is that the third and seventh of the G7 chord (B and F) are the seventh and third of the D♭ chord, and they will still resolve inward (provided there is good voice leading) to C and E.

vertical Another, more general way of saying "harmonic." When you look at a piece of music vertically, you're seeing what notes happen at the same time, creating chords: a column of simultaneous sound, or harmony.

voicing Refers to the vertical organizing of pitches to make a chord or sonority. *Close voicing* means pitches that are close together, such as a tonal cluster; *open voicing* means pitches that are spread farther apart. A voicing can also refer to a vertical organization of pitches without a clear chordal identification.

walking bass A bass line that moves in a scalar and/or chromatic fashion from chord to chord. Frequently found in jazz.

Afterword

I was a teenager when I heard an a cappella recording of the premier choral jazz ensemble, the Singers Unlimited, for the first time. That experience transformed how I thought about music. Hearing unaccompanied voices consistently singing six-part jazz chords in tune opened my eyes and ears to the possibilities of a cappella group singing. It removed the artificial restraints I had placed on the harmonic capacity of unaccompanied voices.

I was enlightened again when I heard this harmonic language being further expanded by Mark Kibble in the early 1980s. He was developing an approach that would eventually become the signature sound of the vocal group Take 6. One of the groundbreaking features of his arranging style was to approach the bass vocalist as an instrumentalist. This meant giving the bass singer a "walking" rhythmic pattern akin to that of an upright jazz bass player, or having him sing onomatopoeic syllables to capture the thumping style of an electric bass player in an R&B-flavored arrangement.

Perhaps the most exciting innovation of contemporary a cappella groups is the addition of a designated vocal percussionist or beatboxer. Deke Sharon is credited with the popularization of this development, which has become a mainstay on college campuses in the US and in a cappella communities around the world.

If man was made in the image of God, it then follows that the human voice is God's instrument, which accounts for the pathos and power that attends a cappella singing. Whether in the context of congregational or solo singing, choral or doo-wop, jazz or pop, blues or barbershop, no instrument can match the human voice's ability to blend, word-paint, harmonize, growl, slur, turn, shake, dip, snatch, slide to, fall off, or bend even a single note. Deke Sharon and Dylan Bell understand the nature of this power and have poured a wealth of professional experience into this practical guide to a cappella arranging. May everyone who reads this book be inspired to affiliate, or deepen their affiliation, with an a cappella community and sing, sing, sing!

Cedric Dent, PhD
Professor of Music, Middle Tennessee State University
Take 6, Member Emeritus

Music Permissions

Black Horse And The Cherry Tree
Words and Music by Katie Tunstall
Copyright © 2004 Sony/ATV Music Publishing UK Ltd.
All Rights Administered by Sony/ATV Music Publishing LLC, 8 Music Square
    West, Nashville, TN 37203
International Copyright Secured   All Rights Reserved
Reprinted by permission of Hal Leonard Corporation

Christmas Time Is Here
from A CHARLIE BROWN CHRISTMAS
Words by Lee Mendelson
Music by Vince Guaraldi
Copyright © 1966 LEE MENDELSON FILM PRODUCTIONS, INC.
Copyright Renewed
International Copyright Secured   All Rights Reserved
Reprinted by permission of Hal Leonard Corporation

Dive into You
Words and Music by Austin Willacy and Garth Kravits
Copyright © 2001 None More Black Music and JoJoLouMusic
All Rights Reserved
Reprinted by permission of Austin Willacy and Garth Kravits

Drive My Car
Words and Music by John Lennon and Paul McCartney
Copyright © 1965 Sony/ATV Music Publishing LLC
Copyright Renewed
All Rights Administered by Sony/ATV Music Publishing LLC, 8 Music Square
    West, Nashville, TN 37203
International Copyright Secured   All Rights Reserved
Reprinted by permission of Hal Leonard Corporation

musicPRO guides

Quality Instruction, Professional Results

978-1-4584-1657-5	A Cappella Arranging	$29.99
978-1-4768-1701-9	The Best Jobs in the Music Industry	$24.99
978-1-4234-9279-5	The Complete Pro Tools Shortcuts, second editon	$29.99
978-1-4234-9671-7	The Complete Pro Tools Shortcuts, second editon – Spanish edition	$29.99
978-1-4234-6339-9	The Craft of Christian Songwriting	$24.99
978-1-4584-0374-2	Desktop Mastering	$29.99
978-1-4234-6331-3	The Desktop Studio	$27.99
978-1-4234-4343-8	The Drum Recording Handbook	$29.99
978-1-4234-9969-5	The Future of the Music Business, third edition	$29.99
978-1-4234-4190-8	How to Make Your Band Sound Great	$29.99
978-1-61774-227-9	Making Your Mark in Music: Stage Performance Secrets	$29.99
978-1-4234-3850-2	Mixing the Hits of Country	$59.99
978-1-4234-9944-2	Modern Guitar Rigs	$24.99
978-1-4234-8445-5	Moses Avalon's 100 Answers to 50 Questions on the Music Business	$19.99
978-1-4584-0289-9	Music 3.0	$24.99
978-1-4234-5458-8	The Music Business Contract Library	$24.99

978-1-4234-7400-5	The Music Producer's Handbook	$34.99
978-1-4234-3874-8	The Musician's Guide to Brides	$24.99
978-1-4234-8444-8	The Musician's Video Handbook	$34.99
978-1-4234-5440-3	1000 Songwriting Ideas	$19.99
978-1-4584-0039-0	Pro Tools Surround Sound Mixing, second edition	$39.99
978-1-4234-8896-5	The Recording Guitarist	$24.99
978-1-4234-3483-2	The Reel World, second edition	$27.99
978-1-4234-9278-8	Rockin' Your Stage Sound	$24.99
978-1-4234-8448-6	Secrets of Negotiating a Record Contract	$19.99
978-1-4234-8847-7	Sibelius	$29.99
978-1-4234-6341-2	The Studio Musician's Handbook	$34.99
978-1-4234-5699-5	Succeeding in Music, second edition	$24.95
978-1-4234-9236-8	The Touring Musician's Handbook	$34.99
978-1-61780-557-8	The Ultimate Church Sound Operator's Handbook, second edition	$39.99
978-1-61780-559-2	The Ultimate Live Sound Operator's Handbook, second edition	$39.99
978-1-4584-7449-0	Welcome to the Jungle	$24.99

Prices, contents, and availability subject to change without notice.

Hal Leonard Books
An Imprint of Hal Leonard Corporation
www.musicproguides.com

1012